Laity Mobilized

Church Growth Series

Church Growth in Mexico: Donald McGavran, John Huegel, Jack Taylor

Wildfire – Church Growth in Korea: Roy E. Shearer

New Patterns of Church Growth in Brazil: William R. Read

Church Growth in Central and Southern Nigeria: John B. Grimley, Gordon E. Robinson

God's Impatience in Liberia: Joseph Conrad Wold

Tinder in Tabasco: Charles Bennett

Latin American Church Growth: William R. Read, Victor M. Monterroso, Harmon A. Johnson

Laity Mobilized: Neil Braun

Man, Milieu, and Mission in Argentina: Arno W. Enns

Laity Mobilized

Reflections on Church Growth in Japan and Other Lands

by

NEIL BRAUN

WILLIAM B. EERDMANS PUBLISHING COMPANY
Grand Rapids, Michigan

Library of Congress Catalog Card Number: 68-56119
Printed in the United States of America

CONTENTS

FOREWORD

In this book Neil Braun has made an important contribution to contemporary science of missions. He sees clearly and states convincingly that the Church has to move out of its clerical structures in a radical way. Propagating the Gospel is not even largely the concern of the ordained ministers and missionaries. If it becomes such, the Church ordinarily ceases to grow. Propagation of the Gospel is a chief business of the laity. It is in the laymen of the Church – the ordinary Christians – that the divine life begins to impinge on the life of the world.

Mr. Braun writes from the Japanese setting, as is quite natural for him, a missionary to Japan, to do; but he is speaking to the Church in all six continents. Some of his illustrations come from the slightly growing Church in Japan, but they are applicable in many countries. Clergy-dominated Churches can be found in numerous places and in all, one of the steps essential to renewal and growth is for ordinary Christians to undertake ceaseless, effective evangelism.

All the other good things which churches and Christians should be doing, to serve mankind and improve the framework of the social order, can be better done with *more Christians.* Then, too, as II Corinthians says so well, "as grace extends to more and more people" it increases "thanksgiving to the glory of God." The service of man and the glory of God are both advanced by the mobilization of the laity for evangelism and church growth.

This book should be widely read both at home and abroad, in many lands, by ministers, missionaries and laymen.

November 1, 1970

Donald McGavran, Dean
School of World Mission and Institute
of Church Growth, Fuller Seminary
Pasadena, California 91101

INTRODUCTION

This book seeks to answer the question: How can all the people of God in Japan (or any other land) be mobilized for winning that nation to Christ in our day? It records the results of intensive research and reflection upon this crucial question. This quest has been forced upon me as an evangelistic missionary during more than a decade devoted to church-planting efforts in a rural section of Japan noted for its slow and difficult church growth.

To the writer, as to most present-day missionaries and pastors, to "plant a new church" has been a concept which included a number of unexamined presuppositions. It meant, I thought, evangelizing until a sufficient number of converts had been won to make possible the financing of a trained pastor's salary and the construction of a building. It gradually became clear, however, that in rural Japan it is almost impossible to plant many churches when the task is so defined. Moreover, even in the urban areas the multiplying of new churches seemed far slower than it ought to have been when measured against the degree of receptivity to the Gospel manifested by city people.

The conviction slowly grew in my mind that there was something wrong with our conception of church planting. About that time a book came into my hands which told of the work of lay preachers in the Methodist Church in England. A new door seemed to be opening in answer to much prayer. Did not this pattern of church life have something valid to say about our problems? Stimulated by a colleague, I re-examined the writings of Roland Allen. From this study came a review of those aspects of his thought which seemed pertinent to the Japanese situation. This mimeographed report is, to my knowledge, still the only representation of Allen's thought in the Japanese language.

Further reflection and study led me to the conviction that the experience of the Church, both in success and failure, teaches that not only is it essential for some laymen to be recruited and trained to assist professional clergy in leading the churches, but that large-scale growth depends upon mobilizing as far as possible the entire believing community for the task of evangelism.

Entering the School of World Mission and Institute of Church Growth at Fuller Seminary in 1965 provided me with a long-awaited opportunity of doing systematic research related to these problems. During this period of study and reflection, it became clear that the problems with which my fellow Christians throughout Japan were struggling had been faced, identified, and analyzed by keen missionary minds decades ago. The Church world-wide, by virtue of her long and wide experience, possesses a vast store of knowledge. Some sections of the Church have in times past found fruitful answers to these dilemmas. And here and there in the world today are to be found Churches which are leaping over and around barriers to growth against which so many of us futilely beat our heads.

The tragedy is that this knowledge is hidden from so large a part of the missionary world, and to an even greater extent from the younger Churches. It is scattered in half-forgotten volumes, or it is lost in the archives of the denominations. In the explosive world in which we live, Christians do not have time for the luxury of trying out in isolation methods which have been repeatedly analyzed in the laboratories of the experience of the Churches. This volume endeavors to bring together what has been discovered concerning the mobilization of the laity.

The book is written against the backdrop of the Japanese scene. The precise way in which the overall argument develops has been inevitably influenced by the unique conditions which characterize that country. It has seemed wise frankly to acknowledge this. Nevertheless, I am confident that the main theses of these pages are applicable to the missionary situation the Church encounters most places in the world. I am hopeful that readers in other lands will see the relevance to their own situations.

Since, however, the argument does assume a particular form owing to the special circumstances prevailing in Japan, it may be well to briefly sketch some aspects of the situation there.

(1) Japanese Christianity is an urban phenomenon. Three-fourths of all Japanese Christians reside in the cities, though over a third of

the population is composed of the farming communities, and many others live in small towns.

(2) In Japan people tend to become Christians as isolated individuals. Seldom does the Gospel move along family or group lines, as is often the case in Asian countries and in Africa.

(3) The Church in Japan possesses a numerous, trained, and able Japanese clergy. Not a few of the positions taken in this book have been carved out during animated and stimulating discussions with keen Japanese pastors of several denominations.

(4) Nearly every church in Japan has its own salaried pastor. The missionary or pastor in Japan is astonished to read of the pastor in Africa, India, or the South Pacific who has five, ten, or even fifty congregations under his care. The way all branches of the Church live and work in Japan, together with the way Japanese books, television, and other media portray the Church, has formed in the minds of both non-Christians and Christians an image which makes it difficult for them to conceive of a congregation without a professional pastor.

(5) Japan has probably the highest percentage of literates of any nation in the world. The world-wide shortage of an adequate Christian vernacular literature is not true of Japan. A recent compilation of all Japanese-language books related to Christianity required a full-length book. Moreover, many of these books are the work of Japanese writers.

The argument of the book proceeds along missionary and existential lines, rather than along those of systematic theology. The specifically theological sections come in the second half of the volume.

Because the book is slated for translation into Japanese, and because the approach to endeavors for Christian expansion advocated throughout is unfamiliar to Japanese Christians, I have taken pains to reference the argument rather more than may seem necessary. I would particularly call the attention of readers in Japan to the frequent references to the writings of such men as Stephen Neill (Anglican) and Lesslie Newbigin (Presbyterian serving as Bishop of the Church of South India). No more outstanding leaders are active in the missionary world today than these two famous writers. They may safely be regarded as leading authorities in the field of mission. That the argument of this book finds inspiration and support in their writings is evidence that what is contended in these pages is not extremist, and that what we are presenting is not merely an argument coming out of one particular Christian denomination.

Some readers may be disappointed that the book does not advocate any fixed church polity or attempt to define theologically the ecclesiastical position of laymen who share in the pastoral work of the churches. The omission is deliberate. As a reading of the book will evidence, almost all branches of the Church, and all varieties of church polity, have at some times and places found it possible to introduce sufficient flexibility into their organizational structures to permit greatly expanded participation on the part of laymen in the pastoral and leadership functions of the Church. This is an immensely encouraging fact. Most readers will have preferences, as does the writer, in matters of organization and polity. But it is deeply reassuring that the major aim of the book is capable of being realized in almost any of the various organizational patterns within which Christian men have served their common Lord.

The references will indicate the writers to whom I am particularly in debt. I owe much to Dr. Wilbur Harr, who first awakened my interest in the Batak Church. Dr. Moses Crouse read some of the theological sections. I am most grateful to Dr. Alan Tippett, under whom most of my reading was done. This was especially fortunate in that his missionary experience was with a Church in which laymen who preach far outnumber the professional ministers. I am also indebted to Dr. Donald McGavran for his encouragement and valued counsel. Nevertheless, the positions taken in the book are my own, and I am solely responsible for them. I must add that without the encouragement of my wife, and her repeated typing of the manuscript, the work could not have been carried through to completion.

A glossary of Japanese terms used in the text appears as Appendix A. The book makes considerable use of church statistics. Every effort has been made to gather accurate statistics and to use them responsibly, but because of the vexing questions involved, the matter has been discussed in Appendix B.

All Scripture quotations have been taken from the Revised Standard Version unless specifically stated otherwise.

With respect to the use of the words "Church" and "church," the capital letter is used for nouns referring to denominations or the universal Church, and the small letter for adjectives or for nouns referring to the local congregation. The word "church" as used throughout refers to congregations rather than to buildings. When the latter are intended, the meaning is clearly specified.

The anthropological system of reference is used. In parentheses placed within the text itself, the author's last name is listed and the year of publication, plus the page and volume numbers where necessary. The reference can be readily identified by turning to the bibliography. In this system, footnotes are usually confined to comments.

Neil Braun

CHAPTER I

AN UNCHANGING MANDATE

The Church grows slowly in Japan. Though church historians frequently say of the Church in Japan that its influence upon the social and moral life of the nation is out of all proportion to its size, almost everyone admits that, as a whole, church growth in Japan *is* slow (see chapter thirteen for exceptions).

Many Japanese Christians and not a few missionaries are perplexed and discouraged. Drummond (1961:452-455) speaks of the "stalemate that appears to have come over Christianity in Japan in its task of witnessing to the nation as a whole." Reporting on Hendrik Kraemer's lecture series in Japan, the article records that he was "aware of the present stalemate and of its depressing effect on Christian morale." Some Japanese pastors say the Church is up against a stone wall. Some missionaries assert that we must patiently work on, in the hope that one day the "wall" will crumble.

While this book takes a decidedly more optimistic view of the situation, the foundational truth we must keep ever before us is that we are under an unchanging mandate. This book on the evangelistic mission of the Church, written with the ofttimes baffling Japanese scene in mind, offers opportunity to see this truth in even clearer focus. If we are Christ's, we are the Church. We are the very ones by whom Christ beseeches men to be reconciled to God. Our commission does not change because the circumstances are either easy or hard.

GOD'S PEOPLE AND THEIR MISSION

The events recorded in the tenth chapter of the Acts of the Apostles led to one of the great spiritual advances in the religious history of man. Immediately after seeing a strange vision, the meaning of which was not immediately clear to him, Peter was visited by messengers from Cornelius, a Roman army officer and a Gentile. The experience that followed at the residence of Cornelius, under the leading of the Holy Spirit, brought to Peter–and through him to the infant Church–a momentous new way of understanding the divine purposes.

This same Peter had confessed Jesus as the Messiah at Caesarea Philippi (Matt. 16:13-28). That event represented a sharp turning point in the ministry of Jesus. All three synoptic gospels declare that Jesus now, for the first time, began to speak of the cross to His disciples. That this confession was of great importance to Jesus is shown by the warm benediction He bestowed upon Peter: "Blessed are you, Simon. . . ." He drew attention to the finger of God active in these events: " . . . flesh and blood has not revealed this to you, but my Father who is in heaven."

Heretofore Jesus had not been able to build upon the shifting moods and loyalties of the multitudes. But now that the disciples had come to recognize Him as the Messiah, He was able to form them into the foundation upon which the future development of His mission was to be based.

Bishop Charles Gore has shown the crucial nature of this passage. It marked a turning point in the sustained efforts of Jesus to form "a reconstituted Israel" (1924:47-50). There are numerous signs in the gospels of the intention of Jesus, as the Messiah, to fashion a people about Himself. These early disciples would be the first of the many who would carry on and complete the calling of Israel, the chosen people of God.

What was Jesus' motive in thus making new the ancient people of God? The answer to this question lies in the purpose for which Israel had been called out and made into a people in the first instance. What lay in the heart of God through all the long years during which Israel was being refined, instructed, and trained in His ways? Hints are to be found in the Old Testament as to how this question should be answered, e.g., the blessing of Abraham in Genesis 12:1-3. Perhaps the clearest statements are in the "Servant Songs" of Isaiah

(43:10, 11; 42:5-7; 49:3-6). Speaking in the last of these three passages, the Lord addressed fallen Israel, lying under the heel of the conquering Babylonians:

> It is too light a thing that you should be my servant to raise up the tribes of Jacob and to restore the preserved of Israel; I will give you as a light to the nations, that my salvation may reach to the end of the earth.

The mysterious election of the obscure Hebrew tribes is now seen to have been the first act in the unfolding drama of history: the story of the God of love whose mighty works are designed to bring salvation to all men everywhere.

The purpose of Jesus Christ in gathering a people to form a reconstituted Israel was not different from that ancient purpose of God. He carefully instructed His disciples in the spiritual principles according to which His kingdom would operate, and trained them in the kind of ministry He wished them to exercise (Luke 9:1-10; 10:1-22). The culmination of His work and thought was the cross. The resurrection was the crowning act in the series of mighty works by which God brought salvation to men. The groundwork now having been adequately laid, the risen Christ was able fully to reveal that burning purpose which had sent Him into the world:

> All authority in heaven and on earth has been given to me. Go therefore and make disciples of all nations, baptizing them in the name of the Father and of the Son and of the Holy Spirit, teaching them to observe all that I have commanded you; and lo, I am with you always, to the close of the age (Matt. 28:18-20).

Peter's experiences in Acts 10 must be viewed against this background. In the early days after the Ascension, the first Christians did not fully recognize the revolutionary implications of this last command of Jesus. The early chapters of Acts indicate that in the period following Pentecost, the disciples limited their evangelism to Jews, as they had done during the ministry of Jesus.

We may surmise that this too was of God. The Book of Acts reveals that a very large number of Jews became Christians in those early days. When at length the Gospel began to leap across racial boundaries, it did so from among a sizeable and rapidly growing body of believers. The transforming and empowering grace of the ascended Lord was visibly at work in the midst of this host of converts, increasing the fervor and confidence with which they carried on their witness. Thus equipped, the new faith could embark upon its conquest of distant worlds.

But one more giant stride was necessary. Because God's love for men is without partiality, Christianity could not become a world faith until Jewish Christians were released from the bonds of anti-Gentile prejudice. Still another mighty act of God was required before the fetters which bound the Gospel could be shattered.

As Peter related the story of Jesus, the Holy Spirit fell upon the receptive Gentile listeners as He had upon the Jewish Christians on the day of Pentecost. Peter and his Jewish companions were amazed when they beheld uncircumcised Gentiles, who kept not the law, receiving the same grace as they themselves had received. As they reflected upon this astonishing development, they were irresistibly driven to recognize the sovereign act of God Himself. Long-standing prejudices fell away. A new hymn of joy was sung in heaven and earth as Cornelius, his relatives, and his friends were given to the waters of baptism.

Shortly after this the band of Christians set out on its journey of world winning. These individuals had been formed into a people by the Lord Himself. Much growth was yet to come, but a great step had been taken when they were purged of Jewish prejudices. They began to perceive that the love of God is for all men and is not limited by racial, cultural, or class differences.

A new variety of men had come into being. This same Peter wrote many years later to Gentile Christians who had never seen Jesus Christ:

> But you are a chosen race, a royal priesthood, a holy nation, God's own people, that you may declare the wonderful deeds of him who called you out of darkness into his marvelous light (I Pet. 2:9).

These realities have not changed though many years have passed. All who are called into the fellowship of Jesus Christ, whatever their race or station in life, are formed into His people. (The concept of "the people of God" is the subject of chapter eight.) They constitute a "race" whose history goes back nearly four thousand years, and are the chosen instrument, by the will of God, to bring to men everywhere the message of the love of God and the forgiveness of sins through the work of the cross.

GOD'S PEOPLE IN JAPAN

This is the reality which underlies the existence of all Christian people in Japan or in any other land. They did not choose Christ, but He chose them, and He intends that they bear fruit. When men become Christians they are given a number of vocations, but none is more fundamental than the vocation of being witnesses to the Light.

We need to be summoned back again and again to this basic matter. The present-day difficulties of winning Japan for Christ must not be allowed to turn us away from our calling. God our Saviour desires all men to be saved and to come to the knowledge of the truth (I Tim. 2:4). Every prejudice, excuse, self-defense, and rationalization which hides this from us must be pruned away. We are called to be obedient to the Lord of men.

It will become apparent that this book owes much to Hendrik Kraemer, but at this point we must express some disappointment with what he is reported to have said in his lectures during his extended visit to Japan in 1960:

> Aware of the present stalemate and of its depressing effect on Christian morale, he sought to turn the eyes of the Christian community away from the barometer of church membership statistics. He tried to change the present emphasis, centered almost entirely on the local congregation, to the possibilities of creative effort in wider spheres that could also help to create more favorable conditions to the reception of the Christian Gospel (Drummond 1961:455-456).

Admittedly, the concentration upon the local congregation needs correction but not in the form of de-emphasis. The Church grows only as local congregations grow and multiply. Nor can we agree with Kraemer's attempt to divert attention from the barometer of growth statistics. The Book of Acts is not ashamed of counting converts (2:41; 4:4; 5:14; 6:1-7); nor should we be. In a city of 100,000 persons, whether 50,000 are reconciled to God or only 500 is not a matter of indifference to Him. People are never "mere statistics." They are persons created for an eternal destiny, men for whom Christ died. We need to know whether we are fulfilling Christ's purpose for them or not.

In the "Christian" West, writers in increasing numbers are calling for a de-emphasis upon individual evangelism and for greater involvement of the Church in political activity and dialogue with the power structures of society. Such writers emphasize the need for making the Church truly Christian.

We may grant a large degree of validity in such demands being directed at the Church in the United States. There over 60 per cent of the population are church members, and many children not counted as members attend church with their families. Forty-five percent of those affiliated with the Church attend services regularly.

Unfortunately, what may be right for the United States may not be at all relevant to the church situation in a country like Japan. Because Japanese Christians compose less than one per cent of the total population, the task of compelling importance is to make Christians of the people. Those who would direct the energies of the tiny Churches of Asia into social action are guilty of cultural overhang. Writing out of the luxury of a situation in which there are active churches on every hand, they chart a course of Christian action which could easily lead Churches in different circumstances into great peril.

Certainly Christians must be concerned with the impact of their faith upon the societies in which men live. The ministry of our Lord impresses upon us that His followers have a vocation to relieve the sufferings of men. Although that vocation cannot be fulfilled by evangelism alone, major changes in the non-Christian society can be built only upon the foundation of large numbers of remade individual lives. Evangelism is pivotal even for those concerned about social reform. We ought to be profoundly thankful for heroic individuals like Kagawa.[1] Others of his tribe, while not so renowned, are part of the evidence for the truth and relevance of the Faith. But, in general, the impact of Christians upon Japanese society is feeble. It will continue to be so until a substantial part of the populace becomes forthrightly Christian. Hara, writing as Secretary of the United Church of Christ in Japan Research Institute on the Mission of the Church, has stated:

> In contrast to conditions in Europe and America, where the churches have already built up a pattern in society, home, and individual, the churches in Asia and Africa exist as a very small minority and their influence upon society is almost non-existent. Thus the front line of our mission is making but very

slow progress, a problem which we feel very keenly in Japan (1964).

In non-Christian lands, to divert the Church's limited energies from evangelism may be to drive them to spiritual suicide. In a day when populations multiply at an awesome rate, stagnant Churches may be engulfed. Not only do they fail to carry out their divine mandate, but they diminish as a factor among the powers which shape the social structures of the nation.

This is not to assert that evangelism can be divorced from right living. Bishop Pickett (1960) has pointed out that large-scale conversions among rural people in India often resulted from the influence of the changed lives of Christians. But this is a somewhat different matter from the kind of participation by the Churches in political and social action which some writers are currently demanding. It is occasionally asserted that when the Church manifests in this way an active interest in social justice and other pressing problems of modern life, people will be drawn to Christ and the Church will grow. This is an attractive theory, but when men are asked to support it with specific case histories, they are unable to do so.

Not only is it difficult to find objective evidence for the contention that engagement in social action leads to church growth, but it is possible to point to sizeable Churches which are much concerned about social action but do not grow. The evidence from round the world suggests that growth is fostered or hindered by other factors. This writer does not believe that engagement in social action precludes growth, but that when growth does occur, it does so because other conditions have been fulfilled. The Churches which grow are those which intend to grow, which work hard for growth, which possess the spiritual enthusiasm and stamina necessary to achieve growth, and which utilize the right methods of obtaining growth.

We must succumb neither to the difficulties of evangelism nor to theological trends which would call us away from the task of reconciling men to God. The slow growth of the Church in Japan is due not only to the disinclination of the Japanese to become Christians, but to the cumbersome and faulty way in which the Church goes about its task. The same is true of many lands. A far greater harvest would be reaped if we adapted our organizations and methods to divine imperatives and worldly realities.

CHAPTER II

EVERY CHURCH A CHURCH PLANTER

> For not only has the word of the Lord sounded forth from you in Macedonia and Achaia, but your faith in God has gone forth everywhere, so that we need not say anything (I Thess. 1:8).

During the years 1945 to 1962, a remarkable case of expansion took place in Central Nigeria (Grimley and Robinson 1966:138-157). In 1945 a Church of the Brethren congregation established some years before in a village called Lassa, beside the Yedseram River, had eighty-eight members scattered across several villages. Under the blessing of God the Lassa congregation began to grow. In 1951 it was able to foster the birth of a new church in nearby Gulak, giving up thirty-five of its members in order to do so. This became a pattern.

The Gulak congregation founded a church in Mboro in 1958, signing over 102 of its members. Mboro subsequently started two additional congregations. In 1958 the Lassa Church began S. Margi, and three new congregations owe their origin to the latter church. Lassa also began Kwaka in 1958 (a new congregation has since been started by Kwaka), besides engaging in many other evangelistic and church-planting endeavors. The 88 members of 1945 had grown to 4,619 by 1963, with twice that many persons related to the churches (Grimley and Robinson 1966:138-157). In such ways is the will of Christ still being carried out in some areas of the world.

Christ commands that the nations be discipled, baptized, and taught His commandments. The Great Commission is thought by some to enjoin only proclamation of the Gospel. Our task is to witness, we are told, and whether or not men respond is not our concern. But such an interpretation is open to serious question. Our Lord has commanded us to baptize and to teach. People should be baptized only if they have been actually converted (not merely preached to), and they are taught only when believing men are associated with one another. The Church, the fellowship of God's people, therefore, is clearly implied in the Great Commission.

What is the loving purpose of God for one hundred million people in Japan? If we take the New Testament for our authority we must say that God desires that all men have an opportunity to hear the Gospel, and that He desires their salvation. When we reflect carefully upon the question of how Christ's redemption can come to the millions of any land, it becomes evident that this can happen only when churches in sufficient numbers are planted in every community. The New Testament makes clear the unvarying desire of God that all men find salvation and attain to an understanding of the truth, and this requires that vast numbers of new churches be planted everywhere.

Not that the mechanical multiplication of "churches" could fulfill God's purposes. Men are not robots to be seated in neat rows in prefabricated church structures! To "plant churches" must be understood to involve the transformation of many real persons as, in the midst of the suffering and perplexities and joys of real life, they move out of the realm of darkness into the light of the Son of God.

Two further considerations compel us to the conclusion that the multiplication of churches in large numbers is essential to the fulfilling of God's will for Japan or any other nation.

The first is that *only as the number of churches is multiplied does the Christian part of the overall population increase.* Statistics from all over the world support this statement. These are Latourette's figures for all Protestants in Japan (1944:390-399):

Year	Churches	Communicant Members
1882	93	4,987
1888	249	25,514
1913	877	89,347

It will be observed that the increase in the total number of members (still only a tiny percentage of the population) is related to a large increase in the number of churches.

The same principle may be seen at work in the postwar era. Figure One shows comparative growth rates for four groups of churches: United, Episcopal, Baptist, and Lutheran *(Kirisutokyō Nenkan* 1964:431). At present the United Church and the Episcopal Church are much larger than the other two, and attention should be called to the fact that, depending upon the definition of "members," some sources list United Church and Episcopal Church membership at considerably higher levels. Whichever set of figures is accepted, the argument is not affected. Note that the Baptists and the Lutherans show a continuing increase in number of congregations, and consequently in their total number of adherents. The result is that they constitute a steadily increasing percentage of the national population. Meanwhile, the two larger groups are in danger of becoming a steadily smaller percentage of the growing national population. The graphs suggest that their slow overall growth is related directly to the fact that they are planting few new congregations.

The lesson is clear. If Churches are to grow, they must multiply new congregations. Between 1953 and 1963, the several Baptist Churches in Japan increased their number of congregations from 59 to 177, or 300 per cent. Membership increased by 287 per cent to 13,022. Had the Episcopal Church planted new congregations at the same rate during that period, its 1963 membership figure probably would have been 53,000 instead of 31,000. Based upon the same formula, the United Church figure for 1963 would have been 195,000 instead of 103,000. The total Protestant figure would have been 366,000 instead of 251,000.[1]

That this principle is valid for other countries, and for Churches with widely varying experiences, is attested by the two sets of figures below.[2] The British Methodists have for many years labored among continual difficulties in Burma. Today an autonomous Burmese Methodist Church carries on despite many hardships. On the other hand, the Baptist Church in Brazil, an outgrowth of Southern Baptist missionary work, has enjoyed a remarkably fruitful ministry for many years.

Methodists in Burma

Year	Worship Centers	Adult Membership	Total Community
1947	30	1,360	2,256
1949	42	1,757	2,915
1951	63	2,271	4,222
1953	66	3,118	5,275
1955	108	4,371	8,084
1957	105	4,491	7,761
1963	105	5,345	9,654
1965	120	6,100	10,681

Baptists in Brazil

Year	Churches	Members
1882	2	50
1890	5	500
1900	30	2,000
1910	110	9,200
1920	210	19,200
1930	440	34,000
1940	740	59,000
1950	1,000	100,000

Note in both cases the close correlation at every point between the increase in total number of believers and the rise in the number of congregations. This is true despite the fact that these Churches differ greatly in size and rate of growth. The principle seems to operate even when the average size of the congregations varies somewhat from decade to decade.

A friendly and intelligent critic has suggested to the writer that the recent history of Roman Catholicism in Japan might well cast doubt on the assertion that the multiplication of new congregations is the secret of church growth. An examination of statistical totals of the Catholic Church,[3] however, seems to give further weight to the position herein taken.

Figure One

Growth in Number of Churches and Men

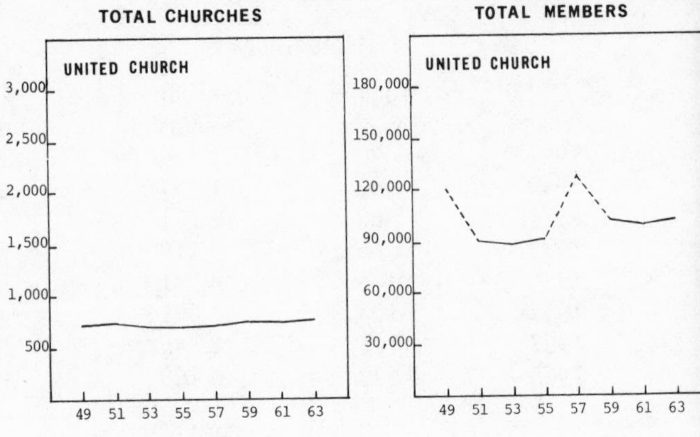

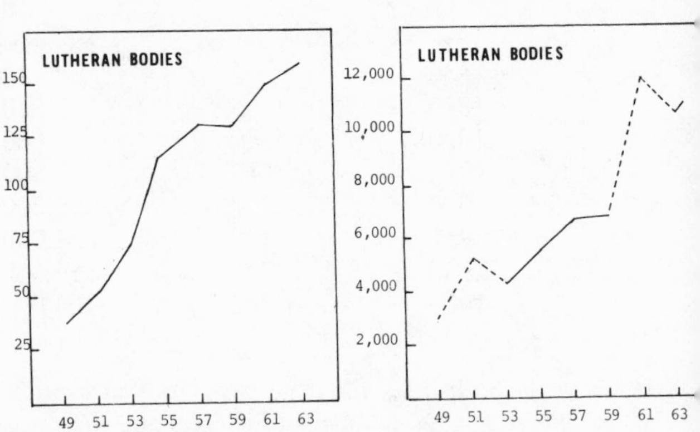

Graphs above reflect comparative percentage growth. That is, any increase of 15 percent (or any other given figure) in the number of churches or members will be reflected by the same angle of ascent in the line of growth in any of the above boxes.

ur Traditions in Japan, 1949-1963

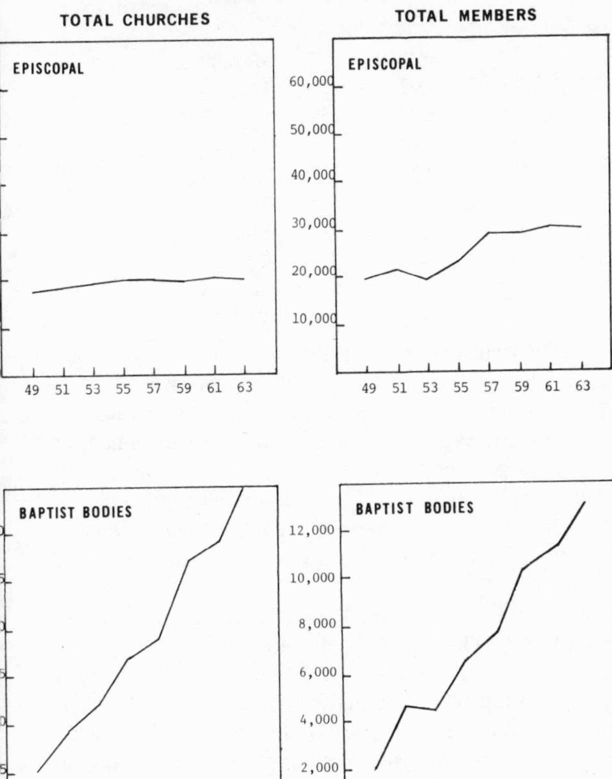

Graphs based upon statistics found in Kirisutokyō Nenkan (Christian Yearbook) 1964. Dotted lines indicate statistics which appear to be in error. The real degree of growth is exhibited by the solid lines. The statistics given by Kirisutokyō Nenkan for total attendance at Sunday services for the various Churches support the assertion that the solid lines above exhibit accurately the real degree of growth. Note that depending upon definitions of "members" some sources give considerably larger figures for the United Church and the Episcopal Church. The rate of growth of these two churches, however, is not greatly affected by this difference.

Year	Churches	Members
1950	497	141,286
1952	445	174,527
1954	650	218,457
1956	725	246,232
1958	811	261,454
1960	1,028	301,901
1962	1,044	323,599
1964	888	305,832
1966	993	333,265

Actually, a year-by-year analytical study of the statistics of each and every congregation, covering a period of one or two decades, would be very revealing in terms of showing the percentage of growth resulting from the establishment of new churches, and that resulting from the enlargement of older ones. It would not be easy to acquire the statistics for such a study, but a capable statistician in one of the larger Churches could make a most valuable contribution to church growth research by publishing the results of an analysis of this kind.

This writer does not assert that the enlargement of existing churches is unimportant. There is here no disposition to deny that building up older churches can lead to growth in a Church as a whole. But objective study of the actual growth and non-growth of Churches round the world seems clearly to indicate that enlargement of existing congregations is not the most important factor in the history of growing Churches. The multiplication of new congregations is the high road to large-scale growth in the number of people the Church of Christ can shepherd for her Lord.

The assertion that "a major secret of growth is the multiplication of new congregations" must not be interpreted naively. It is not contended here that the indiscriminate planting of new congregations will of itself result in the growth of a Church. There is need of much further research into the question of how the planting of new congregations leads to overall growth. It may be that answers to this question will vary from country to country, and from place to place within a country. Some statistics in Japan seem to indicate that a Church may find its long-range growth threatened if too many widely scattered congregations are planted too rapidly. Especially would this seem likely if expansion were based upon subsidies from a central headquarters or a foreign mission. But the facts are not yet sufficiently known to permit dogmatizing, and these necessary qualifications must not be allowed to obscure the importance of the multiplication of new congregations to a Church's growth.

The second reason many new churches must be planted is that a vast number of people must be served. How many people can be served by one church? In America over 70 per cent of the population, including children, is related to the Church and there is more than one church for each 1,000 persons. Although it is true that most churches in any country do not in actual fact serve as many as a thousand persons, let us suppose that in order to bring to all people the opportunity for salvation and meaningful church life, one church is needed for each 1,000 persons. What meaning does this have for Japan?

Yonago is a city of 100,000 in Tottori Prefecture. Following the above principle, if the blessings of Jesus Christ and His Church are to be brought to that city, 100 churches will need to be established there! There are now less than 15 Christian groups in the city, and over half of these are not able to serve as many as 75 persons, much less 1,000.

Another way of becoming aware of the need for multiplying churches is to consider the tremendous number of villages and small towns in the countries of Asia and Africa. In 1937, Kagawa estimated the number of villages in Japan at 12,000 (W. Paton 1939:Vol. 3, 196). Because of recent administrative changes, it is difficult to determine how many small, distinct communities there are today, but the number is not likely to have decreased.[4] A great many churches are required to minister to such large cities as Osaka and Nagoya. Add to this the countless villages and towns which need at least one church and sometimes more, and it becomes clear that only a grand-scale church-planting enterprise can fulfill the will of God for Japan.

The problem is further complicated by the fact that churches in Japan are almost always small. As long ago as 1938, the Rev. Zoji Goshi pointed out to the International Missionary Council conference at Madras that the average attendance at the largest Sunday morning service in Japan was only 289, and that it was difficult to attain an average attendance of 100 (1939:151).

Those familiar with the life of the Church in Japan today know that the situation has not changed. Even in such great cities as Tokyo and Osaka it is rare to find a church with an average attendance exceeding 200. An attendance of 100 is the mark of a fairly strong church. Away from the great cities the churches are much smaller. For example, in the part of the country with which this writer is most familiar, the best churches have perhaps 60 in attendance (with a very rare church reaching 100), and most churches have 35 or less at the main worship service.

This characteristic of Japanese Christianity is of long standing and it is true of every denomination. This need not dishearten us, but it does call for resolute thinking about strategy. To those who think to win Japan by the formation of large congregations we ask: Why advocate a policy which, regardless of denomination, the most able pastors and missionaries have been unable to make work anywhere in Japan during a full century of Protestant effort?

Surely no one would object if churches of four or five hundred members began to multiply. It may be that when one or two million Japanese have become Christians such churches will appear. Until then, if we are realists, we must plan on the winning of Japan by means of vastly multiplying the number of smaller churches.

If church growth and the carrying out of Christ's will in any land do, in fact, depend on great multiplication of churches, Christians must clarify their objectives and concentrate their energies on that which is central. Once leaders recognize this as a central goal of the body of Christ, they will begin to consider concrete measures by which this goal can be achieved and will then be ready to jettison the hindrances to the accomplishment of this objective.

THE NEED: MISSION-MINDED CHURCHES

Brazil is considered the most successful of Southern Baptist missions. By 1961, the Baptists numbered 186,595 members (Read 1965:192). Among the leaders of the large and vigorous Baptist Church in Brazil, none has stood higher than the Brazilian pastor, F. F. Soren (1869-1933). His influence was felt throughout his denomination as it grew from 1,932 members in 1900 when he began his ministry in Rio de Janeiro to 38,960 members at the time of his death in 1933 (Bratcher 1938:50-51).

He is perhaps best known for his leadership of the great First Baptist Church in Rio de Janeiro, which he pastored for thirty-two years. He instructed church members in evangelism, taught lay preachers how to deliver effective sermons, and gathered around him a group of loyal and able deacons who enthusiastically supported his leadership. His vigorous evangelistic ministry not only brought his own church from a membership of 178 in 1901 to 575 in 1933, but resulted in the planting of at least ten new congregations in the vicinity. Some of these congregations in turn started still others. The combined membership of these churches in 1933 was 1,315 (Bratcher 1938:50-57). Crabtree reports that the First Baptist Church led in the planting of fifteen churches in Rio de Janeiro and the surrounding countryside, and that some of these planted from one to five other churches (1953:190-191).

This kind of vision and spirit must become characteristic of churches, pastors, and missionaries everywhere in Japan. To every church and Christian a task has been given: the winning of Japan for Jesus Christ. As we have seen, this must be accomplished through the planting of thousands of new churches in communities all over the land.

The evangelization of Japan awaits the rise of missionary vision and passion in local churches. Every church needs to recognize its evangelistic responsibility for the people around it. Melvin Hodges, executive secretary for Latin America of the Assemblies of God Foreign Missions Department (one of the fastest growing missionary enterprises in the world today) believes that every church should consider itself responsible for all people in the area halfway to the next church in each direction. That responsibility, it should be noted, can never be fulfilled simply by converting a few individuals from nearby neighborhoods and persuading them to commute to "our church." Only by planting new churches where people live can the grace of God be brought to them.

Aside from certain heartening exceptions, this missionary spirit is lacking in most churches in Japan. Many churches do have an evangelistic vision. Christians in such congregations are concerned about leading friends and relatives to Christ and persuading them to join their church. This is good, but a missionary vision which looks beyond one's own church to the task of planting congregations in nearby communities and everywhere in the land is a vital necessity.

This lack may in considerable measure be traced to the stance taken by missionaries, past and present, though it would be unfair to place all the blame upon them. Missionaries have not sufficiently taught that the Great Commission of Matthew 28, which brought them to Japan, is also binding upon each Japanese Christian and church. Missionaries have unwittingly taught by their policies that pastoral work is the responsibility of the churches, and evangelism and church planting the work of the mission. It must be seen that the gift of faith given by God to an individual or to a church brings the recipient under the same Commission, the receiving of which is a mark of the people of God.

The great Indian leader, Bishop Azariah, argued that once a foreign mission has established work in a given area, that mission must not go on doing the work of evangelism while ignoring the existence of the infant churches it has founded. It must recognize a vocation to "perfect the saints unto the work of ministering." The neglect of this principle, Azariah held, has resulted in great harm to the evangelistic work of the Church of Christ. The churches in each place should be taught that they bear the responsibility of multiplying congregations and evangelizing the area (Paton 1939:Vol. 3, 41-46).[5]

Because existing churches in Japan seldom start new churches, the chief way congregations are multiplied in many communities is by the arrival of new denominations. In Yonago, for example, there are perhaps fourteen Christian groups. Each represents a different denominational background. (Even the two United Church congregations are from different backgrounds.) Most of these groups are new in the city, but some of the churches have been there for many decades; yet no denomination has established more than one congregation in this sizeable city.

One sometimes is given the impression that there are pastors and churches which would not welcome an attempt to plant a new church of their denomination in the same community lest it compete with their own. Happily, this is not true of all.

Wide-awake churches foster house meetings in various places, some of them quite distant from the sponsoring church. But even then believers and pastors do not as a rule seem to desire that these house meetings develop into independent churches. Offerings received at the house meetings are channeled into the parent church treasury, and converts are baptized at the parent church and received into its membership. This is quite proper in cases of people who live near the sponsoring church, but it is a hindrance to the spread of the Gospel in Japan that this practice is almost invariably followed even when converts live in places distant from the parent church—places which desperately need the presence of a church.

Japanese pastors have long contended, and rightly so, that foreign missionaries must not seek to control pastors and churches in Japan. Now pastors and churches need to perceive that they must not seek to control new groups which they form. Just as pastors and churches do not belong to foreign missionaries but to the Lord, so new, small congregations do not belong to pastors and parent churches, but to the Lord.

The importance of the economic strain felt by relatively small churches must be fully taken into account, however, when attempting to understand why pastors and even laymen find it difficult to encourage house meetings to develop into independent churches. How can a pastor expect converts he has baptized to contribute to an independent treasury, when this may mean that the man will have less money with which to feed his children or to send them to school?

The economic problem in a number of ways constitutes a roadblock of major proportions in the way of multiplying new churches. When a Japanese church considers planting a new congregation in its vicinity, it is immediately confronted by three problems: (1) the need of a pastor–it is difficult to find a suitable ordained pastor for a small new church; (2) the pastor's salary–it is hard to win enough converts in the early days of a new church to pay the pastor's salary; and (3) a church building–land prices and building costs in Japan are prohibitive. Facing such formidable obstacles as these, how can churches with modest financial resources be expected to found new congregations?

The following chapters investigate possible solutions to this threefold dilemma.

METHODS FOR STARTING NEW CHURCHES

The most common method of starting a new church in Japan, as in many other countries, is for a Church or Mission to send one or two professional clergymen to the locality and subsidize their activity. In areas where no churches exist, or where the existent churches are not missionary, this is doubtless one method which may be followed. But as a method it is clumsy, slow, and inordinately expensive. In addition, it seldom involves the laity, being almost wholly clergy-centered. This way of multiplying churches can never win Japan.

A great need exists for developing more effective methods of enabling local churches to start new congregations. Chapter fourteen sets forth a number of ways in which this can be done. The keen minds in Japanese Christianity can contribute to our knowledge and skills in this matter if the need is recognized. Proposals must be simple and practical, they must not require large sums of money, and they must involve the whole people of God, not just the clergy. The local churches must be involved not only in fund raising, but in all phases.

Pastors and church members must resolutely rid themselves of the grave misapprehension that the real responsibility for multiplying churches rests upon their officials in Tokyo or Osaka. Church headquarters may formulate programs for planting new congregations, but these programs should be designed to involve local churches. If denominational leaders attempt to evangelize Japan by gathering funds from the churches to employ missionaries to start new congregations in various parts of Japan under their direction, they will be making the same mistake as the Missions against which Bishop Azariah protested. Under the present circumstances, however, in which almost the only church growth which takes place occurs within the several denominations, it is often necessary for denominations to send missionaries, whether indigenous or foreign, to areas in which they do not as yet have churches. We must recognize this necessity, but it must not be allowed to hide from us the still greater importance of establishing churches which can and do start other churches. Denominational and regional leaders must find ways in which to inspire and assist local churches to carry out their missionary task.

CHAPTER III

A PAID PASTOR IN EVERY CHURCH?

> "Pastor, when I wrote to you I asked you to make me five prayer-fellows here in Sawadani, and you have made twenty-seven. What can I do now? I cannot preach, and in any case it is hardly a woman's work; and yet we cannot leave these souls alone, we must have meetings for them" (Gosden 1957:80).

In these words Sumi San, in the book, *Upon This Rock,* expressed her astonishment and dismay to the evangelist she had invited to her remote village in Okayama Prefecture. The book records the amazing story of how a church, through this humble midwife, came into being in a Japanese village, reputed to be one of the most difficult social units in Japan in which to establish a church. Fortunately, the Sawadani Christians had a wise advisor in Pastor Tatsumi Hashimoto, who told them they could carry on with leadership from among themselves, with occasional visits from regular clergymen. The church prospered for some time in this way.

PASTORS AND CHURCHES IN JAPAN

It is not surprising that Sumi San and the new converts in Sawadani found it hard to imagine how they could carry on without a salaried pastor, or that they felt they could not be a real church until they secured such a pastor. It is regarded as axiomatic by the vast majority of Christians in Japan, both laity and clergy, both Japanese and missionary, that any real church must have a salaried pastor. Listening to the conversation of Japanese Christians, one realizes that this "axiom" is not even questioned: As a school has teachers, as a hospital has doctors, so a church has a paid pastor.

Furthermore, the pastor in any given church serves only that one church. The kind of church life of which we hear in Africa or India, in which one pastor may be in charge of ten to fifty churches, is utterly unknown in Japan. There are rare cases where a pastor is in charge of two congregations, but usually this is regarded as an unsatisfactory situation which must be tolerated only until each church can have its own salaried pastor. Moreover, another proposition that is not even argued is that only clergymen who have studied at theological school and are, or hope to be, salaried should be ordained.

The ratios of clergy to worship centers on pages 36 and 37 show the remarkable difference between Japan and other countries in this respect. It is likely that Japan has a higher ratio of clergy to churches than any other country in the world.

Nor is this a new development. The pattern has persisted from the very beginning of Protestant Christianity in Japan. In 1882, Cary reported that there were 93 organized Protestant churches in Japan. As against this, there were 49 ordained preachers, 100 assistant preachers and catechists, 37 Bible women, and 145 missionaries (1909:163). In 1900, the number of organized churches was 416. Ordained ministers numbered 306, unordained ministers and helpers 518, Bible women 289, and missionaries 502 (Cary 1909:163, 296).

Of course, the assumption that any real church will have a salaried pastor is not peculiar to Japan. It is the unexamined assumption of many Protestant denominations round the world. At Jerusalem, in 1928, the proposed constitution of The United Church of Christ in the Philippines was announced. One section read:

> The Policy of the Church shall be that every pastoral charge shall have, as far as possible, a pastorate without interruption, and that every effective minister shall have a pastoral charge (International Missionary Council 1928:269).

In Japan today, the feeling that every church must have a paid pastor makes it difficult for a local church to plant new churches in its vicinity. It also makes it hard to plan for the planting of churches in rural districts, where only small groups of believers can be won. Who will pay the pastors?

We must ask: *Is it true that there must be one paid pastor for each church?* Again, *Is it true that all pastors must be salaried?*

THE NEW TESTAMENT CHURCH

The question of how patterns of leadership developed in the New Testament Church is discussed in greater detail in chapter nine, but here we must briefly anticipate our position.

In the New Testament, the leadership patterns of the Church were in the formative stage and were still quite flexible. The practice of one paid clergyman heading each church was not mentioned by Paul and his contemporaries. We know that some congregations met in the homes of believers in various cities. From time to time these churches were visited by traveling apostles, evangelists, prophets, and teachers. In at least some cases, several elders were appointed from among the believers to serve as leaders in local churches. Regular salaries are not mentioned in this period of the Christian Church, although leaders did from time to time receive support from believers. It is well known that Paul made tents for a living and did not regularly accept remuneration from the churches. It is not unlikely that in this Paul drew his example from the Jewish rabbis. Rabbi Hillel, who founded a well-known rabbinic school, worked at felling trees. The occupations of other rabbis are also known, though it seems that still others were exclusively engaged in the study of the law (Vischer 1965:39).

It is remarkable that while in modern Churches problems of finance occupy a prominent position in any discussion of evangelistic outreach and the multiplying of new congregations, the New Testament shows little concern for such matters.

THE POST-APOSTOLIC CHURCH

Some scholars insist that it was hundreds of years after the apostles before it became a regular practice for clergymen to receive their full support. Recent research has considerably clarified the patterns which prevailed during the first few centuries of the Church's existence (Vischer 1965:36-54; Ream 1956:420-428).

Socrates tells of Spyridon, a bishop in Cyprus, who worked at tending sheep. According to Sozomen, Zeno of Gaza was a linen weaver, although he had responsibility for a large and wealthy church. William Ramsay wrote:

> It is certain that priests even late in the fourth century ordinarily lived by practicing some trade, as Basil, *Ep.* 198,

Figure Two

Ratio of Clergy to Worship Centers

Presbyterian Church (Korea)
1956
2,048 Churches
941 Ordained Clergy

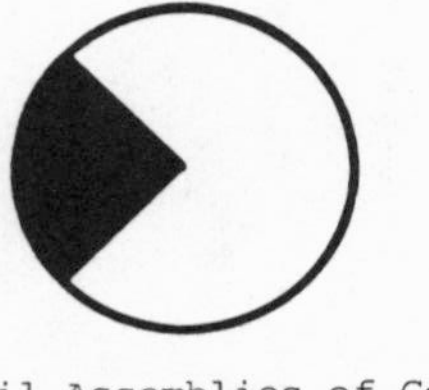

Brazil Assemblies of God
1955
1,200 Organized Churches
3,000 Preaching Points
1,064 Pastors

Christian and
Missionary Alliance (P.I.)
1962
618 Worship Centers
81 Ordained Clergy

Methodists in
Great Britain
1961
13,250 Worship Centers
4,371 Ordained Clergy

Protestant Episcopal
Church (U. S.)
1951
7,116 Churches
6,473 Ordained Clergy

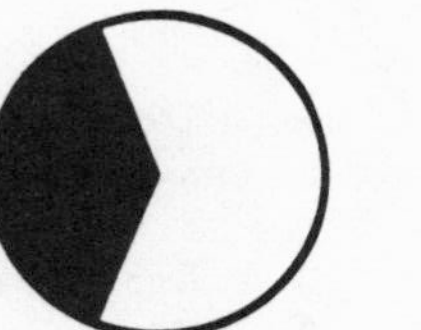

All Philippine Protestants
1938
1,284 Churches
493 Ministers

All Japan Protestants
1882
93 Organized Churches
49 Ordained Clergy
100 Assistant Preachers

All Japan Protestants
1900
416 Organized Churches
306 Ordained Ministers
518 Unordained Ministers

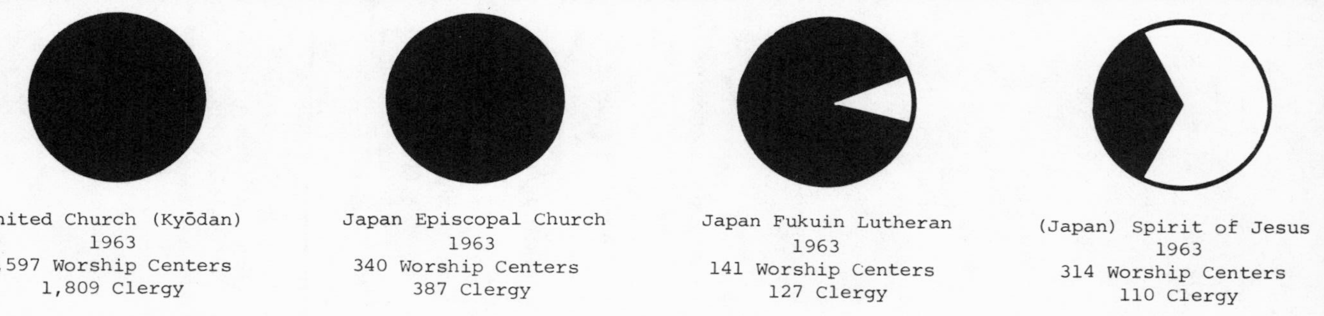

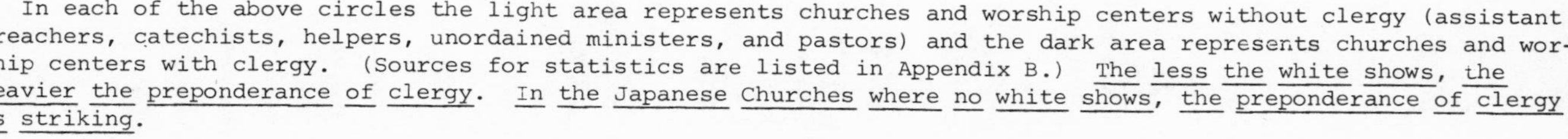

United Church (Kyōdan)
1963
1,597 Worship Centers
1,809 Clergy

Japan Episcopal Church
1963
340 Worship Centers
387 Clergy

Japan Fukuin Lutheran
1963
141 Worship Centers
127 Clergy

(Japan) Spirit of Jesus
1963
314 Worship Centers
110 Clergy

In each of the above circles the light area represents churches and worship centers without clergy (assistant preachers, catechists, helpers, unordained ministers, and pastors) and the dark area represents churches and worship centers with clergy. (Sources for statistics are listed in Appendix B.) The less the white shows, the heavier the preponderance of clergy. In the Japanese Churches where no white shows, the preponderance of clergy is striking.

says, "the majority of them ply sedentary crafts, whereby they get their daily bread" (Ramsay 1908:389).

In the fourth century, Chrysostom described the life of the rural bishops of Antioch:

> These men you may see sometimes yoking the oxen and driving the plough, and again ascending the pulpit and cultivating the souls under their care; now uprooting the thorns from the earth with a hook, and now purging out the sins of the soul by the word (Ream 1956:424).

The *Apostolic Constitutions,* a Church order which is thought to have been prepared in Constantinople or Syria about A.D. 380, directed the younger clergy:

> You shall provide at all times for yourselves and for the needy, so that the Church of God may not be encumbered (Vischer 1965:45).

Canon 19 of the Council of Elvira, *circa* A.D. 300, forbade bishops, presbyters, and deacons to leave their areas of residence for purposes of trade, but permitted trading itself:

> In order to secure their livelihood let them send a son or a free man . . . or whom they will, and if they want to trade, let them trade inside the province (Ream 1956:422).

In the fourth century, debate did not center upon whether clergymen should earn their own living or not, for many were doing so, but rather upon what sort of occupations were suitable for them. It was urged that they be freed as much as possible from the necessity of doing secular work, and that work not be permitted to take a clergyman away from his diocese. It was thought that trading was not a proper occupation for members of the clergy (Vischer 1965:50).

It was only gradually that clergymen began to receive their full support. It came to be more and more important that they be able to give their full time to pastoral work, with their needs met by the congregation. The bishops were the first to be freed from the necessity of employment, and later the presbyters and deacons (Vischer 1965:40-71).

Even in our own day these ancient patterns are practiced by the Orthodox Church in rural Greece. Here it is common for a farmer, respected by his neighbors and nominated by the church members because of his devotion, to become a priest. A man who has had some experience serving in various ways in the church is given a few weeks training at a monastery, after which he is ordained by the bishop. He continues to serve in his own village church, but now as a priest. The same practice is common in Balkan countries, among ancient Churches of Egypt, Ethiopia, and South India (Vischer 1965:84-85).

It is not my purpose here to argue that these patterns invariably work for the health of the Church, but only to survey what has been the practice of Christians in history. It is abundantly clear that the pattern of each church having its own paid pastor is required neither by the New Testament nor by the history of the Christian Church. It is true that salaried clergy have an indispensable role to play in our day. When the needs of the churches in any country or area require the services of professional clergy, there can be no convincing objection to their employment. On the other hand, when the expansion of the Church is hindered by the attempt to place a salaried clergyman in every church, it must be asserted that there is nothing in Christianity which requires such a practice.

THE DILEMMA: HOW TO PROVIDE PASTORAL CARE

Presentations of missionary work frequently leave the impression that the evangelism which secures the initial decision to follow Christ is the main business of mission. Such evangelistic effort, however, always requires the follow-up of pastoral work among the converts. People who have left their old religions and sins to follow Christ become discouraged and fall away if they are not shepherded.

The need for pastors is indisputable. We do not question that every church needs pastoral care, or that it needs someone to administer the sacraments. The real question is: Who may properly be considered a "pastor," and who may properly administer the sacraments?

The greatest problem in the world-wide missionary work of the Church may well be the problem of how to provide pastoral care for the millions. The immensity of the problem becomes apparent when we consider the vast populations which might be won for Christ if they could be effectively shepherded.

All too often this fact is hidden from Protestants because they think in terms of how to provide pastors for their own members only. But if Jesus Christ is the image of the invisible God, then what shall we make of the record,

> As he landed he saw a great throng, and he had compassion on them, because they were like sheep without a shepherd; and he began to teach them many things (Mark 6:34)?

Should we not think of God as looking with compassion upon the confused and drifting multitudes in every land and earnestly desiring that they be gathered as a flock and shepherded? We must learn to think in terms of whole nations and the spiritual needs of whole populations.

In some places in the world, great people movements occur in which thousands or even tens of thousands, over a period of years, declare themselves ready to become Christians. In such a situation, the problem soon becomes one of how to teach and shepherd such great numbers of responsive people.

Surveying the problems encountered in situations of rapid growth among receptive peoples, some Roman Catholic theologians speak of the "law of strangulation." When such large numbers are baptized that one priest must have the care of thousands of believers, many of whom he can see only occasionally, genuine growth tends to be stunted because meaningful pastoral care can no longer be provided.

Augustin Tellkamp, a German theologian, wrote in 1950 about this problem. He proposed the increasing of the number of indigenous priests, and a world-wide strategy of transferring priests to the places of most acute need. Seven years afterwards, the papal encyclical *Donum Fidei* gave sanction and authority to these proposals. That these proposals, as valid as they may seem, are not sufficient to the need is evidenced by the recent Vatican Council decision to revive the permanent diaconate. It is doubtful whether even this expedient will shore up the sorely overtaxed system of depending upon professional clergy only for pastoral care.

The Roman Catholic Church, since it thinks in terms of whole nations, sometimes appreciates the immensity of the problems that face the Church more fully than do Protestants. A writer in a Catholic periodical points out that 85 per cent of the thirty million people in the Philippines are Catholic. The separation of Church and State in that country has created enormous problems for the Catholic Church. The new constitution forbids the teaching of

Catholicism in the public schools. This was formerly the way in which many received religious instruction. There is such a critical shortage of priests that the ratio of priests is only one to 15,000 Catholics in the land. Of elementary school children, only 12 per cent today receive any religious instruction. The remaining 88 per cent live in *barrios* or towns where no priests or churches are found. The result is the possibility of a "massive de-Christianization" (Pezzota 1965:88-92).

Roman Catholicism attempts to take into its ranks all who will enter, while adhering tenaciously to its system of providing pastoral care exclusively through a professional clergy. As a result, its "Christians" are sometimes, as in parts of Latin America, hardly a step away from paganism.

Most Protestant Churches, too, find themselves committed to a system of pastoral care through salaried clergy, which greatly restricts what they can do. To bring people to a more biblical level of spiritual experience requires so much of the limited number of clergy the Churches can train and finance that large portions of the population must be neglected, even though they may be highly receptive to the Christian message. Neither approach can be regarded as satisfactory.

Protestants in Africa and Asia are being forced by circumstances to face up to this dilemma. In some places large numbers of converts crowd into the churches. In East Africa, Lutheran pastors must serve an average of eight churches each, while Presbyterian and Methodist pastors are in charge of 15 or 20 churches each. The average Anglican priest in Kenya and Central Tanganyika has 20 to 25 churches under his care.

In India, missionaries have attempted, sometimes with the help of catechists, to act as pastors for scores of towns. Converts are baptized, but frequent reversions take place because subsequent pastoral care cannot be given. Paton reports that in China, in the Anglican diocese he knew, there were only 35 clergy (not all of whom were engaged in parish work) to move among 250 congregations. The result was that people ready for confirmation waited in vain to be confirmed, and Christians who desired the privilege of the Eucharist could not receive it for lack of priests (1953:48).

The debate about pastoral care in the Anglican communion tends to focus on the problem of the Eucharist because church life is built around this celebration. Paton remarks about the anomaly of a Church which holds a high doctrine of the ministry and frequently observes the sacraments but which, because missionaries "exported to China our own torn and mutilated Western post-medieval Christian tradition," could not make the sacraments available to the people. It is not surprising, he concludes, that Christians sometimes moved into nearby Plymouth Brethren congregations, which enjoyed a warm spiritual fellowship and a breaking of bread every week.

Stephen Neill holds that in many Indian villages there is need for a worship center in almost every street. In these places the believers should have the privilege of the sacraments, but overworked ministers, responsible for fifteen or twenty thousand souls, cannot provide them. He thinks each such little group should have its own lay ministers, whose livelihood is earned in ordinary occupations, but who have been ordained for the administration of the Lord's Supper to the people. He believes this would be nearer the primitive Church as it is reflected in the New Testament and other Christian writings of that age (1957:66).

The difficulty of insufficient clergymen multiplies because of the increasing occupational competition from industry and government service. The situation in a country like Africa grows steadily more precarious and that, alas, in a day when great numbers of people can be won to Christian faith. Bishop Lesslie Newbigin, until recently Director of the Division of World Mission and Evangelism of the W.C.C., has declared: "The non-Roman churches of Africa are perilously near the point of no return in the matter of the pastoral ministry."

The pattern of church life imported into these lands from the West, with a salaried pastor in each church, simply does not cope with the situation the Church often faces in the world today. In some places temporary alternatives are fast becoming outmoded. Bishop Neill reports that in Tinnevelly, India, where he spent many years as a missionary, 50,000 pupils were studying in some 700 village schools. More than half the pupils were non-Christians. Many of these schools were mission sponsored, with a Christian teacher. But now the government is increasingly taking over these schools, and it is clear that this way of meeting the spiritual needs of great numbers of people cannot long survive (1957:62-63). What shall take its place?

No relief appears on the horizon. If the Churches find themselves unable to keep pace with the hectic demands of today, what will happen in the decades that lie ahead? Whereas it formerly took hundreds of years for the world population to double, at the present rate of increase it will take only thirty-five years. In thirty-five years the population of India may be one billion! In Africa, Asia, and Latin America, an already severely taxed Church will be faced with staggering new population increases. How are world missions to avoid being inundated by this situation? Is there any solution short of breaking new ground in the matter of providing pastoral care?

The use of catechists is one maneuver which has been widely attempted. Alexander de Rhodes, a Catholic missionary who had intended to go to Japan, went instead to Viet Nam in the seventeenth century. He acquired an excellent knowledge of the language and won many converts. He encountered increasing persecution and several times had to leave the country; finally, he was permanently banished. Before he left he instituted the policy of organizing a body of celibate teachers called "catechists." They were trained, though not so thoroughly as priests. They were not ordained. These men were greatly used, so that though there were only two priests in the country after de Rhodes' departure, the work continued to grow. By 1658, no less than 300,000 converts are supposed to have been won. Neill considers this an exaggeration, but holds that it was certainly a large number (1964:195-196).

Since that day, the catechist has played a most important role in missionary work. Sometimes these workers have been called by other names such as lay-readers, or church agents. Often a large number of catechists worked under the direction of one missionary or indigenous pastor. Catechists frequently outnumbered the ordained clergy. In one section of the Gold Coast (now Ghana) in Africa, a large Church with a Christian community of 50,000 had come into being by 1949. The missionary in charge had a team of three ordained pastors and 160 catechists (Sundkler 1960:156-157).

Sundkler estimates that in 1938, among Protestants, there must have been nearly 40,000 catechists in Africa south of the Sahara. Those who understand the modern missionary enterprise realize that in most parts of the world the catechist has been in the front lines of the battle for the souls of men. In countless villages and towns, such instruction and church life as millions of Christians have had, has been possible only because of the catechist.

Yet there have been many and increasing problems. Catechists have usually been unordained and unable to administer the sacraments. When paid with foreign money, problems of professionalism and struggles over control have frequently arisen.

Salaries have often been insufficient, with resultant discontent. It has not always been clear whether catechists were clergymen (they were not ordained) or laymen (they acted like full-time ministers). The decreasing subsidies from supporting Churches in the West in more recent times have meant an increasing burden for the indigenous church. In some countries catechists may be enlisted only with difficulty because of the small stipend.

For these and other reasons, the use of catechists is being questioned in many quarters. Sundkler reports that except for some denominations in southern sections of Africa, the tendency among Protestants in most of Africa south of the Sahara is to dispense gradually with the catechists. Efforts are being made to replace them with teams of laymen working in combination with ordained ministers (1960:39, 65, 156-157).

The problems related to ministering to vast numbers of people are staggering indeed. Increasingly they are compelling missionary leaders to re-examine prevailing practices and to seek new solutions.

Sidney Clark was a British businessman who retired early in life to give himself to the study of world-wide missions. He was a great believer in constructive surveying of the work yet to be done. In the two decades before World War II, he devoted careful study to a large area of North China, and became convinced that ordinary methods could never suffice for the need. The immense population, scattered in countless villages, deeply impressed upon him the fact that the Western pattern of a highly trained and salaried clergy could never enable the Church to fulfill its mission there. Only as multitudes of humble laymen were set to providing pastoral care for the churches could there be hope of adequately serving the people. He wrote, "The China Survey enables us mathematically to prove that unless such men, during the next 25 years, do the work, in a large measure it must remain undone" (1928:26).

By the time of the Madras Conference in 1938 there had been a definite shift from assumptions hardly questioned at Jerusalem a decade earlier. Voices were heard insisting that it is entirely unrealistic for rural pastors in the Orient to be assigned one church each. J. Merle Davis had, by this time, made several surveys of the economic problems of the indigenous church. Only when pastors serve circuits–large circuits–and are assisted by lay preachers, Davis insisted, can the work of the church possibly be financed and evangelism extended to unreached parts. Another statement asserts that the indigenous churches are quite unable to bear the financial burden the Western pattern of the ministry entails. In some places, he held, clergymen who earn part of their own living provide a partial answer. However, under such circumstances the minister cannot do all he is asked to do. A better solution is for one well-qualified minister to supervise a number of churches, assisted by lay helpers.

David Paton calls attention to the increasing number of voices within the Church of England who ask whether the ever more difficult problem of securing enough clergy of sufficient quality is not a sign that God is leading the Church to adopt different patterns. Ought not the norm, he asks, be to organize teams of voluntary clergy, working in concert with their fellow believers and assisted by a smaller group of highly trained clergymen (D. Paton 1965:14)?

Stephen Neill makes an urgent call for flexibility in concepts of the clergy. He feels that the pattern of the salaried ordained minister or catechist in each church must remain the norm, as no adequate alternative has been suggested. But this system, he concedes, has broken down under the strains of our time. We must be prepared to modify our practices in order to meet the needs of Church and people.

Lesslie Newbigin, on the other hand, feels that the situation into which the Church has been thrust demands a fresh examination of the Word of God. The biblical doctrine that the Church is always a missionary community may well lead us to the conclusion that in some circumstances the essential ministry is nonprofessional and the professional ministry the supplementary one.

In the years since World War II these issues have been discussed with increasing intensity. The Willingen Conference in 1952 asked that these questions be made the object of research. Five years later the assembly at Ghana repeated the demand. In 1962 a small paper entitled *A Tent-Making Ministry* grew out of the work of the Division of World Mission and Evangelism of the W.C.C. Other publications have followed, and further studies are planned.

NEED FOR PROFESSIONAL CLERGY

It is not my purpose to argue that we should dispense with the professional clergy. The writer himself is part of the salaried clergy and carries on his work in good conscience. Not the use of salaried clergy, but its abuse, is what we must deplore: the limiting of pastoral care and ministerial service to professionals.

There are several reasons why professional clergymen are needed. If unpaid men from small congregations are assigned responsibility for the pastoral care of the congregation, they eventually come to feel need of the help and instruction of trained professional clergy. Roland Allen made the interesting observation that some years ago in India traditional village leaders, called *chaudri,* were entrusted with spiritual responsibilities in the churches. For a time they were paid, but payment was discontinued when experience showed that salary tended to create a professional class. Subsequently, the *chaudri* serving in this way increased to thousands. These men went at the work in a way different from regular clergy and grew very close to the people. When real responsibility was given them, they welcomed the assistance of the paid clergy in a new way.

A professional clergy is needed to help the churches keep abreast of a fast-changing society. Sundkler asks whether the Protestant Churches will be able to keep pace with the problems in Africa rising out of rapid urbanization. The situation in Japan also threatens to get out of hand. The Church needs specialists assigned to research such matters who are at the same time in touch with the people in the churches.

The issues of pastoral care and the defense and proclamation of the faith are not simple. The Church needs not only academic theologians but some leaders who are free to move around in a way which people engaged in ordinary employment cannot do.

RELEVANCE FOR JAPAN

In 1904, the Church of Japan (Presbyterian) Synod wrestled with the problems of self-support. Part of the difficulty lay between the Church and the cooperating missions on the question of control. A proposal to dissolve local churches which could not become self-supporting in two years was defeated by only two votes. The following year action was taken to disallow groups which could not be financially independent to be organized as churches. Such groups were to be placed under the direct control of the presbytery (Cary 1909:334).

Today, as at the beginning of the century, a group of believers can be gathered in most communities in Japan. But it is difficult to gather enough believers to provide sufficient funds for the regular support of a pastor and his family, plus the expenses of a church building and other costs of church life.

As a result, evangelism and church multiplication in Japan today are weighed down and hedged in by the tyranny of money. Mindful of the problem of providing pastoral care, church planters avoid communities in which a reasonably large number of converts cannot be expected, even where small groups certainly could be gathered.

These problems are not limited to Japan. The evils which result from imposing Western patterns of salaried clergy are felt in many lands. In many instances Churches of the West have been able to maintain a salaried clergy in each congregation only because the livelihood of the clergy has derived from the government. In America, the great wealth of the nation puts enough extra money in the pockets of Christians that even small churches usually can afford to pay their pastors. But in most countries of Africa and Asia, neither of these conditions applies.

In India, because the clerical patterns of the wealthy Churches of the West were imported, a pastor may have to oversee twenty or thirty scattered villages. It requires many groups of believers to maintain his salary. Because the regular clergy are too few and the catechists not ordained, congregations are deprived of the sacraments.

In Japan, the insistence upon a paid, trained clergy creates an even more serious problem. The people not only are deprived of the sacraments, they are deprived of the Gospel itself. We insure that believers may have pastoral care and may receive the sacraments at the high cost of limiting the number of converts in countless communities in every part of the land. The necessity of limiting evangelism to localities from which a goodly number of converts can be expected means that thousands of communities never receive the Gospel of Christ at all.

The fast-growing and militant Buddhist sect, Sōka Gakkai, vigorously announces its intention to win Japan, but one seldom hears Christians talking in this fashion; they seem to have no such plan. Perhaps they are not convinced that it can ever be done. Is not this the consequence of being limited to a system—the *one-paid-pastor-per-church system*—which can never suffice to plant Christian churches in every village and neighborhood of the land?

Masahisa Uemura (1858-1925) was one of the great Christian leaders of Japan. He believed strongly that missionaries from abroad could never carry out the evangelization of Japan, that this must be done by Japanese. He insisted upon administrative control of the Church by the Japanese themselves. In these things he was surely correct. But today we must add the further insight that Japan can never be won by professional clergy, Japanese or foreign. Only the entire body of Christ, most of whom are not clergymen, can do that.

CHAPTER IV

A FLEXIBLE AND MOBILE MINISTRY

If the *one-paid-pastor-per-church* system is not required by Christian doctrine, and if it limits the spread of the Church everywhere in Japan, as well as in many other lands, what must we do? What other ways are there of providing pastoral care, the blessings of the sacraments, and warm Christian fellowship? In this chapter we examine briefly case studies from several countries in which various patterns of church leadership have been utilized in ministering effectively to large numbers of converts. Although it is unlikely that any of these patterns could be used in other countries without modification to prevailing conditions, valuable insights may be gained from this kind of study.

THE METHODISTS IN ENGLAND

Methodists have always stressed the leadership potential of laymen. From the time of Wesley, members have been gathered into small groups called classes, each with a class leader, and congregations have often been ministered to by unordained lay preachers. Methodist lay preachers have been, and still are, much more numerous than the regular clergy. For example, in 1860 the Primitive Methodist Church in England (which in 1932 became part of a reunited Methodist Church) reported 675 ministers, 11,384 local preachers, and 132,114 members (Norwood 1966:301-307).

A charming little book about the life of the Methodist Church in England today is John Lawson's *Green and Pleasant Land.* For much of the following information I am indebted to Lawson, who as a Methodist minister has spent most of his life in rural circuits. The book reflects the love for his work of a thoughtful clergyman who knows his Church, its successes, and its failures.

In the rural sections of England, especially, the Methodist system continues to prove its effectiveness. Perhaps 90 per cent of the Free Churches in English villages are Methodist. Though other independent churches (usually Baptist or Congregational) are frequently strong in the towns, the two churches most likely to be found in the villages are the Anglican parish church and the Methodist chapel. Other independent churches have not been able to find a way to survive there in these days of religious decline in England. The clergy of the Anglican Church can still be maintained in rural places because of government support and various funds surviving from former days. We may surmise that since 60 per cent of all Methodist pulpits are filled by lay preachers each Sunday morning, it is the lay preacher that makes rural Methodist church life economically possible.

These congregations are grouped into circuits. Though some circuits are composed of but one church, a rural circuit will usually contain from ten to fifty congregations, extending as far as twelve miles from its center. Circuits appoint their ministers (subject to the approval of the Conference); they are responsible for recruiting and overseeing the work of lay preachers, and have numerous other responsibilities as well. Usually a circuit is located around a country town and is served by two to six ministers who receive their stipends from circuit funds.

Circuits are usually worked by "sections," for which one minister is responsible. A minister will have charge of five to twelve congregations. He usually preaches three times on Sunday and conducts weeknight meetings which are usually, but not always, within his section. All other services are led by lay preachers who preach successively in different places within the circuit according to a "circuit plan" drawn up by the ministers. Ideally a lay preacher can carry out his assignments if he prepares one or two sermons each quarter.

A minister may visit a congregation on three to six Sundays in a quarter, at which time he often administers the sacraments. He may also be in the village one night in three weeks for visitation and an evening meeting. Stronger village congregations may have from 25 to

40 in attendance, though there are many villages where as few as three or four persons gather.

Lay preachers, often assisted by the nearest minister, undergo a course of study in the Bible, Christian doctrine, and public speaking. In a circuit visited by this writer in 1966, training classes were taught by a science lecturer of a nearby university, himself a lay preacher. Candidates must pass qualifying examinations, and are then accredited as lay preachers.

These men and women often develop into effective speakers, although they usually present a different kind of sermon from that of the minister. Attendance in the villages normally is as good at services led by lay preachers as at those led by ministers. The recruitment of effective lay preachers is a key matter and determines to a great extent the health of the circuit.

One interesting feature of the system is the "circuit chapel." Their status is unofficial, but nevertheless real. This larger church is located in towns, one or two in a circuit, and is often regarded as a sort of mother church. Villagers enjoy an occasional rally with a large audience in this more spacious building, and an opportunity to preach in this dignified place is a coveted privilege for lay preachers. The village congregations look to this church to help them find circuit ministers, to provide a number of the lay preachers, and to underwrite a good part of the budget. Thus, although the prestige privileges of these larger churches are high, they must bear a rather heavy burden in sharing their personnel and financial resources.

One of the strengths of the Methodist churches and some independent churches has been the large degree of lay participation. Lawson believes that one main reason their congregations often contain a somewhat higher proportion of men is the satisfaction of having an office to fulfill.

These are not easy days for Christians in England, and it would be inaccurate to assert that British Methodism is not wrestling with formidable problems. But these are common to all denominations, and the high degree of lay participation in church life is no small help to Methodism as it seeks to cope with the difficulties. Recent statistics list 3,408 clergymen, over a thousand "supernumeraries" (retired ministers), and 22,000 lay preachers as serving 10,942 churches. (See Appendix B.)

METHODISTS AND BAPTISTS IN THE UNITED STATES[1]

During the nineteenth century, the Methodists and Baptists

forged far ahead of all other Protestant groups in the United States in size, despite the fact that at the beginning of the century they were a minor part of the religious landscape. They continue to be by far the largest Protestant bodies in that country today. What are the reasons for this great growth?

The first humble Methodist preachers immigrated to America shortly before the Revolutionary War. Wesley had not originally thought of America as an area for Methodist effort, but in answer to appeals for help, eight missionaries were sent between 1771 and 1774. Of these, all but Asbury had returned to England by 1778.

The first Methodist conference was convened in 1773 and ten circuits were set up from New York to Virginia, with a minister in charge of each. Clearly the Methodists intended to use in America the system which had served them so well in England. It proved wonderfully adaptable to the different circumstances of the new country.

In any community in which there were a few believers, a class would be organized, with a class leader having spiritual responsibility for members of the class. A class normally had about twelve members and met once a week. Ranking above class leaders were the exhorters and next the local preachers. (The terms "lay preachers" and "local preachers" are synonymous.) Their work was supervised by the circuit minister and the quarterly meeting. Licenses of local preachers were renewed annually. After 1789 they could be ordained as deacons. Care was taken to insure that only worthwhile candidates were thus ordained.

From the first, Methodist growth was rapid. By 1785, when the American Methodist Episcopal Church was formally organized, members numbered 14,988, with 83 ministers, and the circuits had multiplied to 43. Methodism had not yet penetrated north of Long Island Sound, but within six years all settled parts of the new nation east of the Alleghenies had been covered by Methodist circuits. The burning zeal and constant itineration of circuit riders carried the Methodist message everywhere.

As the population moved westward on the frontier, the Methodists went with them. Two circuits were forming in Tennessee by 1782, and in 1784 a circuit appeared in Pennsylvania. In 1786 these three circuits reported 1,210 members. By 1800 at least fourteen circuits had been inaugurated west of the Alleghenies. The Indiana Territory was reached in 1805. By that time an Ohio district had been organized, and it contained five circuits, two of which extended some distance into what is now part of West Virginia and Kentucky. In the last decade of the eighteenth century, Methodism penetrated New England, Mississippi, and Louisiana. In 1811 the two westernmost circuits were in Illinois and Missouri and reported a total of nearly 700 members.

In 1800 Methodists west of the Alleghenies numbered 2,622 whites and 179 colored. By 1811 there were 29,093 white members and 1,648 colored. The number of circuits had increased from nine to 69 and the ministers from 14 to 100.

The momentum of growth did not diminish with the passage of time. By 1840 all the populated sections of the United States, including California and Oregon, were covered by Methodist circuits, districts, and conferences. The Methodist Church was by far the largest in the country, numbering 852,908 members. Even in New England, where Methodists encountered their greatest difficulty, they were second only to the Congregationalists.

The itinerating circuit rider and the flexible Methodist system made it possible for Methodists to claw a foothold wherever the slightest opportunity existed. Often the circuit rider would make his first call while a new settler's cabin was still under construction. An early circuit rider came into Kentucky by way of the Ohio River. He made his way to Semin Kenton's Station, and three miles from that place found the cabin of the Stevenson family. Welcomed there he preached, and organized a class before leaving. At the end of the year, 91 members were reported in the circuit. At times circuit riders met strong opposition, had their horses stolen, ran into financial embarrassments and other difficulties. But soon a string of small classes would be formed, and a circuit had begun.

We shall not deal with the growth of the Baptists in detail as in many ways it resembles that of the Methodists. Methodism grew faster until after 1850, but Baptist growth from 1800 to 1960 is unparalleled. From a little over 100,000 in 1800, they were approaching 20 million by 1960 (Gaustad 1962:55). Figure Three indicates the rapidity of their growth over the years. Roman Catholic growth was larger, but was due in great measure to the coming of Catholic immigrants from Europe.

A major reason for Baptist growth is that they found a method of providing pastoral care for the population as it fanned out toward the west. This was the justly famous Baptist farmer-preacher.

The Baptist preacher was a man who had moved west with others of similar social station who were seeking improved opportunities (Sweet 1964). When a man felt a call to preach, he would tell the church. He would then be asked to preach; and if his sermon indicated promise, he would be licensed to preach in that church or perhaps in a small area around it. If, after some experience, he showed improvement, he was licensed to preach in the association (the group of Baptist churches in an area). If he seemed not to improve, he was advised to discontinue preaching.

A preacher might spend five or six days a week working his own land. He would preach Sundays and occasional weeknights, and conduct funerals and other services. The churches frequently were small, and a log cabin sometimes would serve as a church's home for several years.

A new church often would be formed when a farmer-preacher moved into a community. Sometimes there were several preachers in the same congregation. Licensed preachers often preached at several churches within an association, after the manner of Methodist local preachers. Many Baptist churches were begun by these men, sometimes at great personal sacrifice. Often a licensed preacher would be asked to assume regular charge of a congregation, at which time he would be ordained. Ordained preachers could administer the sacraments; licensed men could not.

Though he largely supported himself, he sometimes received small sums of money. (It was not uncommon for the preacher to receive assistance.) Church members helped him plant and gather his crops, aided in time of family sickness, and in other ways helped him gain time for thinking and preaching.

The farmer preacher enabled the Baptists to surmount the economic barriers to growth. As the frontier moved west, many small communities were formed. It was very difficult in these sparsely populated places to find enough believers to support a fully salaried clergyman. But when pastoral care could be provided by men who needed little or no salary at all, small churches could be established in almost every village and farming community. The multiplication of churches and the provision of pastoral care became a spiritual rather than a financial problem.

The amazing growth of the Baptists and Methodists in America in the 180 years since the Revolutionary War is of deep interest to those who would inquire into the reasons why Churches grow. There

Figure Three

NUMBER OF CHURCHES SIX U.S. DENOMINATIONS

	1750	1850	1950
Congregational	•••	••••••••	••••••••••••••••
Episcopal	••	••••••	•••••••••••••••••••••••••••••
Presbyterian	•	•••••••••••••••	•••••••••••••••••••••••••••••• ••••••••••••
Lutheran	•	•••••••••	•••••••••••••••••••••••••••••• •••••••••••••••••••••••••••••• ••••••••••••
Methodist		••••••••••••••• ••••••••••••••• ••••••••••••••• ••••••••••••••• ••••••	•••••••••••••••••••••••••••••• •••••••••••••••••••••••••••••• •••••••••••••••••••••••••••••• •••••••••••••••••••••••••••••• •••••••••••••••••••••••••••••• •••••••••••••••••••••••••••••• •••••••••••••••••••••••••••••• •••••••••••••••••••••••••••••• ••••••••••••••••••••••••••
Baptist	•	••••••••••••••• ••••••••••••••• ••••••••••••••	•••••••••••••••••••••••••••••• •••••••••••••••••••••••••••••• •••••••••••••••••••••••••••••• •••••••••••••••••••••••••••••• •••••••••••••••••••••••••••••• •••••••••••••••••••••••••••••• •••••••••••••••••••••••••••••• •••••••••••••••••••••••••••••• •••••••••••••••••••••••••••••• •••••••••••••••••••••••••••••• •••••••••••••••••••••••••••••• •••••••••••••••••••••••••••••• ••••••••••••••••••••••••••

Each dot represents approximately 200 churches

can be no doubt that the ability of these two denominations to encourage a flexible pattern of the ministry, including the use of leaders usually regarded as "laymen," is a chief reason for their growth.

In 1780, there were 745 Congregational, 490 Presbyterian, 450 Baptist, 405 Episcopal, 235 Lutheran, and a bare handful of Methodist churches in the United States. With the exception of the Baptists and Methodists, these Churches all insisted upon a paid clergy with high academic qualifications.

In 1760, Ezra Stiles, in a book called *Discourse of Christian Union,* estimated that the population would double every twenty-five years and predicted that by 1860 there would be 7,000,000 Congregationalists. Unfortunately, the Congregationalists did not keep pace with the population, and were more like 1,250,000 in 1860 (Gaustad 1962:59).

The problem was that a sufficient number of qualified clergymen could not be found or trained to meet the tremendous need and opportunity. Stressing an educated ministry, the Congregationalists, Episcopalians, and Presbyterians tended to draw their members from the upper classes. The great majority of people, as in every nation, were lower in the social scale.

Moreover, a flexible pattern of ministry and church organization was much better equipped to deal with the fluid, ever-changing frontier situation, with its mobile and often sparse population. The more rigidly structured church systems were unable to cope with this new challenge. It was not that the Churches which fell behind were unconcerned about the souls of men. They formed societies whose purpose was to reach the westward-moving populace, and some of the spiritual giants of the day were in their ranks. But they were tied to a system which hindered their meeting the demands of the times for mobility. The Episcopalians, Congregationalists, and Presbyterians have not to this day regained the positions they held in 1780.

Due allowance must be given the fact that church growth is always a complex matter, and we must recognize that other factors influenced the ability of the several Churches to grow. The Episcopalians were dealt a severe blow by the Revolutionary War. Many of the clergy were sympathetic to the English cause and returned to England after the War. Some Churches tended to be limited to certain groups: the Lutherans to Germans, and the Presbyterians to Scotch-Irish communities. The Methodists and

Baptists, on the other hand, found entrance into the lower classes of all races and groups. Moreover, the basically non-authoritarian polity of the Methodists and Baptists, some argue, was more suited to the spirit of the new country than that of the other Churches. Nevertheless, the decisive importance of providing a practicable form of pastoral care for the millions must not be overlooked when enumerating major causes of the growth of the American Churches.

It was fortunate for the future of America that these two great Churches grew as they did. The nation was in danger of secularization. In 1800, less than 10 per cent of the population were church members. By 1910 the figure had grown to 43 per cent, and by 1960 to about 60 per cent (Neill 1957:57).

It would be naive to compare frontier America with Japan. The frontier was turbulent and mobile. The Japanese rural scene is sedentary: people in a village may be using irrigation systems begun by their ancestors a thousand years ago. Americans on the frontier had drifted from Christianity and were recalled to it. The Japanese live in a tightly knit Buddhist-Shinto society which has for a millennium and more been structured around ancestor worship. But one thing is similar: the need for a flexible kind of church organization and form of ministry which can enable the Church to gain a foothold, survive, and on occasion grow, in any community where 4, 8, 12, or 50 are receptive to the Christian Faith.

THE LUTHERANS IN NEW GUINEA

New Guinea is the world's second largest island. Almost unreachable valleys girdled by high mountains are the home of perhaps two to three million people[2] divided into small tribes. It is reported that there are approximately 500 different languages spoken on the island.

In 1886, the first missionary of the Neuendettelsau Mission arrived. The work was carried on by German missionaries until World War I, when American and Australian missionaries joined the Germans.[3]

In the early days, students from some of the tribes attended schools founded by the missionaries. Though not baptized, they returned to their homes to oppose or put in doubt certain pagan practices inherited from the ancestors. The tribal elders saw that their world was being threatened and opposed the students. In 1899, when the first converts were baptized, the missionaries thought the breakthrough had come. Instead, to their dismay they found that the converts were completely cut off from their tribes and could no longer influence their people. Moreover, tribal loyalties exerted overpowering pressures upon the converts.

One of the missionaries, Christian Keysser, pondered long over the stalemate that resulted. The mission, fortunately, did not have the money to create Christian villages. This procedure, not uncommon in other missionary work, has often so isolated Christians from their people as to make further evangelism extremely difficult. At length Keysser hit upon the idea of persuading whole tribes to move into Christianity together.

He gradually learned how this could be done. When adults came to believe in Christ and desired baptism, Keysser would advise them to wait until the whole tribe, including the elders, was persuaded. The inquirers, longing for baptism, often became ardent and effective evangelists. They would interpret unusual events in the tribal life prophetically as God's warnings to the people. Gradually they wore down the resistance of the elders.

When Keysser felt the people were ready, he would sponsor a great feast. According to tribal custom, this gave him the authority to request a decision concerning Christ. If the decision were favorable, many were baptized, and the way was open to win the entire tribe.

On the great day of decision, the people would perform a series of symbolic acts by which they manifested their intention to become Christians. Dramas, songs, dances–planned by the people themselves without consultation with the missionaries–graphically portrayed the great change in tribal life.

Thus, in a way so congenial to the peoples, tribe after tribe was won. Not all the missionaries were immediately or easily convinced of the rightness of this approach. But as time passed, it became clear that such "tribal conversions" produced as good, or better, results in the personal lives of the converts as the individual conversion method, and in far greater numbers.

Keysser emphasized that Christians are called to evangelistic work, and the churches have taken this very seriously. New congregations are desirous of sharing in this ministry. An effective means of evangelism has been the sending of evangelists to untouched tribes. The evangelists take up residence near a village, learn the local language, and gradually win the confidence of the residents. Amid frequent trials and sometimes dangers, they win the tribe to Christ. In 1956, there were 914 such evangelists. The number had grown to 1,200 by 1960.

This missionary work is considered the responsibility of the congregations, and they support the evangelists from their treasuries. The elders supervise the evangelists by making occasional visits to the areas where they are at work.

Space does not permit detailing the truly remarkable transformations which have taken place in tribal life. We can pause only long enough to call attention to the way pastoral care was provided from the time of the first converts in 1899 until 1960, when the Church numbered 208,000 members, with about 800,000 under the influence of the Mission. Frerichs (1957) states that in 1956 there were 163,222 living Christians, 914 evangelists, 89 pastors and assistant pastors, 2,164 elders, and 209 missionaries (including 84 wives). It is worth noting that this Church is about half the size of the entire Protestant membership in Japan.

In pre-Christian times the whole community participated in the tribal religious life and, as much as possible, the Church preserved this pattern. Emphasis was placed upon the whole community being responsible for the spiritual life of its members. Evening prayers were based upon a pre-Christian gathering. Ordinary church members took turns leading. Confession of sins, before Communion, served as a means of maintaining spiritual power and discipline. Certain persons were appointed by the community to hear confessions; missionaries and pastors also served in this capacity.

The people had been accustomed to the leadership of tribal elders, so it was only a short step for them to accept the idea of elders in the church. Elders were trained, with some difficulty, in the Christian meaning of service, and were given both social and religious responsibility in the congregations. Since there have been no pastors in the villages, pastoral care has largely devolved upon the elders in each church. Elders visit the sick and pray with them, settle quarrels, and watch over those in danger of going astray. In harmony with tribal custom, the elders lead with the consent, support, and cooperation of the Christian community. At public meetings, the elders usually lead in speaking, although any members of the congregation may speak and it is not uncommon for them to do so. Missionaries and teachers also bear preaching responsibilities.

For many years there were no pastors, in the Western sense, but in recent decades attention has been given to the training of pastors. The need for more trained leaders has grown as the people have increasingly come into contact with the modern world, and able persons from among the elders and teachers[4] of the churches are being given additional training.

The value of emphasis on participation of the laity in church leadership was demonstrated during the Japanese occupation of World War II. The remaining missionaries were interned and the pastors scattered, but the laymen gathered their relatives and friends and continued services through those trying years.

Here, then, is a large and flourishing Church in which pastoral care has been provided primarily by unpaid leaders from within the congregations, with the assistance and direction of a much smaller number of missionaries and pastors.

THE BATAK CHURCH

One of the most remarkable stories in modern missionary annals is that of the growth of the Church among the Bataks in Sumatra.[5] To those savage but able people, in 1861, came missionaries of the Rhenish Mission, one of whom was Ludwig Nommensen, a towering figure in the history of missions. Fierce opposition was met in the early years, but when a number of chiefs were won to the faith, the tide began to turn. Available statistics reveal the extraordinary growth of this Church. (See Appendix B.)

Year	Members	Ministers	Teacher-Preachers	Presbyters
1866	52			
1876	2,056			
1891	21,779			
1911	103,538	29	659	1,125
1930	273,000			
1938	400,000	65	1000	7,500
1950	540,000	90		
1962	691,463			

The growth of the Church is continuing. Warneck estimated the population in 1911 at between 600,000 and 700,000 (1911:22). The overall Batak population is estimated now to be somewhat in excess of 1,500,000 (Cole 1966:271). Many sections of the land have become completely Christian. This Church has had a remarkable record of financial support, and has accepted responsibility for the winning of all Batak people, sending out a large number of missionaries. It is one of the few Churches in the world which has been able to win Moslems in appreciable numbers.

How has pastoral care been provided for this enormous number of converts? Contrary to the practices prevailing in most Churches in the world, pastoral care in the Batak Church has been built on the principle of wide participation in leadership functions. From early days unpaid elders (presbyters) have played a most important role in the local churches. Tribal chiefs have also been given recognition and authority in the church: they have had responsibility in church government and discipline, in dealing with quarrels among believers, and for construction of church buildings.

The number of missionaries has never been large, though they long occupied a prominent position in the Church. Briefly stated, the organization at the time of the Madras Conference in 1938 was as follows: the entire field was divided into five districts. A missionary was in charge of each district, with his four or five Batak clerical colleagues in charge of the sub-districts. The churches in the villages, which averaged 500 members each, were led by teacher-preachers, who in turn were assisted by unpaid presbyters who had spiritual responsibility for twenty-five families each. The districts sent representatives to the annual Great Synod, and a representative Federal Council acted as an interim committee.

Almost none of the ordained ministers were in charge of a single congregation, but they itinerated constantly between the eight to fifteen churches for which they were responsible. They conducted the sacraments, arranged retreats and classes for the training of the teacher-preachers and presbyters, and gave advice concerning the affairs of the church and community.

The teacher-preacher was, and still is, an indispensable figure in the life of the Church. He usually was licensed as a teacher by the government after seven years of schooling and was made a teacher-preacher following two more years of training. After ten years of experience, especially well-qualified men could take two years further training and then be ordained.

Many of the teacher-preachers received a salary from the government, which was augmented by the Church. They were in charge of the village school as well as the village church. Where schools were not government sponsored, they were financed by the churches.

The teacher-preachers, under the direction of the ordained ministers, assumed responsibility for church services and catechetical instruction. The assistance of the unpaid presbyters made it possible for pastoral care to be given to the entire community at a cost within the capabilities of the church.

Though the Rhenish Mission is not a denominational organization, Lutheran influence has been strong. In 1952 the Batak Church joined the Lutheran World Federation.

It would be unwise to attribute the outstanding record of growth of this Church to one cause. The Bataks are a virile and capable race. They had a community code, called the *Adat,* which was pure enough in its moral connotations to be continued–when given Christian dimensions–as the social code of Christian communities. For many years there were no competing denominations. The school system worked well as part of the evangelistic program.

Nevertheless, it is clear that this great story would never have been recorded had the Rhenish Mission insisted on the *one-paid-pastor-per-church* system, limiting pastoral care to that provided by highly trained clergy. The pressures of a people movement influx forced the missionaries to provide pastoral care through a graduated system of leaders, paid and unpaid, who remained close to the people. This made it possible for the many thousands who were receptive to the Christian message to believe in Christ and become responsible members of His Church.

It would be impossible to transfer this system *en toto* to Japan, and yet it is highly suggestive for those in Japan who desire to prepare the Church there to shepherd the millions. As we have seen, the flooding into the congregations of great numbers of converts pressured the Batak Church into making pastoral care available through the participation of thousands of unpaid or slightly paid laymen. The Church in Japan can deliberately choose to do the thing that necessity laid upon the Batak Christians. Surely there are many other lands where the Church could greatly profit from a careful study of the history and growth of the Batak Church.

Beyerhaus and Lefever (1964:85-86) seem to react unfavorably to the small number of ordained ministers (only 90 in 1950 to minister to a community of 540,000). They apparently also consider it regrettable that a minister was "more of a district or circle superintendent than a local shepherd 'calling his own sheep by name.' " They call attention to the difficulties the Church encountered in the early 1950s. With government subsidies cut off, funds were insufficient for salaries. Some ministers had to supplement their income through outside employment, with the result that they had less time for church work. A proposal to meet this problem through a tax to be levied on all members was rebuffed by the churches.

But these authors do not seem to consider the alternatives to the leadership and pastoral care system employed in the Batak Church. They do suggest that when the number of ordained ministers was insufficient to permit regular provision of the sacraments for the huge membership, evangelists and teachers should have been ordained. They seem to approve of the stance of the early missionaries in regard to indigenous leaders, commenting that "no attempt was made to follow slavishly the Western pattern of the ministry" (1964:77). But one searches in vain for recognition of the fact that the large growth experienced by the Batak Church would have been quite impossible if the missionaries had insisted upon the kind of ministry they had known in Germany. Despite the problems of the 1950s which Beyerhaus and Lefever mention, the Church has continued its growth, as the statistics show. Though the various kinds of leaders who have shared in the pastoral function as sketched in this chapter are mentioned, the authors do not seem to recognize adequately that this flexible approach made possible a scale of growth often denied to Christians working among potentially receptive masses in other places. Since they do not view the matter in this context, it is difficult to assess the validity of their objections.

PENTECOSTALS IN BRAZIL

Although the countries of Central and South America have been nominally Roman Catholic for centuries, the Catholic Church there has not been characterized by the vitality of that Church in other lands. Huge numbers of people are alienated by anti-clericalism and political factors. The religion of many others is scarcely recognizable as Christian. The number of Protestants is growing at a remarkable pace in Latin America, a fact that is attracting widespread attention in both the secular and religious press.

What is not so widely known is that much of the Protestant growth, especially in Chile and Brazil, is Pentecostal. If their present growth rate is maintained over the next forty years, the Latin American Pentecostals will have become one of the great Protestant Churches in the world.

A recent book by a Presbyterian missionary to Brazil has for the first time accurately revealed the actual shape of the leading Protestant Churches in Brazil (Read 1965). This book deserves a careful reading in Japan, as well as in other countries of the world. The following account is based upon it.

In Brazil today, the Pentecostals are beyond question one of the fastest-growing segments of Christianity in the world. The Southern Baptists in Brazil also have had a remarkable history and Brazil is their most fruitful mission field. Their present communicant membership is nearly 250,000. Yet there are probably more than six times as many Pentecostals. In this section we shall briefly describe the two leading bodies from among the numerous Pentecostal denominations in Brazil.

The *Congregacao Crista no Brasil* was, in its early years, largely a movement among Italian immigrants. It began in 1910 when two humble missionaries, whose native tongue was Italian, went from America to Brazil. They did not remain long, but one of them made many visits to the country over a long lifetime. These missionaries succeeded in starting some churches, especially in São Paulo where the greatest growth has occurred.

Though in its early years it was restricted to the Italian-speaking community, the growth of the *Congregacao* has been rapid. By diligent research, Read was able to obtain the following statistics:[6]

Year	Cumulative Baptisms	Net Growth
1920	18,000	
1930	45,804	
1940	87,008	50,223
1950	188,477	105,838
1960	303,025	223,663

There is a mammoth mother church in São Paulo which the members everywhere regard with mixed feelings of awe and pride. Baptisms, by immersion, are conducted there every fifteen days. On a Sunday in November, 1963, Read saw 130 baptized at a service attended by 3,000 people. In the first ten months of that year, 3,801 had been baptized at the mother church alone.

The astounding thing about this large Church is that it does not have a single paid pastor! In fact, one of the reasons the *Congregacao* does not engage in fellowship with the Assemblies of God is that the latter employ paid clergy. The churches are led by elders, who are called *anciaos.* Several are elected at the annual assembly at the mother church, as the church waits upon the Holy Spirit for guidance. The elders are able men who have responsible positions in Brazilian economic life. Since funds are not needed to support the clergy, all income is used for the poor or for the construction of buildings.

A strong effort is made to involve every member in the missionary task. Elders and others who go out for evangelistic work pay their own expenses. The *Congregacao,* according to Read, holds its members better than most Churches. It is statistically only a little smaller than the combined total of all Protestants in Japan.

Many criticisms are leveled against the *Congregacao* by other Protestants. The evidence would seem to indicate that some are justified but many are not. But the relevant point for Christian leaders in Japan and other countries is that a Church can be built up and achieve rapid growth without a single paid clergyman.

A detailed account of the astounding growth of the Assemblies of God in Brazil cannot be undertaken here. Accurate statistics for fast-growing Churches are hard to come by, and the Christian world is much indebted to William Read for the painstaking care with which he has compiled the figures which are summarized in the table below. The reader is referred to his book (1965) for an explanation and defense of these figures.

Year	Active Members
1930	14,000
1943	60,000
1948	104,836
1951	200,000
1956	312,749
1957	345,943
1960	500,000
1962	702,750
1964	950,000

Since 1934, the average annual rate of growth has been about 23 per cent. The figures show a truly astonishing increase in numbers during the last decade.

How is it done? Many factors must be considered in accounting for this kind of growth. For the immediate purposes of our study, we wish to lay emphasis upon the effort to get everyone to participate in church life and in evangelism. There are jobs and opportunities for leadership for all. Pastors are constantly on the lookout for members with the spiritual gifts the church needs, and the Church carries out a vigorous and widespread training program.

A considerable number of the congregations are large, but many others are small. Frequently it happens that members in a city will flock to the big church for Sunday services but carry on the rest of the time in small churches in or near the city.

Read reports that in 1955 there were 1,064 Brazilian pastors, 5,108 lay preachers, 1,200 organized churches, and 3,000 preaching points. Here again is underlined the necessity for flexible organizational patterns which welcome unpaid preachers in large numbers and encourage the utilization of the gifts of all the people of God. Freed from the mind-set which requires a highly trained and salaried pastor in each church, Pentecostals in Brazil and other Latin American countries display an amazing ability to multiply new churches and disciple responsive population units. Their non-rigid procedures enable them to sweep past economic roadblocks and to gather large numbers of people into churches. They not infrequently do this in the same areas in which other denominations find themselves fenced in by economic problems and tied down by the cumbersome and time-consuming process of attempting to train along Western lines a clergy to serve in a young Church.

* * * * *

In this chapter, although we have emphasized the importance of flexible patterns of ministry, we have refused to attribute the remarkable growth of the Churches described to this factor alone.

Receptivity to the Gospel is another important factor. No system of church life, however excellent, will lead to large in-gathering if the populace continues impervious to the appeal of the love of Christ. We dare not overlook the unseen work of the Holy Spirit. This study has established, too, that other factors—the zeal, the spiritual power, and the willingness of Christians to make great sacrifices for their fellow men—are essential to great advances in church growth.

Nevertheless, the evidence presented in this chapter clearly demonstrates that a pattern of ministry which includes the use of unpaid preachers (or elders, or presbyters, or whatever name they may bear) as part of the plan for providing pastoral care for all who are willing to receive it, is one indispensable factor in unshackling the Church for battle. In such diverse lands as England, America, Sumatra, and Brazil, the Churches which have experienced large-scale growth have been Churches which adopted flexible and graduated levels of pastoral leadership. Churches which have not done so have experienced modest growth or no growth, even when working under essentially similar circumstances. Even when populations are potentially responsive to the Gospel, rigid adherence to sedentary and institutionalized church organization will inhibit the Church from winning them in large numbers.

CHAPTER V

SOME RECENT MODIFICATIONS OF MINISTRY

In addition to the cases examined in the previous chapter, there are Churches in a number of places in the world that are currently practicing forms of ministry which represent departures from the familiar forms of the West.

These new practices are so varied that they are difficult to categorize. In most cases their justification is the shortage of clergy in the face of the need to provide pastoral care for numerous churches. But leaders in some places contend that it is good for pastors to have employment in the workaday world in order to bridge the gulf between clergy and laity.

We may distinguish two alternatives to the familiar pattern of the full-time ordained clergy: (1) Those leaders who serve the church without remuneration. Some such men have had seminary training, others have not. (2) Those who receive part of their income from the church. Again, some of these are men with seminary background, some are not. In each of these groups are found both ordained and unordained persons.

PART-TIME MINISTRY IN LATIN AMERICA[1]

Both of these types may be found in Latin America, very commonly among the Pentecostals but not confined to them. About half the Presbyterian pastors in Brazil are part-time clergymen. Most of these men are theologically trained and take employment for economic reasons. Opinion in this large Church is divided as to the desirability of this practice. Younger ministers tend to feel that engaging in secular work keeps a pastor closer to society. Lay leadership is considered desirable during the "house meeting" stage of new churches but usually an ordained minister eventually takes charge.

In 1963 the Southern Baptists in Chile had 10,000 adult members, 100 churches, and 200 preaching points. Of the 62 full-time pastors, 80 per cent were seminary trained. The Baptists regard the term "lay-pastor" as contradictory, but 100 *encargados,* who were unpaid but carried out pastoral functions, were serving in the churches.

Some friction arises between the pastors and the *encargados.* The *encargados* defend their rights, and three have been recently ordained. (The Church's policy is that only those for whom there is financial support may be ordained.) The seminary-trained clergy consider it improper to ordain "untrained" men even when support is available.

The Baptists in both Chile and Argentina place great emphasis upon lay training. In Argentina, 75 per cent of the churches are led by part-time ministers, many of whom are not seminary trained. Trained ministers tend to be full-time; untrained ministers, part-time. There is a feeling that untrained men would find it difficult to utilize effectively the greater amount of time available to them should they become full-time ministers. The sentiment in the denomination is growing that untrained men can no longer cope with the problems of the day, and that the Church must move on to a full-time trained ministry. It will be interesting to see what happens to Baptist growth in Argentina if this conviction rules the future.

Webster reports that it is generally recognized that the fastest-growing Church in Argentina is the Plymouth Brethren.[2] As in other lands, the Brethren in Argentina do not have ordained clergy, nor do they pay their local church leaders. The Argentina Church, however, supports 18 salaried missionaries. In addition, a much larger number of unpaid missionaries are active, some of whom are exceptionally able men. Local churches are led by elders. Each congregation has four or five men trained to take responsibility for evangelistic work.

In the Brethren pattern, there is a main church, or assembly, which normally has around it four or five branch meetings. The latter are not considered churches, and the service of communion is not practiced there. As a branch meeting grows in strength, it requests independence and becomes an assembly. For a limited period, an officer from the sponsoring church acts as overseer. The new assembly proceeds to sponsor its own branch meetings, and so the work grows. In 1963 there were 260 assemblies.

The Mennonites in Uruguay are convinced that in South America the part-time clergy are best suited to the situation. Full-time clergy, they hold, tend to get out of touch with the common people. The Mennonites usually have three or four "ministers" in each congregation. Each one preaches about once a month. When there is a need for ministers, the bishops point this out to the church. After fasting and prayer the church votes on candidates, who are asked if they sense in this the call of God. Throughout a probationary period the candidate preaches and considers the matter; when he recognizes a call he is ordained. Ministers are trained in a theological school for urban charges and are given training in a trade at the same time so they can support themselves.

Webster finds that part-time ministers are being widely, but not everywhere, used in Latin America. They are used more commonly by indigenous Churches than by those related to missionaries from abroad. Expanding Churches use them the most. He notes that Churches which have many part-time ministers tend to move toward gaining more full-time ministers, and that Churches which have only professional ministers are showing interest in the part-time ministry. Generally, the part-time clergy want to be full-time clergy.

ANGLICAN LAY PRIESTS

It is intriguing that in several places in the world Anglicans are now beginning to use part-time clergy. Exceptionally able men who have not attended seminary are made priests. Some of them continue in their professions. Perhaps the best known of these is Dr. William Pollard, nuclear physicist and, since 1947, Executive Director of the Oak Ridge Institute of Nuclear Studies in Tennessee, who was made a priest in 1954. James Chang Ling Wong was for many years superintending engineer for a large firm in Hong Kong. In 1960 he was elected to the episcopate and is now rendering outstanding service as Bishop of Jesselton in North Borneo. The way has now been opened in the Anglican Churches of India, Pakistan,

Burma, and Ceylon for the ordination of men who continue in their secular occupations (D. Paton 1965:89-93).

CHURCH OF SOUTH INDIA EXPERIMENTS

A good deal of ferment and creative thinking in the area of pastoral leadership has taken place in some sections of the Church of South India in recent years as that Church has sought to cope with such staggering problems as general poverty, decreasing subsidies from the West, widely scattered congregations, and a vast populace to evangelize.

In 1953 a significant statement was prepared under the auspices of the diocese of Madura (Newbigin 1953). The statement noted that the Synod had in 1952 proposed "that in the CSI the diaconate should be a distinct form of ministry, not simply a stage preliminary to the Presbyterate; and that it should include both paid and unpaid workers; and that there should normally be at least one ordained deacon in every congregation."

The statement pointed out that most pastors had responsibility for ten, twenty and even fifty congregations–manifestly more than any one man could handle. As a result, paid unordained helpers, supported by government grants or mission subsidies, had been employed to assist in the congregations.

This system, it was asserted, developed out of certain propositions taken for granted by eighteenth- and nineteenth-century missionaries: (1) that all clergy must be full-time and salaried; (2) that the clergy should have a theological education comparable to that common in the West, and (3) that the clergy should be supported from offerings received from the believers.

But the Western patterns for the clergy simply have not been able to cope with the vastly different conditions in India. For this reason, the custom has developed of depending upon subsidized agents who have had only minimal training. The result is that untrained preachers have in practice done most of the preaching, while ordained ministers best trained for preaching have been burdened with trying to provide the sacraments for numerous congregations and with administrative work.

The statement goes on to point out several grave defects that have arisen from this system, asserts that it is remote from New Testament practice, and calls for action by the several dioceses to provide genuine pastoral care for village congregations. It specifically asks that they especially "consider whether they would favour the ordination of voluntary presbyters after suitable training, and–if so–under what conditions."

Under the leadership of Bishop Newbigin, the diocese of Madura undertook an experiment of considerable scale, involving villages in which only limited evangelism had been done. Under the plan, men who were unanimously nominated for appointment as deacons by the congregations in which they were to serve were to be ordained and given full authority to conduct the sacraments. Six were chosen in the first instance: one a tanner, two drummers, one a "head-cooly," one a woodcutter, and one a retired school teacher. They were given three and one-half years of in-service training. The first ordinations as deacons were in 1959, and the men were subsequently ordained as presbyters.

In twelve years, the number of village congregations in the area quadrupled. It is reported that the congregations are proving to be more securely grounded in the faith than those who have been under the care of professional teachers and catechists. It is regrettable that this provocative experiment has not been continued, though elements of it are reported to be still in effect.

An important article by Iber Priestley reported on a major experiment in India involving the participation of laymen in leadership and pastoral functions (1956:412-419). The British Methodists long carried on a work in Hyderabad, South India, which is now part of the Church of South India. Under a strong missionary leader, Charles Posnett, a trained and paid evangelist was placed in nearly every Christian village. At the height of this program, evangelists numbered 800, largely supported from abroad. After World War II, new feelings of Indian independence and diminished resources made it impossible to maintain the old system.

Over a period of several years the C.S.I. carried on a careful survey of the field. This led to the redividing of the area, which included 800 villages with Christian congregations, into 34 pastorates. These were in turn subdivided into parishes, with six to ten villages in each.

Originally it was planned that there should be a superintending minister for each pastorate and a staff of three or four paid workers, including an ordained minister, for each parish. However, despite increased giving on the part of the Indian Christians, funds sufficient to pay even such a reduced number of workers could not be realized.

It became apparent that the Church would have to rely upon lay leadership. The work had been Methodist, and in accordance with the traditions of that body, considerable numbers of local preachers, stewards and class leaders were already serving. A Board of Voluntary Workers was established in 1953 and a comprehensive training program conceived. It called for training on local levels, as well as parish, pastorate, and central courses. It was hoped that groups of volunteer workers would develop in each church, and that some with proven ability could receive additional training as local preachers, evangelistic workers, and social service workers. From these a number would be selected for increased pastoral responsibility and receive training (three years) as lay deacons. From among the lay deacons, well-qualified persons would be chosen and trained as honorary ordained ministers. Lay representation on governing bodies was increased, and a strong effort was made to increase the giving of the believers.

Within a few years hundreds of people had received training. Honorary ordained ministers had begun to appear. The plan was to assign one honorary minister to each parish as suitable men were trained and appointed. These men would be different from seminary-trained ministers, but not unprepared for their work. Many excellent lay leaders were being recruited and trained in the towns, although it was proving more difficult to recruit leaders in the villages. Even though the number of foreign missionaries had greatly decreased, and subsidies from abroad had declined, the work had not been curtailed. A new church pattern, under God, was taking shape around the voluntary workers in local churches and the Indian minister.

In an interview with Priestley (then Bishop of the Hyderabad Diocese) in the summer of 1966, this writer was told that there were then over 1,000 persons in the diocese who had received the Bishop's Certificate for satisfactory completion of a lay training course. Most of the trainees were enrolled in the "Pastoral Assistant's Course," in which they learned how to conduct family prayers, visit the sick, and perform various services under the supervision of other leaders. Some pastoral assistants were recognized as "lay preachers," a role somewhat similar to the local preachers of British Methodism.

The practice of appointing as lay deacons selected persons who undergo training two months annually for three years was being continued. These workers were authorized to take charge of local congregations, under the supervision of the pastorate presbyter.

Because of the widespread lay participation in leadership capacities, the number of constituents per presbyter in the Hyderabad Diocese was in 1966 the highest in the Church of South India. Stated another way, this means that each trained and salaried clergyman was able to serve a much greater number of people than would be the case if virtually all pastoral responsibilities rested upon him. In addition, he could receive his salary from a treasury supported by a much larger circle of believers.

This writer was deeply moved and impressed by the enthusiasm and dedication manifest at a Lay Training Institute he visited with Bishop Priestley, near Hyderabad. Here humble village laymen, who were in many instances one of two or three persons in charge of a local congregation, were undergoing further training. The Institute was conducted under the direction of Rev. Joseph, the pastorate presbyter. This vigorous clergyman was serving a pastorate of 2,500 members comprising 23 recognized congregations (including several new ones), plus smaller unrecognized groups.

* * * * *

This all-too-brief survey reveals developments from which we may take heart. We are made aware that there are courageous souls in many parts of the world who are willing to question established custom and to seek solutions to present-day dilemmas. That such experiments are taking place both in the main-line Protestant Churches and in the smaller and sometimes newer bodies is highly reassuring. We cannot doubt that here is one place at which the pressure of the Holy Spirit upon the Churches is being felt, as He seeks to equip them to carry out His loving purposes everywhere.

CHAPTER VI

MANY MEMBERS IN ONE BODY

Christians in Japan, America, and many other lands have known only that form of church life which is led by resident salaried clergymen. The minister preaches every Sunday, he administers the affairs of the church, he conducts the sacraments. The laymen perform various services in the church, but the most important functions are carried out by the pastor. Christians who have experienced only this pattern of church life find it exceedingly difficult to visualize any other. The tendency is to assume, without questioning, that church life cannot be structured any other way.

We cannot know with precision the life of the churches in the days of St. Paul, but it is certain that it was different from that with which we are familiar.

The Church for many centuries has gathered the various spiritual gifts into one man: the pastor. But in New Testament times the gifts were shared. The life of each church was blessed both by persons in its own membership who had differing gifts and by itinerating persons who possessed still other gifts. In Ephesians 4:11 and I Corinthians 12:28 we catch a glimpse of a day before the wide gulf between clergy and laity had been opened. Instead of one man in a church being expected to be expert in almost everything, the gifts of many persons were exercised for the benefit of all. Note that "pastor" is but one of the kinds of leader mentioned. From Acts 20:17-38 we learn that pastoral responsibility in the church at Ephesus was exercised not by one man, but by a group of men. It is, moreover, widely recognized that the remarkable growth of the early church was largely dependent upon the fact that every believer was a witness.

The mobilization of all the people of God for the winning of Japan and many other countries of Africa, Asia, and Latin America, may well depend upon a return to these New Testament principles. The passivity of the laity owes largely to two facts: (1) their potentialities are not developed and are not even fully perceived, either by the clergy or by the laity themselves; and (2) very little scope for the realizing of their potentialities exists due to the largely unquestioned assumption that most leadership functions in the church are to be exercised by the clergy. Often the highest understanding of the function of laymen attained to is that they can be excellent "helpers" of pastors.

Yet the Church's own experience points to the fact that an active laity is the secret of power. Whenever there is a place in the world where a Church is characterized by biblical faith and great power, where large numbers of people are being led into faith in Jesus Christ, it will be found that there are many ordinary people who, fired with love and zeal for Christ, are volunteering their time and energy for His cause.

There can hardly be many problems of greater importance for the Church than that of enlisting widespread participation of Christian laymen in its evangelistic and leadership tasks. The experience of powerful religious movements declares that the discovery of well-defined and meaningful leadership roles, and the training and appointment of large numbers of ordinary folk to fill these roles, is of decisive importance in achieving this kind of participation. This is a secret of which the early church was not unaware.

We can and should learn from other men. South Africa and Korea have been the scenes of two important adventures in church growth in which leaders of various kinds have played a most significant part. To these stories we now turn.

METHODISTS IN SOUTH AFRICA

In chapter four we dealt with the Methodist Church in England and America, paying special attention to the lay preacher and the circuit system. Methodist organization, which is patterned after the British (as distinguished from the American) Methodist Church, is similar everywhere in the world, though there are minor variations.

As to organization, circuits are governed by the quarterly meeting, a body which is formed of the circuit clergy, the lay preachers, class leaders, and representatives of the congregations. A superintendent minister oversees the circuit.

The next organizational level is the district, which is governed by the synod. A chairman superintends the work of the district and acts for the synod between its sessions. The conference is the highest authority in the Church. Among other things, it has responsibility for the recruitment, training, discipline, and stationing of the clergy.

Sundkler describes the offices for lay leaders as they are practiced in South Africa (1961:135-138). They have exercised much influence over other Churches, including Sundkler's own Lutheran Church.

The class system is the foundation of the Church's organization. A class has from ten to twenty members and is presided over by a leader elected by vote of the leaders' meeting upon the nomination of the superintendent minister.

The officials of the leaders' meeting are called stewards. They cooperate with the ministers in all matters pertaining to the spiritual welfare of the church and are men of influence in the congregation and circuit.

While these unpaid leaders have responsibility for the lower parts of the organization of the churches, there are three grades of unpaid workers who engage in preaching. Persons who feel called to serve by preaching are appointed as *exhorters.* If they serve worthily, they may next be appointed as *preachers on trial.* These are persons who feel led to become lay preachers. They are examined "as to their spirituality, knowledge, and general suitability" before they are eligible to become lay preachers. Candidates must pass a test based on the catechism and one on fluency in reading the Scriptures before being appointed.

Suitable persons are in time made *lay preachers.* These workers carry preaching responsibilities in the circuit churches and preaching places. Candidates must have been preachers on trial for at least twelve months, read prescribed literature, and passed an examination on knowledge of the catechism and Scripture.

In 1940, there were 2,150 exhorters, 3,933 preachers on trial, and 8,915 lay preachers in the Methodist Church in South Africa. It is easy to see that such an army of unpaid workers, led and instructed by a well-trained professional clergy, would constitute a powerful force for the evangelism of a country. No wonder other Churches are influenced by this kind of mobilization of human resources!

PRESBYTERIANS IN KOREA

The Presbyterian Church in Korea is justly famous. Its record is one of the great dramas of the modern missionary era. The amazing growth of this Church in the midst of almost continuous political turmoil and economic hardship has been chronicled in a valuable book by Roy E. Shearer (1966). The following account, except as otherwise noted, is based upon this book.

Presbyterian missionaries began work in Korea in 1884. The first convert was baptized in 1886. By 1890 there were 100 members. Slow growth continued until about 1895, when large numbers of people began to flood into the churches. The statistics below give an indication of the rate of growth in communicant members:

Year	Communicant Members
1895	300
1900	3,914
1905	11,036
1910	39,384
1920	69,025
1930	87,186
1940	112,276

It should be noted that the figures listed are for *communicant* members. Much larger figures must be visualized for the number of believers. A comparison of available statistics indicates that the Christian *community* figures are about three times those of *communicant* members. Shearer reports that Dr. Samuel Moffett estimated the Presbyterian community in 1961 at 775,000.

A number of factors–which it is beyond our purpose to detail here–are important for understanding this unusual record of growth. For example, there is the matter of the weakened condition of Korean religion, coupled with a high degree of receptivity to the Christian Gospel. There is also the fact that in the days of Japanese occupation, to be a Christian was at times an effective way of expressing Korean sentiments of independence and patriotism.

It is frequently asserted that the famous Nevius Plan for missionary work was the primary reason for the Presbyterian success. But Shearer points out that although the Presbyterians employed the Nevius Plan everywhere in Korea, the rates of growth varied greatly according to area. The most striking growth took place in North and South Pyongyang. Although the same policies were followed in other parts of the country, church growth there was, until after World War II, modest. Apart from the Pyongyang area, the Presbyterians (who used the Nevius Plan) grew at a pace roughly equivalent to that of the Methodists (who did not follow Nevius). The unusual receptivity to the Gospel on the part of the people of Pyongyang, and their zeal in wimning others to Christ once they had themselves become Christians, must be taken into account in attempting to assess the reasons for the remarkable Presbyterian growth in Korea.

Nevertheless, it is undoubtedly true that the Nevius Plan did play a most important role in Korea. Even though many Koreans were responsive to the Gospel, the large ingatherings which have occurred might have been missed had the work been conducted in a different manner. Here we wish to refer to three factors which seem to us to have been of great importance in the remarkable growth achieved by Korean Presbyterians. These factors are directly or indirectly related to the Nevius Plan.

1. Lay Evangelism

From the early days of the work a large portion of the evangelistic ministry has been carried out by laymen. In 1895, a missionary reported that laymen were distributing Christian books and preaching to the people in the villages of their areas. These laymen would organize converts into groups and instruct them as best they could. In time such groups would request missionaries to come and instruct them further. In Shearer's words, "the Church began to multiply ahead of the missionaries." There were, by 1898, churches the missionaries had seldom or never seen. So fast did the churches multiply that missionaries were occupied with instructing the Christians, to the point that they could not give themselves to evangelism. A missionary found on his first visit to a village that all the people were already Christians and were maintaining family worship, though no church was yet organized, and the people had not previously seen a missionary.

This pattern has appeared repeatedly through the years. From 1948 to 1958, in a district in southwestern Korea which had not before seen such rapid growth, communicant membership increased from 14,818 to 40,781. Christians would walk out on Saturday to invite their fellow villagers to attend the churches. Relatives and family members were won. Missionaries were kept busy simply baptizing and instructing the converts.

2. Training for All

The Nevius Plan prescribed intensive training in the Bible for all believers. This policy is largely responsible for the vigorous lay participation which has characterized the evangelistic and church life of Presbyterians in Korea.

Although the training program began on a very small scale late in the nineteenth century, within twenty years it had become one of the most remarkable enterprises in missionary history. Chapter eleven relates the various aspects of this educational system in more detail.

3. Diversified Ministries

A book by Soltau has an important section on the graduated leadership policies of this Church (1954:53-73). Whenever a new group came into being, a number of persons who were held in general respect would be selected from among the new Christians, and appointed temporary leaders. At first these appointments were made by the supervising pastor or missionary; later, as the church grew, they were elected by the members. It was impressed upon these men that the responsibility for the growth of the church in faith and numbers rested upon them. Missionaries were repeatedly astonished at the willingness of people to assume responsibility and the way in which this experience hastened their spiritual growth.

At least five offices which shared in pastoral responsibility were established:

Elders. An office held in high respect by Presbyterians everywhere. In Korea this office carried more dignity and responsibility than in the United States. Elders frequently sat on the platform with the pastors, conducted prayer meetings and Sunday evening gatherings and, with the pastor, dealt with discipline and other emergency problems. The first ruling elders were appointed in 1902. In 1938, 2,713 men were serving in this office.

Preparatory Elders. Often appointed in the early days of a church from among the older persons who had become believers. It was understood that this officer usually looked forward to appointment as elder when the church had grown to sufficient size. This practice educated the new believers in the selection of the right kind of leaders.

Deacons. Appointed from among both men and women. They had responsibility for the finances of the church and also conducted services in nearby villages, as well as in the homes of believers.

Exhorters. Larger churches were divided into districts of from five to ten families, with one male and one female *exhorter* being placed at the head of each district. They visited the families, called on the sick, held meetings in their homes, and consulted with the pastor about the people in their districts.

Bible Women. Selected and employed by the church. They received support commensurate with their needs, either in grain or money. They assisted the pastor in calling, visited the sick, and did evangelistic work among the non-Christian homes in the community. Many were widows of strong faith. (Though Soltau does not mention it, others were converted sorceresses who played an important part in the battle with Korean animism.) Many received training at Bible institutes. They made a tremendous contribution to the work.

In 1938, it was reported that the 3,000 Presbyterian congregations were supporting 599 ordained and 777 unordained pastors, and 675 local evangelists. In addition, there were 19,839 lay leaders and 32,183 Sunday School teachers serving without pay (C. A. Clark 1939:156).

We may summarize by saying that Presbyterians in Korea (1) allowed wide scope for lay participation in important leadership functions at several levels, (2) engaged in church expansion in a way which made it essential to depend upon lay leaders, (3) rigorously trained the believing community so that leadership potential in the churches was uncovered and developed, and (4) resolutely recruited able unpaid leaders and appointed them to well-defined tasks. (It ought not, of course, to be overlooked that missionaries and Korean pastors vigorously exercised their ministries as well.)

Examination of rapidly growing churches elsewhere affords substantiation of the principle which the history of Korean Presbyterians urges upon concerned Christians everywhere: a major secret of power and of church growth is the recruiting and training of large numbers of people for responsible places of leadership in the congregations.

A BUDDHIST COMPARISON

That this principle is not limited to Christianity, and is as true in Japan as anywhere, is currently being demonstrated in the amazing growth of Sōka Gakkai. In 1950 this militant pseudo-Buddhist sect was an obscure body of about 5,000 members. Today its leaders claim over 13,000,000 adherents, and it has become a power to reckon with in the nation's politics.

The organization of Sōka Gakkai is effective enough to be the object of study by political bodies, including the communists. It was largely the invention of Toda Josei, the organizational and promotional genius who played the key role in Sōka Gakkai's march to prominence.

The religion is structured along military lines. At the top is the president. The organization includes a board of directors (*rijikai*), an administrative section (*daikanbu*), general branches (*sōshibu*), branches (*shibu*), districts (*chiku*), squads (*han*), groups (*kumi*), and the family units.

Each of these levels of responsibility means opportunity for the participation of many persons. Especially is this true of the *kumi* level. *Kumi* vary in size from five to 25 members and often incorporate family units. Each *kumi* has a group leader. A women's chairman and a trained member of the Education Department are also frequently active. When one recalls that Sōka Gakkai claims a membership of 13,000,000, this means there probably are as many as 500,000 group leaders, plus a large number of other local leaders! Note that these persons are all unpaid. We also hear of guides (*tantōin*) who have responsibility for other persons in matters of faith. There are ingenious devices for maintaining a series of personal relationships between converters and those converted.

The Education Department is unique in that it has teacher-members in every part of the country. Four ranks of teachers are recognized: assistant lecturer (*joshi*), lecturer (*kōshi*), assistant professor (*jokyōju*), and professor (*kyōju*). Each rank has its required courses of study, and all candidates for these offices must pass examinations. The *joshi,* for example, must be familiar with the two major periodicals of the movement, the *Shakubuku Kyōten* (Manual for Forced Conversion), and certain writings of Nichiren.

By the early 1960s, the number taking qualifying examinations for these offices annually exceeded 100,000. Members of the Education Department, according to their rank, may be active in local *kumi,* or may lecture at periodic rallies throughout a district.

The effectiveness of this widespread participation is not lost on Buddhist leaders of other sects:

> Established religions like Buddhism and Christianity have their professional priests and pastors, and a system whereby they manage, educate, and lead the believers. Thus the believers are put into a place subordinate to the priest and pastor and stop with belief in the doctrines of their religion. Propagation is left to the priest or pastor. On the other hand, it is not like this in the new religions. The moment someone becomes a believer in these religions the responsibility to propagate the faith is given to him. Thus to become a believer is to become an energetic propagator (Ito 1961:39-40).

Sometimes Christians in Japan are heard speaking contemptuously of the competition and desire for advancement among Sōka Gakkai leaders. It would be better to recognize that the desire for achievement and the satisfactions gained from exercising leadership are common to most men. Such human qualities are not evil in themselves. The Church should claim them in the name of Christ. The Church is strong only in proportion to the number of responsible persons it can recruit to a variety of recognized and meaningful leadership offices.

SOME LIMITATIONS OF LAY LEADERSHIP

It must be forthrightly recognized, however, that the appointment of lay preachers, elders, and other laymen to offices and to pastoral responsibility, as advocated in this book, is not a solution to all the Church's problems. Rather, it is likely that their assignment will expose the churches in Japan and other lands to problems and even sorrows they do not now experience.

Neill points out that many professional men are subject to reassignment. When such men act as church leaders, it will sometimes ensue that a church is deprived of leadership just when it needs it most. When a professional clergyman fails to work harmoniously with a congregation, he can be transferred, but this way of dealing with a lay leader who runs into trouble is usually not practicable. Farmers who own land, and doctors or businessmen who have an established clientele, would of necessity stay in the same locations even though their leadership in the church ceased to be constructive.

This writer once talked with a Japanese pastor who had trained several laymen in his church to preach. He reported that at length the church members had decided they could now do without him, and he had been discharged. He decided, he said, as a result of this experience, not to train any more laymen in preaching!

Sundkler records a story of a church in Africa in which there was an influential elder who was a man of means. A young pastor was assigned to the church, but the congregation placed greater confidence in the elder. The latter represented the church at district meetings rather than the pastor. Although other pastors criticized this state of affairs, the young pastor was eventually replaced by an older man (1960:161-162). Of course, similar problems occur under our present system, but it is likely that they will increase as additional responsibility is given to the laity.

Congregations with only part-time pastors may feel that they do not receive enough pastoral care. The demands of employment often take increased amounts of time. The temptation to gain more money by greater expenditure of time is strong. If part-time ministers earn a salary higher than the average member of the congregation, resentments may arise.

Men fully employed may have neither the time for counseling or membership training, nor the opportunity for acquiring the requisite skills. Such are some of the problems which are encountered in Latin America with part-time ministers.

Nevertheless, though the widespread utilization of lay leadership will entail problems such as these, the price that is paid for limiting pastoral leadership to professionals is so great that a missionary Church cannot afford to pay it. Throughout the world in a host of communities are countless millions of people who will never be able to receive pastoral care unless it be from unpaid and humble servants of the Church. Everywhere in Japan there are thousands of towns and villages and city neighborhoods which will in our lifetime have no Gospel witness, no churches, and no pastoral care, unless it be through the work of dedicated, trained, unpaid leaders and ordinary Christians. These urgent needs must be placed on the scales and weighed against the problems which the elevation of laymen to responsible positions may entail.

CHAPTER VII

SURMOUNTING OBSTACLES TO CHURCH PLANTING

Let us briefly review the ground we have covered thus far. It may be expressed by a sequence of seven propositions.

1. We must bring the Gospel of Christ to all the people of each land, to the end that they may be saved.
2. We must vastly multiply the number of churches, in full recognition of the fact that the multiplication of new churches is a central and indispensable factor in large-scale church growth and in bringing salvation to the multitudes.
3. We must provide pastoral care for the multitudes through flexible patterns of pastoral ministry.
4. We must realistically face the fact that, as is true of many other countries of Africa and Asia, Japan cannot be evangelized by the *one-paid-pastor-per-church* system, and that that system is neither required by the Bible nor universally practiced by the Church of Christ.
5. We must recognize that unpaid men can render signal service in helping to provide pastoral care.
6. We must enlarge the borders of the clergy so that more than one type of leader may be acknowledged as part of the pastoral leadership of the Church.
7. We must greatly increase the number of church leaders who participate in pastoral and preaching responsibilities by making room for meaningful and graduated levels of service which include both laymen and clergymen.

It can be seen that the emphasis of the book to this point has been upon the need for restructuring the practices by which the Church seeks to provide pastoral care for the multitudes. As a sort of summary statement of this emphasis, and in support of the arguments already advanced in previous chapters, we turn now to the thoughts of one of the most discerning and influential missionary writers of modern times.

THE ARGUMENT OF ROLAND ALLEN

Probably no other name in the field of missionary strategy is so well known as that of Roland Allen. Such diverse figures as Bishop Azariah, Kenneth Grubb, Eugene Nida, and Lesslie Newbigin have pondered carefully the provocative contentions of this missionary scholar. His writings, now several decades old, continue to challenge thoughtful Christian leaders, not only of his own Anglican persuasion, but of every branch of the Church (1962).

Allen recognized that if the vast populations of such countries as India, Africa, and China were ever to be reached with the Gospel, it would have to be by the Christians of those countries, since foreign missionaries and their indigenous employees could never complete the task. He insisted that spontaneous expansion is the only hope of success.

By "spontaneous expansion" he meant that growth which comes about through the unexhorted and unorganized efforts of Christians to share the good news which they have themselves received. It is a growth which occurs when men are irresistibly drawn to the ordered life of the Church and to the secret of life which they see in it, and which they desire for themselves. It is a growth which leads to the establishment of new churches. The amazingly swift spread of Christianity over the Roman Empire is an example of genuine spontaneous expansion.

Missionaries, he maintained, must lay a foundation which will enable the Christians of China or Africa to evangelize their own countrymen through spontaneous expansion.[1] Two powerful factors are at work to bring about such growth: (1) Men have a natural inclination to share with others a new-found joy, and (2) the indwelling Spirit of Christ, who yearns for the salvation of men, turns that natural inclination into a desire for the conversion of others. When this desire is given genuine opportunity to express itself, there occurs a remarkable surge of power which leads to a rapid spread of the message of salvation.

Strange though it may seem, missionaries themselves have frequently hindered spontaneous expansion. Fearing that the doctrine of the Church might be misrepresented if ordinary Christians were allowed to proclaim the Gospel on their own initiative, they have sought to tie all evangelistic activity to the work of the Mission, where it can be controlled. But spontaneous expansion is something which by its nature cannot be controlled. To control it is to suffocate it.

Spontaneous expansion is continually hindered by our patterns of ministry. Though the system of a salaried clergy is not apostolic, it has become the unquestioned practice in much of the West, and missionaries have assumed that this system is part of the Gospel. So fixed and unconscious is this assumption that the first reaction of missionaries upon receiving reports of conversions and advance is to appeal to the homeland churches to send more money and personnel. When laymen spontaneously gather a group of Christians in a new place, the missionary's first thought is to send a paid clergyman to lead the new group.

The instinctive reaction of missionaries to send a paid agent to lead every new group of Christians causes many unhappy results. It suggests to the converts that the teaching of a paid agent is more weighty than that of the layman who engages in spontaneous evangelism. It suffocates the church instead of helping it, for it teaches the new Christians to depend upon the salaried leader rather than to bestir themselves. Moreover, it makes the spread of the Gospel an economic matter. Christians come to feel that there can be no expansion of the Church apart from the expenditures of large sums of money.

Allen's solution to this dilemma was that each church be provided with its own ministry (in many cases unpaid), usually chosen from among its members, and assigned full responsibility for its own church life. This, he insisted, was the method of Paul.

Missionaries in the modern era, on the other hand, have been very slow to entrust the proclamation of the Gospel to ordinary believers. Allen attributed this reluctance to fear for church doctrine. Unsupervised men of ordinary attainments, it is contended, cannot accurately grasp and express theological issues and will unintentionally misrepresent the doctrine. Allen vigorously denied the validity of such fears. The early Church allowed ordinary believers to preach wherever they went, yet the doctrine was not endangered. It was not, in point of fact, from among humble, nameless teachers appointed to lead new churches that heresy broke out, but from among sophisticated and highly educated Christians in places such as Ephesus and Alexandria.

Paul ordained elders in the churches he had established (Acts 14:23). Allen held that the sacraments were observed in these churches and that almost certainly they were administered by the elders. Leadership was exercised by the elders, who were men of mature years. Paul set not one but several elders over each church. By placing responsibility upon several persons (rather than one) for the church's health and progress, the growth of the whole church together was fostered, and a spirit of mutual responsibility encouraged.

Churches thus equipped need not depend upon outside money to care for themselves or to foster expansion. The way is opened for churches to be planted everywhere through spontaneous activity of Christian believers.

Allen was not opposed to the ministry of salaried clergy, but he argued strenuously in his books against the limiting of pastoral leadership to professionals. In one book he described what would happen if his proposals were practiced in England. Each group of Christians would be constituted a church in which a full church life, including participation in the sacraments conducted by that church's clergy, would be possible. Each church would have several ordained voluntary clergy. (By "voluntary clergy" Allen meant unpaid workers who would be ordained for services in their own churches. He held that the elders of Acts 14:23 and 20:16-26 were "voluntary clergy.")

Professional clergy would serve in three capacities. Some would move among a group of rural churches, each led by its voluntary clergy. Others would pastor parish churches in small towns, meanwhile having responsibility also for several churches in the surrounding countryside which were led by voluntary clergy. Still others would be in charge of large town parishes and would also watch over the several local churches in the town. Voluntary clergy would be active in town churches, also, freeing the head pastor to give attention to nearby churches under his care.

The writings of Roland Allen are perhaps exercising more

influence today than they have for many years. Undoubtedly this is because he draws attention to issues which are now, more than ever before, being recognized as crucial to world-wide missions. A short treatment cannot do justice to the complexity and fullness of his thought. Nevertheless, even the brief summary above contains many ideas which are most important for our study.

A number of interrelated problems call for our attention as we seek to identify ways by which we may surmount obstacles that block the way to an increased multiplication of churches. To these we now turn.

NEED FOR FLEXIBILITY

A review of the seven propositions which stand at the head of this chapter will attest that they represent a sustained argument for flexibility. This is also the plea of the well-known Masao Takenaka:

> I would like to touch briefly on the reform of the structure of the Church in Japan. Both the (Christian) Non-Church Movement (Mukyokai), and the Communists challenge constantly the present institutional structure of the Church. Both operate without heavy investments in buildings; and with few paid or professional leaders. Also some of the new religions like Sokagakkai emphasize the importance of nonprofessional leaders and the establishment of a nucleus fellowship in the milieu of ordinary people. On the other hand, in the Christian Church the rigid normative idea of the institutional church has been kept up, practically saying that unless you have a church building and a full-time professional minister you will not have the Church of Jesus Christ. Here the idea of the tent-making ministry is suggestive. We must find the way to make the Christian Church not a static, building-centered religion but a people's movement, a company of new humanity making a joyful pilgrimage on earth (1964:209).

We can no longer afford the shackles of which Takenaka speaks. If a million Japanese people should become willing to follow Christ in this decade, we would be unable to shepherd them. We would be handcuffed by our own inflexibility.

Neill observes that despite the increasing "depth and intellectual maturity of American religion" today, the Methodists and Baptists—who continue to be the Churches which most effectively adjust to ever-changing conditions–remain the largest Protestant bodies (1957:57). That flexibility in matters of church organization can lead to accelerated growth is a fact which is demonstrated not only by the experience of Christians in America alone, but in a number of other places as well.

Who can read of the daring and fruitful experiments which have in recent years been and are still being carried out in many lands by various branches of the Church without a deep sense of joy? These experiments are found in groups as diverse as Episcopalians and Pentecostals. They are found in conservative bodies, including fundamentalists, as well as in the more familiar Churches of the WCC. We have much to learn from each other. The courage and flexibility which these varied endeavors manifest are fresh evidence that the Holy Spirit is still powerfully at work in the Church, and that this venerable Society of the Unseen Lord is still worthy of our passionate loyalty and dedication. In the strength which comes from above, we can cope with the problems of our fragmented, baffling, turbulent world. Let Christians in Japan and other lands in which the Church remains a tiny minority throw off their fears, move out in the freedom of their Lord, and attempt great things for Him!

How can we achieve flexible church forms which will enable us to move into a new era of greater church growth? The experience of the Church is rich. We are not forced to settle upon a single alternative. From the several case histories recorded in these pages we may learn how various branches of the Church have, in sundry times and situations, greatly multiplied their effectiveness by modifying ecclesiastical patterns to ways more adequately designed to cope with the actual life-situations which the missionary Church encounters.

In the remaining pages of this chapter, we shall discuss several matters which have intimate bearing upon the flexibility our situation so insistently demands, and which weigh heavily upon Christians the moment they move beyond theory and set themselves to the task of planting new churches.

SMALL CHURCHES

In chapter five we discussed the plan for the multiplication of churches of the Plymouth Brethren in Argentina. This involves the establishment of small new groups around a parent church. This method is undoubtedly one of the fastest ways of multiplying churches.

In 1956 the Assemblies of God had one church of less than 100 members in the city of San Salvador, capital of El Salvador (Hodges 1966: 81-82).[2] A large evangelistic campaign was held, followed by intensive after-training, with the result that 250 converts were baptized in the ten weeks following the campaign. Six weeks later 125 more were baptized. Instead of gathering these into one church, the city was divided into twelve districts, with a leader placed in charge of each. People gathered in rented buildings.

Soon there were twelve emerging churches. In the next eight years these twelve established fifteen more churches and 200 preaching stations in and around the city.

Most congregations of this denomination in El Salvador are kept small. Average figures are as follows:

	Baptized Members	Worship Attendance	SS Attendance
Churches	35	65	105
Small Churches	9	17	28

Small churches usually meet in one rented room, thus keeping expenses down. The table below shows the growth rate. Note that in 1965 Sunday School attendance was about one per cent of the total population.

	1953	1960	1965
Churches	74	204	300
Small Churches	193	554	1,000
Members	3,071	6,992	13,000
Average Attendance	4,954	12,936	
SS Attendance	3,556	21,160	30,000
Pastors	82	213	
Local Preachers	184	596	

There is every reason to believe that this sort of evangelism and church multiplication, which is practiced by fast-growing Churches of many varieties in numerous countries, would bear fruit in Japan and in many other places as well. Today small churches, as churchmen in Japan well know, are a drag upon denominational budgets and energies. But flexible patterns of ministry could transform them into an effective organization for an expanding missionary program. However, certain principles must be respected if this is to be achieved.

In chapter two we discussed the necessity of parent churches allowing new groups their independence. There should be a cooperative relationship between the two. Parent churches should teach small churches to govern themselves and to handle their own funds instead of requiring them to send their offerings to the parent church treasury. The small churches should in turn be mindful of the welfare of the church which gave them birth, and in many cases should bear a portion of the pastor's salary. The latter point is of particular importance in a country like Japan, where even parent churches tend to remain small.

When the necessity of small churches is seriously contemplated, however, the problem of pastoral leadership inevitably comes to the fore. Long habit has so conditioned our thinking that we almost instinctively picture a salaried pastor in every church, large or small. This immediately raises a problem: How shall pastors of small churches be financed? In Japan, where few large churches are to be found, this dilemma becomes acute. At this point we must be prepared to do the kind of hard thinking expressed by one Japanese pastor:

> Limited in number, we are challenging this tremendous populace. It will never do to go on thinking that we will not consider anything but that every church, even where only 10 or 20 gather, must have its own pastor. The Japanese love inspiring stories. To follow this kind of policy may seem like an "inspiring story," but it is not evangelism. It is necessary that there be organizing and unifying of the church, and it is also inevitable that churches without pastors come into being (Eguchi 1965:10).

These blunt words of Pastor Eguchi express the kind of thinking we must do in our day. The practice of sending pastors to tiny churches of ten or twenty members and subsidizing them there should, except in the most unusual situations, be discontinued. Pastors should not be subsidized to go to a church where the attendance is less than twenty, and the congregation cannot pay at least 80 per cent of his salary from the beginning. Such difficult assignments often demoralize young pastors just out of seminary. If funds for subsidizing salaries are available, it would be better to assign such men to work for a while in a circuit under experienced pastors or missionaries.

When a pastor goes to such a small church, he tends to overawe the group by his superior gifts, and the abilities and initiative of the people are not developed. If salaried pastors were not sent to tiny churches, both clergy and laity would learn that building up the church is as much the task of the laity as of the clergy, and that the specific role of the clergy is to inspire and train the laity for its task.

But it is not only the clergy which must learn to think new thoughts. We teach more by what we do than by what we say. The way in which missionary and church-planting endeavors have long been conducted by Western missionaries and their converts has effectively conditioned the thinking and practices of Christians in many lands. Because the pattern of *one-paid-pastor-per-church* has been invariably followed in Japan and numerous other countries, most laymen consider it the normal and inevitable pattern. Before the recommendations of this book can be followed, the laity will need to be re-educated.

The hardest task will be to convince Christians in small churches that they can be genuine and sound churches without a salaried pastor. If the clergy and the Christians in larger churches take the attitude that any church that amounts to anything "of course" has a salaried pastor, then the task will be harder still.

For this reason, we need to develop a new way of evaluating churches. The view that a "good" church is one with a large average attendance and budget must be modified. Christians must come to regard a "good" church as one that is able to establish viable new congregations in its vicinity. The modified standards of excellence must declare that regardless of numerical attendance at worship and the size of the budget, a church which cannot bring into being new congregations of believers in nearby communities is spiritually poor. When the issues are viewed in this light, then established churches will soon come to see the necessity for lay leadership. They will train lay preachers. They will carry out evangelistic efforts and church-planting programs. They will allow their pastors to be away on Sunday mornings from time to time to speak in new little churches and will recognize these tiny congregations as real churches even though they have no paid pastor. Christians will have become missionary in their attitudes and practices.

Literature which emphasizes these truths needs to be prepared.

This literature should encourage little churches without professional pastors by insisting that they are one of God's greatest instruments for the salvation of their countrymen, that they are in the apostolic tradition, and that there are thousands of similar churches all around the world. It should speak to larger churches about their missionary responsibility. It should emphasize that for a church to have a salaried pastor entails an obligation to assist other churches which do not enjoy this privilege.

The above lines should not be interpreted as arguing that a tiny church is preferable to a larger one. While we may entertain some misgivings about the spiritual effectiveness of large congregations numbering thousands of persons, hardly anyone, I suppose, would prefer a church of 15 active members to one of 150. A larger church can offer more in terms of leadership and participation opportunities than a small one. All other things being equal, a more balanced faith should be possible in a larger group. Whether it be church music, sports for the men, opportunities for Christian friendship with persons of one's own age, or finding a Christian husband or wife, a larger church affords a richer experience than a small one.

But we live in a world in which, for tens of millions of people, there exists no choice as to the size of church in which they will worship. If they are to know Christ and to drink from the waters of life which only He can give, they will have to do so in a small church. In countries such as Japan, the only opportunity great numbers of people in thousands of communities will ever have of receiving the Gospel is if small churches are planted near their residences. (Of course, hopefully, many such small groups will in the course of time increase in size.) It is essential that Christian leaders recognize this reality and willingly and thoughtfully devise forms of church life and leadership which will enable small churches to come into being, survive, and even prosper. Christian leaders must resolutely set themselves to planting congregations in every needy community.

RATIO OF PAID TO UNPAID CLERGY

If we accept the principle that Churches should appoint lay preachers and other unpaid leaders to participate in pastoral ministry, how numerous should they be? Let us consider some Church figures at random for purposes of comparison.

	Ministers	Lay Preachers
Primitive Methodists in England, 1860	675	11,384
Methodist Church in Transvaal, 1913	36	2,091
Assemblies of God in Brazil, 1955	1,064	5,108
Assemblies of God in El Salvador, 1960	184	596

It will be seen that the ratio varies according to time and place. Only experience can determine what an appropriate ratio will be for a given situation. In any case the number of lay preachers available should be considerably larger than the number of preaching places, so that each place can have a Sunday worship service without placing too heavy a burden on the lay preachers. Moreover, it is safe to assert that lay preachers should considerably outnumber the salaried clergy.

RECRUITING LAY LEADERS

Our Lord has taught us to pray that laborers might be raised up for the vineyard (Luke 10:2). Prayer is the first and most important element in the enlisting of workers for Christ.

There are natural leaders present in any group of people. One of the reasons for the astounding growth of Sōka Gakkai is that it identifies and uses humble people with leadership potential. The Church in Japan too often is content for its membership, many of whom are able people, to attend services and listen to the pastor preach.

If we can learn to create meaningful roles with which people can identify, and if we are expectant, the Lord will inspire many laymen to serve Him in these capacities. It is important that we have graduated levels of leadership roles so that inexperienced persons, including young people, can begin at the level of their present knowledge and ability. If leaders for small groups (like the Methodist class leaders) are elected by the congregation or quarterly meeting, and if eager young people are assigned modest leadership roles in preaching meetings, within two years a stream of experienced laymen who can be trained to serve as lay preachers and elders will begin to appear.

Each clergyman and each church must make this a matter of concern. The Methodists in the Fiji Islands do not think highly of any church that does not have at least two lay preachers in the congregation.[3] It should be made a matter of pride for each church to contribute in this way to the evangelism of its area.

Let the churches in a district plan missionary rallies from time to time, as do the missionary societies in England, America, and other countries, to arouse enthusiasm for world missions. If impassioned speakers present the needs of the unevangelized people round about, and tell how other lay leaders are being used in the vineyard of the Lord, men and women will hear the call of God to evangelistic and pastoral service.

Let ministers take laymen with them when they go out to preaching stations. Let the minister encourage the layman to give a testimony, explain a passage of Scripture, or contribute music, and recognize his contribution. If the minister tells a layman he was blessed by what the layman said, or that he thought the layman's word was meaningful, the dedicated laymen will take this very seriously, and soon will be willing and able to render greater service.

ADVANTAGES OF COOPERATION

For many reasons, not the least of which would be matters such as training and exchange of experiences, work along the lines suggested in this chapter will best succeed where there is cooperation among a number of churches. Our object here is not to argue for any one kind of church polity. Nor is it our present purpose to discuss "cooperation" in the sense of a highly organized ecclesiastical machinery, with committees regularly meeting to discuss all aspects of church life. We concern ourselves rather with the more modest problem of the need for cooperation in a program of evangelistic outreach, intended to steadily plant new churches, and which contemplates pastoral and evangelistic duties being shared by paid and nonpaid leaders.

If the work can be administered by a number of churches, large and small, banded together for cooperative efforts in planting new churches and strengthening older ones, many advantages will accrue. These joint efforts might be conducted along the lines of a Methodist circuit, a small Reformed-type presbytery, or some similar plan. For our purpose we shall borrow the term "circuit."

If, from the first among new groups, offerings are received and 25 to 50 per cent forwarded to the circuit treasury, new Christians will cheerfully accept this as an entirely reasonable procedure. The circuit treasury might then pay the salary of one or more circuit pastors, somewhat after the British Methodist pattern. Or it might assume responsibility for part of the support of the pastor of a nearby church, with the understanding that he devote an agreed-upon percentage of his time to circuit itineration.

If local church elders are to be ordained and lay preachers appointed, wiser decisions can perhaps be made by a circuit than by a local church alone. Probably the agreement of both the circuit and the congregations should be a condition of such actions. Also, if problems of unsuitability or other unpleasantness occur, these can be more easily handled by the larger group than within the narrow confines of one church. If circuit pastors set up preaching schedules for lay preachers which rotate them among the circuit churches, these men will, in many cases, do better work than if they must preach to the same congregation every week. It is difficult for busy working men to prepare an acceptable new sermon every week.

A survey of rural churches in Korea in 1938 showed that the average attendance at preaching services was as follows:

Members of Conference preaching	75
Supplies preaching	41
Lay preachers preaching	62

"Members of Conference" refers to trained clergy. "Supplies" refers to men who had left another occupation to become pastors. They were untrained and served smaller churches. It may be that because of their lack of training, people tired of their preaching and ceased attending. Lay preachers, who did not preach so often to the same congregation, had almost as large attendance as the regular clergy (Felton 1938:Appendix B).

Strong city churches might, as a missionary venture, volunteer to pay one-third or one-half the salary of a circuit pastor in a new or rural circuit, and missionaries could sometimes serve as circuit pastors. When finances permit, several circuit pastors could be employed in addition to the salaried pastors of larger churches in the circuit.

Most men work better in company than they do alone. It is this writer's observation that denominations in Japan frequently have only one church in an area. Especially when they are financially hard pressed, the enthusiasm of pastors often wanes as the hard realities of life bear in upon them. In a circuit, the circuit pastor can serve and itinerate among the churches, encouraging the salaried clergy, the elders, and the lay preachers.

What can a pastor do if he cannot persuade the churches in his area to cooperate in some such ways as these? He need not become discouraged. He can train lay preachers in his own congregation and, with their cooperation, begin new little churches in nearby communities. In some cases he may be able to join with one or two other like-minded pastors in such a venture.

ARE BUILDINGS NECESSARY?

It is a commonplace among Christians in Japan that the chief roadblocks to church multiplication are (1) the exorbitant cost of land and buildings, and (2) the high cost of pastors' salaries. By developing patterns of pastoral leadership which are within the capacity of converts to support, Pentecostals in Brazil and Mexico have simply by-passed economic barriers which block church multiplication in other Churches (McGavran, Huegel and Taylor 1963:118-120). But what can be done about the problem of church buildings in Japan?

This writer is not opposed to church buildings. He has in his own Church proposed the creating of loan funds for church-building programs. He has participated in the establishment of an agency, administered by Japanese Christians, which raises and administers funds for church-building loans. Buildings can help churches grow. But we do great harm to the cause of winning Japan for Christ if we insist that every church must own a building at every stage of its life.

When, about 1957, I visited the Okayama Seishin Church of Okayama City, led by pastor Yoshio Nagakura, I found a thriving church with an average attendance of about 200. It had then one of the largest church budgets in Japan, but for ten years the congregation had met in a rented building, and sat on the straw mat floor.

Missionaries in Japan have unwittingly hindered expansion by their practices regarding buildings. Able to draw on funds from abroad, they have given or loaned large sums of money for the construction of fine church buildings. This has given Japanese Christians the impression that the way to plant a new church is to secure foreign funds for the building. But there will never be enough foreign funds to construct church buildings in every village and town in Japan. This method of church multiplication is doomed the moment the limits of the mission budget are reached. Foreign funds must be used wisely lest they do more harm than good. One of the stumbling blocks to winning Japan today is that many pastors insist that in Japan a large, impressive building is necessary for growth. They have learned this strange idea from missionaries. The stupendous growth of Sōka Gakkai through the use of house meetings, with few buildings being constructed for local groups, shows conclusively that great religious movements are possible without the extensive use of buildings.

The impressive growth in recent years of the Southern Baptists in Japan is in no small measure due to their uninhibited use of American money for church buildings. Borrowing a plan pioneered in Brazil, they have provided land and a building for churches in every prefectural capital city and in many other places. They have demonstrated that bold planning can lead to exciting church growth. Every person concerned for the redemption of Japanese people may rejoice at this record of growth. Two problems present themselves, however: (1) Most denominations do not have the kind of money the Southern Baptists do. This is especially true of those who receive little or no aid from abroad. (2) Even Southern Baptist budgets have limits. If their pastors and laymen have "learned" that new churches can be built only through generous infusions of American money, then a heavy anchor has been fastened onto their vessel which will inhibit their progress in the future. There has now been brought into being a numerous and well-trained Japanese Baptist leadership. It can, if it will, re-educate itself to ways of church multiplying which will work with or without the help of American aid. Japanese Baptists should be aware that just as their vigorous and generously aided Church in Brazil is being far outdistanced by the relatively unaided Pentecostals, so in Japan their growth rate is being far exceeded by the Spirit of Jesus Church, which receives little or no aid from abroad.

Nevertheless, we regard the argument advanced by some that churches should cease owning buildings at all, as extreme. Buildings are not the most important thing, but they are useful.

To be practical, what can be done about the roadblock of high land and construction costs in Japan? Here again, the need is for flexibility. There are many ways in which a meeting place can be provided for a new group. Some can meet in the homes of Christians. Others can rent modest quarters. Sometimes a generous person will make available without cost a small piece of land which the new church can use for an inexpensive prefabricated or other temporary structure. Land may be leased in some situations. Denominations may decide to count the cost of an inexpensive and temporary chapel as part of the "evangelism" expense in a new locality if, as is often true in Japan, the work will be considerably speeded by having a settled meeting place. If men pray and seek divine guidance, there is a way for every new group of Christians to have an inexpensive place to gather during the early years. As the group grows in size and maturity, sacrifice and dedication will be rewarded with more long-term solutions to the problem of housing church groups. The fact that salaries have risen dramatically in Japan since 1950 means that believers have more resources to contribute for building costs than used to be the case.

SUMMARY: AN INDEFINITELY REPRODUCIBLE PATTERN

Essentially what we need is an indefinitely reproducible pattern for church multiplying. We must recast our ideas so that it will become possible for any church, anywhere, at any time, without outside assistance, to start a new church in its vicinity.

We must reject the idea that every church must have (1) a paid pastor, (2) a pastor who has graduated from theological school, and (3) an expensive building. Let it be reiterated that this book does not totally reject any of these, but it does insist that they are not always necessary. These patterns are not native to Japan; they were imported from Western Churches living and working under very different circumstances. They are neither found in, nor required by, the New Testament. They make church multiplication primarily dependent upon money, whereas the New Testament is almost silent on the matter of money for this purpose. In the New Testament church multiplication was dependent upon prayer, fellowship, zeal, sacrifice, and spiritual power. These imported patterns make the Japanese Church heavy and clumsy in its attempts to advance. Only slowly and awkwardly, aided by large expenditures of money from the outside, are new churches being planted.

What we must have is a flexible pattern of church organization and leadership which will permit any ordinary church, led by an ordinary pastor, to start a new church in its vicinity, at any time, without outside assistance.

The several sections of this chapter have made specific proposals designed to foster such flexibility. Whether or not they are accepted in the form in which they appear is a matter for each Church in freedom to decide. But if rejected, Church leaders must answer the question: What then do you propose, in order to make it possible for any church, at any time, anywhere, without extensive aid from the outside, to start new churches for the salvation of people in its area?

CHAPTER VIII

THE *LAOS* OF GOD

In chapter one we dealt with the mandate given to the people of God, tracing the path by which the first Christians came to recognize their identity as the people of God. It remains now to inquire into the theological dimensions of this term as it is used in the New Testament. We must go on to inquire further, in the light of this New Testament concept, how we are to fit those slippery words "clergy" and "laity" into a New Testament framework. If there is a vocation from God to the work of shepherding men, is there also a vocation for those who are not called to be pastors?

Throughout the Old Testament, Israel is constantly referred to as the people of God. Among the especially formative passages are Exodus 19:4-7, Deuteronomy 4, and Deuteronomy 7:6-12. Although Israel as a whole failed to recognize it, there was, as we saw in chapter one, a missionary vocation bound up in her election as the people of God.

The Hebrew term for "people" (*am*), according to Hort, is translated in the Septuagint in most cases (over 1,200 instances) by the Greek *laos.* As such it is used of foreign and heathen peoples, as well as frequently of the Hebrew people. It is in the mouth of God in the expression "My people." In the New Testament *laos* is used of the Jewish people and is also applied to the new Israel. When used in the latter sense, it is, with only a very few exceptions, confined to quotations and borrowed phrases from the Old Testament (Hort 1898:129).

The first Christians regarded themselves as being the continuation of God's ancient people and not merely a movement which began with Jesus. The depth and grandeur of their faith was in no small measure due to this conviction.

Such passages as Hebrews 4:9 and Revelation 18:4 show Christians consciously appropriating to themselves the ancient Hebrew terminology of "the people of God." In Hebrews 8:8-10, the stirring prophecy of Jeremiah is applied to Christians:

> "The days will come," says the Lord, "when I will establish a new covenant with the house of Israel . . . I will be their God, and they shall be my people."

The relationship between the Church and the ancient people of God is clearly reflected in I Peter 2:9, and the purpose of her election pointed out:

> But you are a chosen race, a royal priesthood, a holy nation, God's own people, that you may declare the wonderful deeds of him who called you out of darkness into his marvelous light.

The concept of the early apostolic community taking over the role of Israel as the people of God was set forth half a century ago by Hamilton:

> The Apostles and their company found themselves in a unique position. They and their converts were alone the true people of God. That which had constituted the old Israel was a common devotion to one God. The same tie now bound the believers in Jesus into one; they and they alone were the servants of the true God.
>
> All that belonged to the Israel of old now belonged to the new; what was true of the pre-Messianic Israel was true of the post-Messianic Israel. . . . As the old Israel had been a definite and visible religious society . . . so also the Apostolic band necessarily became a definite and visible society (1912:Vol. 2, 28).

The idea recurs from time to time in biblical theology, especially among British theologians. Streeter pointed out that the early Christians

> did not regard themselves as a new society, but as the ancient "People of God," that is, as that portion of the Church of the Patriarchs and Prophets, which had not yet by rejecting the Messiah forfeited its birthright and cut itself off from the promises of Israel . . . . The Christian position was that by recognizing Jesus as Messiah, they and they alone understood the prophets aright (1929:47).

How did the apostles arrive at this conception? Unquestionably it came from Jesus Himself. In an important chapter, significantly entitled "The Intention of Jesus," Bowman writes: "Jesus wished . . . to teach his people that . . . he would raise up a new congregation of Israel to displace the old one" (1943:214). We may briefly point to three lines of evidence for the view that Jesus intended to form what Bishop Gore called a "reconstituted Israel."

There are *the terms Jesus used,* of which we shall first mention "covenant." As many scholars have made clear in recent years, the concept of the "covenant" was a most important one in the Old Testament. It cannot, then, have been accidental that Jesus chose to use this word in Matthew 26:27-28: " . . . this is my blood of the *covenant* which is poured out for many . . ." (Turner 1953:270).

There is the metaphor "little flock," which is reminiscent of many Old Testament passages which depict God as Shepherd, and the people of Israel as a flock. Jesus applied to His followers a name given throughout the Old Testament to the people of God (Luke 12:32).

It is of great significance that *Christ chose twelve men* to be apostles (Luke 22:30). There can be little doubt that this was connected with the fact that in ancient Israel there were twelve tribes (Turner 1953:269; Bowman 1943:209-216).

There is *the very important passage, Mark 12:1-11.* It is likely that Jesus had the ancient allegory in Isaiah 5 in mind as He related this parable. In any event, the story is manifestly related to His ministry and its relationship to Israel. The owner of the vineyard expected to receive his share of the produce, but the messengers he sent were repeatedly abused and dishonored. He at length sent his son, expecting that at least the tenants would respect him. But their response was to do away with the son and seize the vineyard for their own. The key verse is the ninth:

> What will the owner of the vineyard do? He will come and destroy the tenants, and give the vineyard to others.

The parable signifies the rejection of one people (the unbelieving Jews) in favor of another. The people to whom God had given a great task had failed to carry it out. Hence that task was to be given to "others"–by whom Jesus surely meant those whom He had chosen to be with Him (Gore 1924:46).[1] The enemies of Jesus discerned the thrust of the parable and sought to arrest Him.

It is to this people that the Great Commission was given. Writing many years later, Peter showed that the purpose for which this people was called into being is the missionary vocation (I Pet. 2:9).

THE WHOLE PEOPLE OF GOD[2]

In the New Testament passages referred to above, and in the others in which the expression or the concept "*laos* of God" appears, the entire believing community is meant, and not just a select group within the body.[3] This people of God is the Church, that unique community composed of all chosen by Christ. It is that community in which Christ is Lord, and which gains from that conviction power to act and witness in the world (Kraemer 1958:*Laity*).

The *laos* of God is called to ministry. The word "ministry" in English has come to refer to clergymen or to their work, but in the New Testament *diakonia* (ministry) is not the function of one class. It is a role to which all believers are called. In the New Testament, all are *diakonoi* (ministers). Women are numbered among the *diakonoi* (Rom. 16:1, 3, 4, 12). In I Corinthians 12:4-30 Paul speaks of the different gifts bestowed by the Holy Spirit as "varieties of *diakonia*" (v. 5), and he includes all believers in his picture of the body.

The *laos* of God is called to mission. That chosen race addressed in I Peter 2:9, and which is called to herald the wonderful works of God our Saviour, is not one part of the believing community but the whole. All members of the Church, says Kraemer, the laity not less than the clergy, are to proclaim the "new reality in Christ, to manifest the hope of the world now set forth in Christ." The task of the pastoral leadership of the Church is to enable all believers to fulfill the meaning of their calling. Bishop Azariah's plea at Madras was that "the entire church membership be won for evangelism." For this reason, he desired that once clergymen from abroad, i.e., missionaries, had baptized converts in a district, they place responsibility squarely upon the converts and not ignore them in the continuing evangelism of the area (Azariah 1939:Vol. 3, 41ff.).

The primary and fundamental reality concerning Christians is that they are collectively the *laos* of God, regardless of their function in the Church. Unfortunately, a harmful dichotomy developed early in Christian history. As the Church drew away from the apostolic era, the division between clergy and laity grew steadily wider and the role of the laity ever more subordinate. Eventually that view–familiar to us in the traditional Roman Catholic doctrine that the laity is an inferior class ruled over by the clergy–prevailed almost everywhere. In this view the clergy exercise virtually all authority and, as Kraemer says, "in their collectivity may judge all things, and be judged by none." The laity passively and obediently receive from the clergy the sacraments and guidance in the religious life (1958:*Laity*, 53-55).[4]

Kraemer holds there was a linguistic dimension to this change of emphasis. The word "laymen," he says, is a descendant of the Greek *laikos* which passed into several Western languages in its Latinized form. The word *laikos* does not appear in the New Testament, but it refers to the *laos,* the people of God. The word *laikos* was a term of honor in Paul's day, but it gradually underwent changes in meaning. Liturgies, written by clergymen, came to use this word to refer to the congregation, as distinguished from the priest who officiates (1958:*Laity,* 49-50, 155-156).

The word "layman" now refers to a person who is outside any profession. A "layman" is one who is not qualified to make judgments concerning specialized fields of knowledge. Once a term of honor, it has become a term of subordination. As such it devaluates the expression "the people of God." The same is true of the Japanese term which translates it *hirashinto.* Unfortunately, no solution to this problem of terminology has yet been put forward.

The Reformation rejected many of the concepts which had grown up around the clergy and gave new recognition to the vocation of the laity. Yet, because of the enormous difficulties encountered in forming a new body of leaders from a laity so desperately unaware of its real role, and the other hardships of the day, the gap between the clergy (now frequently called "ministers") and the laity was not adequately bridged. A sharp distinction between clergy and laity remains to plague Protestant life today. In some ways this has become acceptable to the laity, which all too frequently resigns itself to inaction. It is the clergy, they assume, who must both carry the load of responsibility and measure up to the standards of the faith.

ROLE OF THE LAITY

It is impossible to defend from the New Testament such a division of the flock. There are no first-class members (clergy) and second-class members (laity) in the Church as it is seen in the New Testament. In our day we are called to reaffirm the full role of the laity in the Church. Many Christians are coming to see that privileges and responsibilities which have been traditionally restricted to the clergy actually belong to all the people of God.

Hendrik Kraemer has led the way in calling for a theology of the laity to undergird the widespread renewed interest in the role of the layman. Only when the Church recognizes "the laity's essential place and responsible partnerships in the Church's vocation," he says, will a theology of the laity have meaning. The view of the laity's role, all too common today, which allows laymen to be appealed to as a sort of auxiliary army for times of special but temporary need, is no true biblical view (1958:*Laity,* 14, 119).

In considering the different functions of clergy and layman we should never lose sight of the fact that all are people of God. The vocation of the laity is of equal dignity with that of the clergy, and the Body of Christ is healthy only as this understanding is constantly maintained. In Japan we sometimes hear it said that laymen are *bokushi no te to ashi* (the hands and feet of the pastor). This unhappy expression is evidence of the defective theology of the laity often prevalent in the Church. True, there is nothing objectionable about laymen assisting the pastor in his duties, but they are to be regarded as men and women who are also called of God with a calling fully as worthy as that of the pastor. The pastor does not do the work of the church assisted by the layman. All are called: some are given one gift or function, some another.

ROLE OF THE CLERGY

When the biblical calling of the laity is revived, it is inevitable and essential that the role of the clergy also be re-examined. A good deal of this kind of examination is going on today.

We need to ask anew why clergymen are given to the Church. The answer of Ephesians 4:11-12 is that they are given "to equip God's people for work in his service." The Corinthian letters show Paul performing this role with a very troublesome church. The clergy must perceive by faith that every believer has gifts from God, otherwise they tend to regard themselves as the only possessors of divine gifts. They organize the church according to their own plans and shape people's faith according to their clerical concepts of God and His world. If believers manifest new gifts, clergymen sometimes become frightened and try to mold them into the existing stereotyped patterns of church life. But if the clergy can demonstrate Paul's attitude, then they assist believers to recognize and develop and discipline their gifts, with resultant new power for service.

The placing of a comma has a determining influence on the interpretation of Ephesians 4:11-12. Verse 12, which gives the purpose of the offices named in verse 11, is translated in the Revised Standard Version, "for the equipment of the saints, for the work of ministry, for building up the body of Christ." The Authorized Version gives a similar rendering. The comma after "saints" makes it appear that the work of the clergy is being referred to in the phrase which follows. But in fact a number of scholars insist that there is no justification for placing a comma here (Kraemer 1958:*Laity,* 140; Eastwood 1960:110-111).

The Interpreter's Bible, while noting that the words of verse twelve "would apply most fitly to the work of pastors and teachers, and are perhaps meant to be so taken," goes on to state: "The three phrases of vs. 12 are not parallel, as the thrice-repeated *for* of our versions would suggest; in Greek there is a change of prepositions (*pros, eis, eis*). It seems best to take the first two phrases together–'in order to fit his people for the work of service' " (Goodspeed).[5] B. F. Westcott writes:

> A consideration of the scope of the whole passage in which special stress is laid upon the ministry of every part to the welfare of the whole, seems to be absolutely decisive as to the interpretation. . . . The change of the preposition shows clêarly that the three clauses . . . are not co-ordinate, and however foreign the idea of the spiritual ministry of all "the saints" is to our mode of thinking, it was the life of the apostolic church (1952:62-63).

The New English Bible translates: "to equip God's people for work in his service, to the building up of the body of Christ." J. B.

Phillips has it: "His gifts were made that Christians might be built up." Happily, the Kōgotai (colloquial language) translation used by most Protestants in Japan also renders the passage with this sense.

The right meaning, then, is that the work of pastors, teachers, prophets, and evangelists is to equip all the saints so that they may be able to serve Christ. However, Japanese leaders should be alert to the fact that this pivotal passage has long been misunderstood in the West, and that the theologies and ecclesiologies on seminary library shelves are heavily colored by this fact. Thus we find that at Madras, Ephesians 4:12 was interpreted in a clerical sense: "From the time of the Apostles there have been special orders and ministries in the Church, given by God" (W. Paton 1939:Vol. 4, 199). That is true, but it is doubtful if verse twelve is saying that.

The role of the clergy, then, is not so much to do the work of the Church, as to equip believers so *they* can do this work. If this could be fully understood in Japan and other countries of Asia and Africa, and put into practice, the life of the Church would be revolutionized. One recognizes that this will not be easy, for the training of the clergy in the seminaries is not at all designed to prepare them for this kind of role.

The pastor, in this view, may regard his congregation as a field in which there are many diamonds, most of them still hidden, precious gifts which, when discovered and polished, will mightily enrich the Church and manifest the glory of God.

The true glory of the pastor is that he enables the members of Christ's Church to develop their gifts. It is not so much the vocation of the pastor to bring the Christian influence upon schools and hospitals, courts and city halls. Rather, he is called to be used of God to prepare Christian teachers, doctors, lawyers, and politicians to do that.

This book contends for the greater use of many laymen in various capacities to participate in pastoral care and the leadership of the Church. The professional clergy can render one of its most significant contributions by training and stimulating laymen to prepare themselves for this ministry. At Madras, the recognition of this function of the clergy was urged (W. Paton 1939:Vol. 4, 209-210).

This role is actually being played by clergymen in numerous places in the world today. Sundkler (1960) narrates several interesting cases from Africa. At Dābou in the Gold Coast (Ghana) where the Harris movement led to widespread growth of the Methodist Church in years past, 275 catechists gather every Saturday to hear a sermon by their pastor. The next day they modify this sermon according to their respective individuality and deliver it to the congregations under their charge. A student preparing for the ministry at an African theological school writes: "I am interested in the New Testament because it helps me to teach our catechists and elders when I become a pastor." How greatly is a clergyman's vocation expanded when he can come to view it in this way!

Admittedly the above does not exhaust the calling of the pastor, but it does represent a significant aspect of his role.

WHAT WE MUST DO

We conclude, then, that the Church must both theologically and practically reassert the vocation of the laity. The seminaries must teach it. The clergy must believe in it and must educate the laity concerning it. We need to make specific changes in our way of conducting the Church at this point, for we teach more by what we do than by what we say.

Attention needs to be given to the question of how the laity must be enabled to participate more fully in the worship of the Church (liturgy and preaching), as well as in teaching and administration.

THE VOCATION OF THE LAITY IN THE WORLD

The layman is called to serve God in two places, in the Church and in the world. In this book I have intentionally limited myself to the evangelistic and pastoral vocation, what may be thought of as the "church" part of the layman's calling.

But of course both aspects of the vocation of the laity must be fulfilled. The workaday world is the object of God's concern in creation and providence, and the Christian is called to do the will of God in this world. Most of a layman's time is spent at his work and in his home. The church must not excessively multiply meetings to which the same believers are expected to come. To imply that the laity's calling is limited to prayer, Bible study, church work, and evangelism is to distort the concept of a vocation.

Many today seek to place the emphasis upon the laity's role in the world. One voice urges that the Lord wants His people in the world, there to do battle with power politics, smashing the idols that shackle twentieth-century men (Weber 1963:34-35). Another maintains that although there are important tasks within the local church, the concern for Christian service must not be limited to this, otherwise fewer and fewer laymen will be found in the churches (Gibbs and Morton 1964:117). There is much truth in this emphasis, and the Church in any country will neglect it at its own peril. Yet it can be overdone. To emphasize Christian social action at the expense of evangelism is to commit spiritual suicide. It is amazing how many books, devoted exclusively to the calling of the Christian, fail to reach the question of whether men are being converted through the *diakonia* of Christians.

Some Western churchmen seem to be indifferent to whether the Church grows numerically or not. They value Christian action as an end in itself. But in a land where Christians constitute an almost insignificant minority, the Church cannot afford the luxury of this kind of thinking. Few idols of modern life are going to be smashed when only one person in 200 is a Christian. Here the emphasis must be upon evangelism–upon winning the millions for Christ. Japanese Christians dare not neglect their calling in the world, but the great need is for every Christian to be engaged in the task of evangelism. This, be it noted, is also a Christian role in the "outside world."

CHAPTER IX

THE PASTORAL OFFICE

In view of the set policies followed by most Christian Churches for centuries, and the importance attached to such matters by many, it may come as somewhat of a shock to some to find that the New Testament does not set forth one clearly definable doctrine of holy orders.

While most modern Churches have narrowed the pastoral function down largely to educated and salaried ordained clergymen, the New Testament presents a picture of variously gifted persons who share in the ministry of the Word. We read of apostles, prophets, teachers, men who speak in tongues, evangelists, and pastors. We hear also of administrators, helpers, workers of miracles, and healers (Rom. 12:6-8; I Cor. 12:4-11; 14:1ff.; Eph. 4:7-12). No one person or class of persons exercised a monoply of the ministry of teaching or prophecy. The only limitation made was that any contribution must be such as to edify the church (Manson 1948:57-58).

The records speak of the appointment of presbyters (elders) and deacons. Paul appointed presbyters in churches he founded (Acts 14:23). It is important to note that in the New Testament the terms "presbyter" and "bishop" are used to refer to the same office.[1] Many think that the office of elder was almost certainly taken over from the synagogue. This office was obscured somewhat in the New Testament era by the ministry of persons endowed with special charismatic gifts, mentioned in I Corinthians 12 and Ephesians 4; and then, after these had disappeared, by the monarchical bishops, as the latter came to have increased authority. However, when the bishops began to rule over wide territories, the elders emerged again and to this day regularly act as the pastors of local churches. The New Testament evidence concerning the office of deacon does not leave us with a clear definition of the function of this level of ministry (Morris 1964:70-71, 80-90).[2]

In fact, as many writers in recent years have pointed out, the dominant note in the New Testament, so far as organization is concerned, is fluidity. No hard and fast policies emerge, and the picture is rather one of new and flexible arrangements for various situations which arise (Manson 1948:57-65; Grant 1955:823).

Of course, it is probable that this "fluidity" was not intended to be permanent. It is a common characteristic of most group movements before settled forms have been established. Jesus appears to have distinguished between the function of a *disciple* and an *apostle.* Yet the apostles, though originally twelve, were not confined to that number by the New Testament Church. Others were called and sent by the Holy Spirit. The epistles reflect the emergence of more settled forms of ministry, though we are not told much about them. The emphasis is more upon the work to be done than upon matters of position or status. The appointment to pastoral functions is nowhere in the New Testament limited to persons who receive a salary from the Church, or who possess certain educational qualifications. The apostles themselves were men of varied educational levels. Insofar as qualifications are mentioned (I Tim. 3:1-13; Tit. 1:5-9), they deal with matters of character rather than with educational or professional issues. We are left with the impression that it is far more important that the feeding of the flock of God be diligently attended to than that persons appointed should have qualifications of a professional nature.

The New Testament scholar, T. W. Manson, gives his considered conclusions concerning the matter:

> So we come to the settled ministry. It need not be a whole-time job. It need not have been to a theological college. Its only fundamental requirement is fitness and willingness to give the kind of service that is needed in the common life of a colony of Heaven (1948:55).

We conclude, then, that there are no restrictions laid upon us by the New Testament which would preclude the adoption of more flexible forms of ministry and the inclusion of more than one kind of leader for providing pastoral care, as urged in these pages. This is in accord with the words of Leon Morris: "Since there are no authoritative directions for the ministry, we must feel that at least in some respects the ministry is capable of adaptation to the various situations that will arise" (1964:112).

After the first century, more rigid and authoritative patterns of organization made their appearance in the Church, until after some centuries the system now familiar to us in the Roman Catholic Church came to prevail everywhere. It should be noted, however, that even this development did not necessarily preclude various levels of ministry. A letter from Cornelius in the third century concerning the church in Rome, where there were somewhere between 30,000 and 50,000 members, lists the following: 1 bishop, 46 presbyters, 7 deacons, 7 sub-deacons, 42 acolytes, 52 exorcists, readers, and doorkeepers (Manson 1948:70).

After the Reformation, there were departures from the hierarchical system espoused by the Church of Rome. The Reformers rejected the high claims of the Roman hierarchy, and the cleft between clergy and laity was somewhat reduced. Protestants in Europe have not often returned to the flexible stance of the New Testament so far as wide participation in the pastoral function is concerned but, as we have seen, there have been and are today notable and fruitful moves along this line in the foreign missionary work of the Churches.

PATTERNS OF MINISTRY IN JAPAN

So far as I know, no systematic study of the organizational patterns of the churches in Japan has been undertaken. This writer has for some years attempted, in informal conversations with Japanese pastors, as well as missionaries of various denominations, to ascertain what practices are being followed. The impression gained is that a great deal of uniformity prevails, only slightly affected by denominational differences.

One searches the literature almost in vain for information concerning experiments in which laymen have been assigned to the kinds of roles we have noted in chapters four and five. Whether writers are missionaries or Japanese, so far as leadership is concerned, the emphasis from the Meiji Era until today is almost exclusively upon the professional clergy. Missionaries and Japanese ministers occupy the stage. If attention is given to laymen, it is not for the churchly roles they play alongside the pastor, but for special service they have rendered in the educational world, in social service, or in politics.

We have already called attention to the fact that when the Church of South India began to be concerned about ways and means for providing pastoral care, it found that missionaries had as a matter of course instituted in India the patterns of the Western church. This is also true of Japan, notwithstanding the fact that the position and function of the pastor in his church has been shaped by attitudes which run deep in the social character of the people. Prevailing patterns of pastoral care were not developed by the Japanese, but were introduced during the last century by Western missionaries.

Moreover, they were brought to Japan largely by those American denominations which had held to fixed practices regarding the clergy, even though those forms had proved grossly inadequate to the frontier situation. The first four Protestant missions to enter were the Episcopalians, the Presbyterians, the Reformed, and the Baptists. The precedents they established continue uninterrupted to this day.

The student of the Meiji Era (1868-1912) cannot fail to be impressed by the high caliber of both the first missionaries and the early Japanese leaders. The latter were drawn largely from the *samurai* class. A number of dauntless and able leaders quickly arose. In many ways this was a fortunate circumstance, but it had also the effect of overshadowing the nonclerical members of the churches. A pattern was established which has continued to the present.

Since Methodists have always been prominent among Protestants in Japan, it may be asked why they did not utilize there the system examined in chapter four, with its strong element of lay participation. A standard Methodist history, based on original sources, reveals that the familiar terminology was, in fact, employed (Barclay 1957:667-732). We hear of districts, circuits and circuit pastors, and local preachers, but the terms seem to have taken on new meanings. Circuit pastors appear to be clergymen acting alone to lead several congregations. The term "local preachers" seems to be used of salaried workers with limited formal training, or of a post held prior to appointment as fully ordained ministers.

How are we to account for this change? The reason is almost certainly that the Methodism which came to Japan was not British, but late nineteenth-century American. In the nineteenth century, British Methodism introduced its system with good results into such places as the Gold Coast (modern Ghana) in Africa, South Africa (Sundkler [1960] reports 60 circuits with 6,026 class leaders!), the region of India near Hyderabad, Fiji, and other places. Meanwhile, after the middle of the nineteenth century, though in England Methodism continued the circuit system even in the cities, in America it came to be felt that this system was not suited to the urban situation. Though the office of lay preacher still exists in American Methodism, it now plays no significant role in the life of the churches. Moreover, the class system has also been allowed to atrophy, although something like it, under various names, is being attempted in a few churches today. Almost certainly this change explains why Methodist missionaries, who first came to Japan from America in the late nineteenth century, did not introduce their flexible system there.

The first Protestant church in Japan was organized in Yokohama by the Presbyterian Mission in 1872. The familiar Presbyterian plan, providing for a pastor and ruling elders, was written into the constitution. The second church to be organized was also Presbyterian, in Tokyo in 1873, on the same organizational pattern. Ogawa Yoshiyasu, who afterwards became a prominent minister, was the first elder (Cary 1909:76, 99).

In 1876 missionary delegates of the Presbyterian Church in the United States, the Reformed Church in America, and the United Presbyterian Church of Scotland met and formed what came to be known as the "Church of Christ in Japan." The doctrines were based on Reformed catechisms, and the rules of church government were modeled upon those of Presbyterian churches in the West. Three men were ordained to the Christian ministry at the first session of the new body in 1877.

These accounts are representative of those which record the early activities of all the Churches. We hear of the missionary concern, as was proper, for "raising up, as soon as possible, a thoroughly equipped native ministry" (Cary 1908: 147). But the records are silent concerning any considerable or regular use of laymen for leadership in small churches where no salaried clergy could be placed.

We do hear of catechists occasionally. Henry Tucker, bishop of the Episcopal Church early in this century, mentions several congregations which were led by catechists. At one time before he became bishop, Tucker had charge of three churches after the fashion familiar even today in some rural sections of America. But he obviously regarded this as a temporary arrangement to be borne with only until a pastor could be obtained for each. He refers to the good work done by relatively untrained catechists. He recounts how two such men, Nagata and Urabe, outstanding in evangelistic work for forty years, were as a special favor in their old age ordained–not as clergymen, but as deacons (1951:253, 273). This reluctance to count any as clergymen who do not meet fixed educational standards is the same policy we have observed in much (though not all) of American church history.

In sharp contrast to the slow growth of Protestant missions was the rapid growth of the Orthodox Church under the remarkable leadership of the Russian missionary, Nicolai. He first arrived in Japan in 1861. For some years he worked in Hakodate, and in 1873 moved to Tokyo.

By 1883, he reported a membership of 8,863 (including children), 148 organized churches, 11 ordained Japanese priests, 120 Japanese evangelists, and five foreign priests (Brown 1921:619). In 1882 the combined Protestant statistics were: 93 churches, 4,987 communicant members, 49 ordained clergy, and 145 missionaries (Latourette 1944:390-391). In 1900, the Orthodox Church alone reported 26,000 members, and 34,782 in 1914 (Neill 1964:446).

Nicolai from the first intended that his Church should be independent of the Church in Russia, and truly Japanese. To this end, he placed great emphasis upon preparing Japanese leadership, evangelization of Japan by the Japanese, and the active participation of laymen in the administration of the Church.

He introduced two kinds of leader. The congregations were in charge of the so-called "white priests," who received only minimum training. They conducted the liturgy in the churches. The overall work was administered by the "black priests," men who were much more thoroughly trained. This flexible approach enabled Nicolai to multiply rapidly leaders who could give pastoral care. During Nicolai's lifetime, the Orthodox Church was always considerably larger than any of the Protestant Churches, even though its missionaries were never very numerous. If the spiritual level of this Church could have been maintained after Nicolai's death, it is conceivable that its flexible policies regarding the clergy would have led to unprecedented growth. Is there any relation between Nicolai's willingness to use some clergymen with limited training and the fact that this Church, unlike either the Protestants or Catholics, was able to win thousands of converts from among the lower social classes?

Summary. The pattern of *one-paid-pastor-per-church*, a professional clergy of one type with high educational qualifications, was introduced into Japan by Protestant missionaries in the second half of the nineteenth century. This pattern has been consistently followed by virtually all Protestant Churches to this day. Other than the Roman Catholic Church, the fastest-growing Church until 1912 was the Orthodox Church, which introduced more flexible patterns for providing pastoral care.

Although the ways in which the role and character of the clergy in Japan have developed are peculiar to that country, they will not sound altogether strange to Christians in many other lands. For the obvious reason that most of the missionary work of the modern era has been conducted by European or Europeanized Christians who carried with them the ecclesiastical patterns they had learned in the homeland, the Western forms of the clergy seen in Japan are also found in most other parts of the world. One of the major factors which has served to perpetuate these usages is the custom of ordination.

ORDINATION

This book urges repeatedly that (1) the Church return to the New Testament pattern of a variety of roles by which pastoral care and teaching are made available to the people of God, and (2) the gulf between clergy and laity be reduced by admitting persons now regarded as laymen into the pastoral ministry of the Church.

In addition to its useful and valuable functions, the custom of ordination has operated in history to foster fixed patterns for providing pastoral care and the sacraments, and to sharpen the division between clergy and laity.

A strong cry is heard in many parts of the world today for the extension of ordination to part-time and unpaid leaders of modest training who can minister to small churches, especially (but not only) in rural districts. In part this cry arises out of the conviction that every group of believing Christians ought to be able to enjoy regularly the blessing of the sacraments. Many village congregations are currently unable to do this because of the shortage of ordained clergy.

Is it optional whether congregations be permitted the right of receiving the sacraments? The Church in Japan in which the writer serves, upon reflecting that Christ commanded the observance of the sacraments, and that there were several churches in which they were almost never observed because the leaders were not ordained, came to feel that such a policy could only be termed sinful. It then set about ordaining elders from among members of the churches and also authorizing *hokyōshi* (preparatory ministers) to conduct the service of Holy Communion. Christians in many denominations have come to similar conclusions.

Roland Allen argued that we must not place churches in the position of being unable to observe the rites which Christ commanded (I Cor. 11:25; Matt. 28:19) because their humble leaders are left unordained. We fall into this error, he maintained, because we are bound to a tradition from the West which assumes the only clergy possible is trained and paid. Allen's solution is to ordain unpaid, voluntary clergy in local churches (1962:*Ministry* 170-173).

John Lawson, to whom we are indebted in chapter four for an account of English Methodism, urges the augmenting of the lay preacher system by the ordination of "auxiliary presbyters" in churches which do not have salaried pastors. There are many worthy men, he asserts, including businessmen, technicians, farmers, and social workers who, while they may not be able to preach well, could learn to conduct Holy Communion with dignity and feeling. The more frequent observance of the sacrament with the aid of such men would benefit the churches in a number of ways. It would, for example, open up an avenue of significant service for many in the churches. This would in turn help to relieve the shortage of lay preachers. It would, moreover, often enable believers in small congregations to enjoy a more meaningful worship experience. Especially in very small congregations (three to six persons) the service of Holy Communion might often prove more appropriate than a sermon, for it is not easy to preach to such small audiences. Lawson urges careful selection and preparation of men to be appointed to this responsibility (1955:110-117). The proposal is worked out carefully, and the entire section deserves thoughtful consideration.

But is it proper to bestow ordination upon unpaid men who are not seminary graduates?

In the eyes of the Roman Catholic Church, ordination is one of the seven sacraments. Moreover, by definition of the Council of Trent, when the words "Receive ye the Holy Ghost" have been pronounced upon the candidate by the bishop, an indelible character is imprinted upon the individual. He can never again become a layman, and ordination may never be repeated.

The Reformers completely rejected the claims of the Roman Catholic hierarchy, including its doctrine of ordination. Luther held the essential thing to be the call from God to the ministry of the Word. He considered ordination to be a rite by which the congregation expresses its recognition of this divine call, and this rite is conducted by other ministers on behalf of the congregation. According to Luther, no "undefined magical power, or 'special' grace is imparted by ordination"; nor does it bestow any "indelible character" (Eastwood 1960:40-42; Gerrish 1965:418).

Calvin also denied that ordination imparts an "indelible character." With Luther, he emphasized that the rite is a recognition of a divine call. Calvin rejected the idea of a hierarchy in the Church in favor of the full parity of all ministers (Johnson 1961:59-60).

It has been observed that "in the New Testament there is no hint whatever that the celebration of the Eucharist is the prerogative of the ministry" (Hanson 1965:24). Moreover, there is surprisingly little to be found in the Bible regarding ordination.

When we seek to define "ordination," it is to the formulations of the various Churches that we must go, for the New Testament does not present a developed doctrine of ordination.[3] This fact ought to make us cautious concerning rigid ecclesiastical rules based upon the concept of ordination.

Henri d'Espine summarizes the view of ordination which, though unformulated, has generally prevailed in the Reformed Churches of the Calvinist tradition as follows:

> The Church recognizes by ordination the call that God has addressed to one of its members. It grants him authority for the exercise of the ministry within the church to which God has called him. It prays earnestly on his behalf for the graces necessary to the work of this ministry. It ordains him to the service of God, by the laying on of hands, and expresses its certainty that God grants its prayer (1961:122).[4]

We can be sure that in the New Testament the "laying on of hands" did not always mean ordination (Acts 8:17-19; 9:12; 28:8). Did ordination always involve the laying on of hands? We do not know, although it is a fact that rabbis ordained their disciples by the laying on of hands. By the second century this was the universal practice in the Church, which suggests that it was the practice also during the days of the apostles (Richardson 1958:330-331).

Some scholars think John 20:20-22 describes an ordination rite, but this is not certain. Though Jesus appointed the twelve, there is no record of His having ordained them by the laying on of hands.

Leon Morris argues that while it is "highly probable that the apostles ordained men to the ministry . . . this cannot be proved" (1964:58). True, the Seven were commissioned in Acts 6, but it is not certain that an ordination rite was involved, or that an order of the ministry is meant (Morris 1964:58-60, 87-88).

The meaning of II Timothy 1:6 is disputed. Some think it refers to Paul having made Timothy a bishop. Others, without reference to episcopal concepts, hold that Timothy was ordained twice (II Tim. 1:6 and I Tim. 4:14). Morris holds that while II Timothy is often interpreted as referring to ordination, the context suggests something more like modern confirmation, which if true would leave I Timothy 4:14 as the only passage referring to Timothy's ordination (1964:60). What we have, then, is one and possibly two non-definitive references to ordination in the letters to Timothy.

In the same section Morris argues that while it is probable we should understand Acts 14:23 as meaning that Paul and Barnabas ordained elders, the fact that the key word in the passage *(cheirotoneo)* is also used in II Corinthians 8:19, where ordination is clearly not meant, means that the interpretation is uncertain. The word in question bears the meaning of "appoint" only, and does not contain the meaning of laying on of hands.

This is as far as the New Testament takes us. No clear and closely defined doctrine of ordination emerges from the Scriptures. Whatever we may think concerning the vexed problem of who may *bestow* ordination, it is evident that there are no biblical reasons for authorizing or requiring churchmen to insist upon rigid limitations concerning who may *receive* ordination. In particular, we insist that there are no biblical reasons whatsoever why a Church may not ordain unpaid or partially paid clergy, including men who have not attended seminary.

This should not be construed as an argument for jettisoning the rite of ordination. It is both permissible and desirable that this time-honored rite be preserved as a guard of order in the Church and a reminder of the solemnity of the calling to particular pastoral functions. A Church is justified in developing orderly practices regarding ordination and in basing its practices so far as possible upon scriptural principles. It should not, however, in the light of the nature of the scriptural evidence, insist that its formulation is the only possible one. Above all, its formulation should not be permitted to limit pastoral functions to one particular class within the Church, to the detriment of the growth of the flock of God.

When it is proposed that unpaid but carefully selected men of mature years be ordained as one important step toward the flexibility needed to evangelize Japan, some may consider this suggestion novel. Japanese city pastors in settled churches, especially, may experience difficulty in appreciating the need for ordaining other than full ministers *(seikyōshi).* Such pastors should ask themselves whether they favor a continuance of the prevailing static situation in which few new churches are planted, and churches are seldom found in small towns and villages. Unless they do, they should consider how to cope with a missionary situation in which (1) many new churches, which cannot in their early years afford a pastor's salary, are being continually planted, and (2) churches are formed in small communities which may never be able to afford the salary of a full-time pastor. Such churches as these must perforce be led by lay preachers and local elders, aided by occasional visits from *seikyōshi.* Unless local elders are ordained, people in these churches will be deprived of the sacraments for most of the year. If it is asked why that is a matter of serious moment, the answer is that observance of the sacraments is not optional for Christians: Christ commanded they be observed.

Moreover, it is important to break down the unbiblical gulf between the clergy and other members of the Body of Christ, as one important element in the mobilizing of all the people of God in the missionary task of the Church.

The question may arise as to who would conduct the sacraments in a local church which had both salaried ministers and ordained elders. Any church which employs a salaried clergyman surely should regard him as the senior elder in the church. Normally, then, the ministers would conduct the sacraments. But would it not add to a better understanding of the real meaning of the Church on the part of all concerned if occasionally the ministers sat in the congregation while an unpaid elder conducted the service of Holy Communion?

Others may question whether the people will accept baptism from unpaid elders. There is ample evidence from many places in the world that the people will readily accept the ministry of respected elders if the professional clergy encourage and teach them to do so.

AN EDUCATED CLERGY

All this should not be interpreted as an attempt to deny the importance of an educated clergy. Webster points out that in Latin America today an ever-growing importance is being placed upon education by society in general. Uneducated pastors can minister only among uneducated people. The Pentecostals, among others, appreciate this and are attempting to improve the educational level of their clergy (Webster 1964:36-37).[5]

It would be unthinkable to overlook the need for well-trained clergy in a land like Japan. Large city churches must have men who are trained in many areas. Educated clergy are indispensable in order to enable the Church in every part of the country to meet the challenges of the highly literate, materialistic, and energetic society of modern Japan. Furthermore, if the professional clergy are to train unpaid and part-time clergy, they themselves need much training.

This is not, however, to say that every minister in Japan ought to be a seminary graduate. In farming villages, small towns, and among certain types of urban situations, men with educational preparation not too far above that of their parishioners will often prove the most effective leaders.

J. Merle Davis has reported on the work of a strong Congregational pastor in Brazil, the Rev. Joao Climaco Ximenes (1943:100-103). Led by the men's missionary society of 110 members, the church was supporting seven missionaries in its state. Their efforts to plant new churches were aided by the active evangelistic work of the laity.

During the fifteen years of Ximenes' leadership, the parent church had grown from a membership of 100 to 710. Meanwhile, six churches had been organized and were being led by their own pastors, and 18 small congregations gathered with a view to organizing future churches. The method employed was to station an evangelist in a central rural community. A little circuit of congregations would be built up in the vicinity. When they had become strong enough, these several congregations would organize themselves as one church (meeting in several locations) and would employ one trained pastor.

Said Ximenes, himself a man with a full theological education:

> We need a few trained pastors, but very many men who will work close to the humble people of the villages, who understand them, and whom these people understand. The trained pastors must be placed in strategic places where they can be supported adequately and direct the work of the evangelists in the rural field.

Ordination has been widely used as a device for insuring that only well-educated persons are admitted into the ranks of the clergy. Unfortunately it has also insured that in numerous lands many Christians receive neither adequate pastoral care nor the blessing of the sacraments. In Japan it has furthermore developed that there are hardly any churches at all in small towns and villages, though Protestant missionary work has been carried on for a full century!

The actual life of the Church has made abundantly clear that when the Church's endeavors to shepherd the multitudes are structured in this fashion, consequences ensue which can only be described as pernicious. The situation cries for remedy. The potential powers of the Church for providing pastoral care for people whenever and wherever they will respond–whether in great numbers or in small–to the invitation of the Gospel, must be released. Now is the time for men to step forward with concrete proposals designed to free the churches from constricting traditions which are required neither by Scripture nor by the universal usages of the Church. One practical way out of the dilemma in which we find ourselves would be to provide for a graduated series of leaders, including several kinds of ordained men fully authorized to conduct the sacraments.

A SUGGESTED APPROACH FOR JAPAN

We attempt here to illustrate how pastoral care could be made far more effective and available in a land like Japan by listing several categories of workers which might be approved for appointment.

Fully Ordained Ministers (Seikyōshi). This role would continue as at present. The ordination of *seikyōshi* would be recognized everywhere throughout the Church (denomination). Those ordained to this position would be persons who had completed a thorough educational program which met the standards of the ordaining church. Ordinarily, the laying on of hands at ordination services would be done by *seikyōshi* and not by pastor-teachers or other workers.

Pastor-Teachers (Bokkai-Kyōshi). A new role between *seikyōshi* (ministers) and *hokyōshi* (preparatory ministers) would be created. The name *bokkai-kyōshi* (literally, "a teacher who gives pastoral care") might be used, or some other appropriate title chosen. Pastor-teachers would be recognized as qualified to do pastoral work. They would be ordained and authorized to perform the sacraments. Their ordination would be recognized within their district only. Usually two or more pastor-teachers would serve as the pastors of one church, but qualified individuals could serve alone. Persons appointed to this role would ordinarily be unpaid or part-time workers, but there would be no rule against their becoming full-time salaried pastors. Candidates would have to complete a prescribed course of training including classes taught by *seikyōshi* and other qualified persons, supplemented perhaps by correspondence courses. Persons who completed two years of theological school training would also be eligible. Pastor-teachers adjudged as being exceptionally qualified, who gave high-level service for many years, and who completed a significant and rigorous regime of theological studies, could be elected for ordination as *seikyōshi.*

Preparatory Ministers (Hokyōshi). This role would continue as at present. That is, persons appointed to this position (they would not be ordained) would be understood as being under preparation for ordination as full ministers. If denominational opinion permitted, preparatory ministers might be authorized to conduct Holy Communion if no ordained leaders were present in a congregation.

Elders. Unpaid leaders of suitable qualifications would be chosen from each congregation and ordained to the role of elder. They would be qualified to conduct the sacraments within their own church, their ordination being effective among the congregation which elected them. For several reasons, it would be well to practice the rotation of elders.[6]

Additional Workers. Men and women would be appointed to such roles as deacons, lay preachers, and exhorters. Several such schemes are referred to in these pages (see specifically chapters four and five).

These persons would, for the most part, be unpaid, and would not ordinarily be ordained.

A proposal of this nature might require adjustment to fit the needs of each Church. The circumstances peculiar to various countries might necessitate another kind of adaptation. But if this or some similar scheme were adopted, it would both guard the educational standards of the clergy and permit the recruiting of a varied leadership which could provide pastoral care, including the sacraments, for a rapidly growing missionary Church.

The acceptance or non-acceptance of this particular proposal is not a matter of major consequence. The issue church leaders must wrestle with is: How do *you* propose to free the Church to provide pastoral care and the sacraments for people, in whatever numbers, whenever and wherever they can be persuaded to acknowledge Jesus Christ as Saviour and Lord?

CHAPTER X

MOBILIZING THE PEOPLE OF GOD

> The successful expansion of any movement is in direct proportion to its success in mobilizing and occupying its total membership in constant propagation of its beliefs.[1]

All who are Christ's are the *laos* of God, whether they be clergy or otherwise, young or old, rich or poor. This is the pivotal truth explored in chapter eight. In chapter one we saw that this people of God is under an unchanging mandate to bring to men everywhere the saving Gospel of Jesus Christ. How may this people be mobilized for the task to which they are called? We now turn to this question.

If the argument of chapters two through seven is accepted, and persons usually regarded as laymen are trained for and admitted to various levels of church leadership, including those involving pastoral functions, much of the battle will already have been won. In Japanese churches today, the role of the layman is too often limited to bringing to the services his ears to hear the pastor's sermon and his wallet to support the budget. When believers realize that positions of leadership and responsibility are not only open to them, but that God is calling men like themselves to active service, a new participation in the purposes of the Church will become manifest.

In this way the *power count* can be greatly multiplied. This term may be defined as the amount of talent, time, and energy a believer is (actual) or could be (potential) devoting to church leadership.

Let us suppose an inactive thirty-member congregation which

depends solely on the paid pastor (who counts 40) for leadership. In such a church, the *actual*-power count of pastor plus members may total only 80 or 90. However, a potential-power count in that same congregation might show two believers with a count of 35, five with 25, ten with 20, ten with 15, and others with somewhat lower counts. If these individuals were to be mobilized as working members, a potential-power count of 600 or 700 would become actualized. Such a church could not fail to make an impact upon its community.

What are some of the ways in which this desirable goal can be realized?

PRESERVING ORIGINAL ZEAL

There is a new and natural joy manifest whenever men enter a fresh experience. This is particularly true of those who have newly become followers of Christ. If the church is merely a storage house for believers, however, this initial ardor often cools.

The best way of preserving this original zeal is by involving new converts in the work of evangelism. The Holy Spirit delights to help believers do the work which Christ commissions them to do. The joy of heaven over a lost sheep returned wells up in the heart of the witnessing believer and releases power.

This is one of the main secrets of the amazing growth of the Pentecostal Churches in Latin America. They are aware of the way to preserve original zeal, and they practice it assiduously. In Chile, the new convert is immediately assigned to a street preaching band. There he may be subjected to ridicule, and his words may be stammered, but he is urged to tell of his new faith, and he hears the testimonies of other believers as the band moves from corner to corner. If the new Christian shows ability, he may be put in charge of a band. If he continues to develop, he may eventually be made responsible for a preaching point of his church. Some of these people go on to become pastors.

The principle of encouraging the new convert to begin expressing his faith immediately is most important. Freed from old unedifying habits and worship patterns, he should also be led to exercise stewardship of his time and abilities. If he only receives from the church, his potentiality to serve may never be realized. The tendency of leaders to put off the beginnings of the new convert's service until he has developed more finesse must be resolutely avoided. The beginner's blundering efforts at serving should be encouraged.

The kinds of service may vary. In Japan, the evangelistic emphasis may be presented in different ways, but the principle is the same. "What is required is far greater emphasis upon post-baptismal training, in which help in making immediate and sustained witness to Christ is extremely important" (World Council of Churches 1963). At such training classes, something better than vague exhortations to witness can be done. The teacher can ask the convert if there is not someone he would like to try to bring to church or speak to about Christ. Then prayer can be offered for his success. Converts can be taught to pray for the gift of the Holy Spirit, and shown Scripture passages which declare that the Father will give the Spirit to His children.

NURTURING A NEW CHURCH

The surest way to have an active evangelistic church is to avoid a time gap between the initial enthusiasm of conversion and the effective evangelistic witness of the converts. The first days of a new church are of particular importance at this point.

As soon as the first converts have been won in a community, they should be given responsibility in the group and encouraged in evangelistic efforts among their relatives and friends. Even if there are but two or three converts, a training course in personal evangelism may be very profitable.

People who reside in a community can often be much more effective in evangelism than those who come in from the outside. Frequently in Japan, especially in rural communities, when the responsibility rests upon professional clergy (either Japanese or foreign) who visit from the outside, only a small and nongrowing group of scattered individuals is gathered.

Once a few converts have been won in a new community, the evangelists should mold these converts into witnesses capable of winning the community. Because it is desirable that families and social groups enter faith together, literature which tells how Christians in other places won their families and neighbors should be made available. Accounts of how the evangelist or other Christians have bravely endured family opposition or persecution may make thrilling stories, but they work against people becoming Christians in families. In family-conscious Japan, the emphasis in sermons, illustrations, and tracts should be on what Christ does for Christian families, and how families become Christians.

Even in the early stages, clergymen should avoid doing everything for the converts, lest they become passive. The pastor should not make all the decisions, but should consult with the converts. To work in this way will often seem odd and clumsy. It will sometimes take more time and effort, but it should result in raising active, responsible, enthusiastic laymen. The experience of the Presbyterians in Korea shows the wisdom of appointing temporary leaders from among the believers at an early stage and assigning them real responsibility.

The evangelists (lay or clerical) who start the work should not do all the speaking after the converts have acquired a little experience. The latter should be encouraged to hold meetings during the week which they lead themselves. When there are six or more converts and inquirers, it may be well to divide into two groups for some meetings. These groups would assemble when the outside evangelist came. This might help avoid the tendency to become a small, static, ingrown fellowship.

PARTICIPATION

One of the most important tasks of any church's leadership is to secure the most widespread participation possible of all members. One of the secrets of the power and enthusiasm of Latin American Pentecostals and certain indigenous churches is that everyone has a job.

The key to a growing church and an active laity is participation. This principle can be seen operating in Sōka Gakkai. The innumerable small house meetings, each with its own leaders, provide rich opportunities for participation. The difficult studying Sōka Gakkai members gladly do is evidence of the power generated by the experience of sharing in leadership functions.

It is not easy to find a meaningful task for everyone inside the church. Pastors must not merely create busy work. It is at this point that the advantages of small groups merit consideration. Again, evangelistic endeavors offer an excellent area for participation, especially if carried out by groups. The number of jobs inside the church is limited, but the evangelistic task has no limitations. The custom in Japan of having believers preside at worship and give the offertory prayer is an improvement on the pattern of worship seen in many American churches in which the pastor does everything, and the believers (except the choir) are passive.

The Apostle Paul taught that all Christians in a church were responsible for each other. Spiritual responsibility was not delegated to a professional clergyman; the whole group participated in the selection of candidates for baptism, ordination, and other functions.

Drawing upon this idea, this writer has inaugurated in his church the custom of all members interviewing candidates for baptism at a friendly and informal gathering where the new convert tells of his faith. Members encourage him, make suggestions, and tell of their own experiences. Two principles are followed: (1) The convert is not baptized unless both believers and pastor concur, and (2) all accept equal responsibility for the convert's life of faith after baptism. This custom has proved to be a rich experience both for converts and believers. It helps to develop a family spirit and a sense of spiritual excitement among the members. I believe this is superior to the usual custom of having an official board pass on candidates, for often this means merely "rubber-stamping" the pastor's recommendation, and the ordinary members feel no sense of personal responsibility for the new convert. In a larger church, a small group of ten or fifteen people whom the convert knows, or with whom he will be associated, can perform this function.

THE TECHNIQUE OF WITHDRAWAL

Roland Allen has pointed out how Paul, after founding a church and grounding it in the faith, withdrew. This forced the appointed leaders to assume genuine responsibility for the life of the church. Paul did not abandon these churches; he kept in touch with them by letter and by messenger. But he trusted them to the Holy Spirit, and prayed they might prosper (Allen 1962:*Methods*, 151). Allen urged that missionaries do the same.

The principle is sound, and Japanese pastors and missionaries might well practice temporary withdrawal. When the pastor is always present, the members easily fall into the habit of letting him do everything, and sink into passivity. Moreover, the presence of a well-trained and able leader tends to overawe people, and they hesitate to exercise their less developed gifts.

So the pastor should arrange occasionally to be away, including Sundays, preaching in the little churches and engaging in special evangelism. If he frankly discusses this with the members and urges both new and old believers to try their wings, most congregations will readily cooperate. They will happily tell him at the next gathering what was done in his absence. If his absences are not too frequent, they will appreciate his ministry more for occasionally having a service without him. Of course, most of us find it hard to believe things will go right unless we are on the spot to supervise!

EVANGELISM

Any church which can engage a large proportion of its members in evangelism is bound to grow if the evangelism is winsome, balanced, and motivated by love. The Churches in the world which experience great growth are frequently those in which personal evangelism is carried out on a wide scale by unpaid, unordained believers.

Bishop Azariah has pointed out that the church at Antioch, so important to future missionary outreach, was begun by laymen. He also draws attention to the historical evidence which indicates that the rapid spread of early Christianity was due largely to the witness of informal missionaries (1939:Vol. 3, 34-37).

The organized efforts of many laymen have been indispensable in the remarkable growth of the Batak Church. The extraordinary growth of the Presbyterian Church in Korea was in great measure due to the personal evangelism done by unpaid believers. This was true in the early days and in great ingatherings during the 1950s as well. Congregations were gathered in places the missionary had not yet visited. The progress of Protestant missions in South Africa has been largely due to the power of lay evangelism. In this the strong Methodist Church has led the way and exercised much influence on other Churches.

The places in Latin America where rapid growth is today taking place are notable for the involvement of the whole Church in evangelistic outreach. Every Christian is a witness, and new congregations spring up under the leadership of laymen (Hodges 1965:117ff.).[2] The swift and remarkable increase in the size of the Spirit of Jesus Church in Japan (see chapter thirteen) is attributed by its founder, Pastor Murai, to the active witness of its laymen and its trained evangelists.

It is essential that these facts be known to the Japanese Church, both clergy and laity. The Rev. Kanai Tameichiro, President of Japan Biblical Seminary, has stated that one of the reasons "the

Christian Gospel in Japan has not penetrated into the ranks of the common people . . . is that evangelism has become the exclusive function of the clergy. The laymen have come to be just an approving voice or spectators on the side lines" (Drummond 1958:219-220). Toyohiko Kagawa emphasized the great need for lay volunteer evangelists, stressing that the evangelization of 70,000,000 Japanese was something 2,000 Japanese pastors could never do.

The enormous power of a Church with a laity that is aflame with the joy and burden of evangelism is a precious treasure to be sought earnestly. Nothing the professional clergy can do surpasses working for this goal, and a clergyman who is a mediocre preacher and a poor organizer must nevertheless be counted a success if he can inspire the people of God and train them in their evangelistic calling.

How can such a spirit be developed in a church? Some leaders resort to scolding the believers for their lack of zeal. But rebukes are seldom productive of power. Enriching the spiritual life is far more effective. Prayer is of central importance, and especially prayer for the gift of the Holy Spirit, and prayer that begins with personal confession.

Professional clergymen should acquire training in how to assist laymen at this point. Mere abstract exhortations are of little value. Teaching that is practical and concrete in its thrust will be of much more use. Best of all will be joint participation in actual evangelistic endeavors. Clergymen should take laymen with them in church-planting efforts, visitation evangelism, and other endeavors.

Laymen should be assured in sermons, in literature, and in conversation that they can start new congregations. They should be encouraged to set out and attempt church planting. After they have gained some experience, clergymen should avoid accompanying them on every occasion. This was the practice of Jesus. (See Luke 10:1.) Their efforts should be honored and supported. Believers should be encouraged and given freedom to start new Christian groups on their own initiative. They may make mistakes. They may occasionally unwisely start groups which cannot be carried on. But rigid clerical control is the poorest solution for the occasional errors of zeal. It kills spontaneity, and spontaneity is indispensable to spiritual power.

At this point the need for training laymen to preach must be stressed. Also, the importance of freeing pastors from the tyranny of money is clear. If the budget in a mother church is touch-and-go, and laymen spend time starting new churches instead of strengthening the mother church, the paid pastor's position may become intolerable. In such cases the branch churches should contribute to part of the pastor's salary—or if they remit to the district treasurer, the district when necessary should share in the support of a pastor whose church builds up the district by starting new churches.

Japanese laymen can and do start new churches. This writer knows of two churches in his area started by a layman in recent years. Two laymen of still another church are currently pioneering a new congregation. In the Osaka area, Principal Nishimura of the Osaka School for Girls is a church planter. Immediately after World War II, with one earnest believer, he rehabilitated Tennōji Church. Today it has a congregation of 100. In 1946, he began the Tamade Church. A building was constructed in 1951, and about 100 persons now gather on Sundays for worship. In 1957, Nishimura started work which led to the forming of the Minami-Sumiyoshi Church. At the time of this writing, the church is without a pastor, but the congregation of 100 is ministered to by about five elders who are able to preach. Nishimura also began another congregation which after having grown to about 70 members merged with a preaching station of another church. Currently Nishimura is at work on still another new church in an apartment zone (Teranishi 1966). Unfortunately, such cases are rare. When they become common all over Japan, we shall be winning the land for Christ.

AZARIAH OF DORNAKAL[3]

Let us now consider a notable attempt to involve the whole people of God in the spread of the Gospel.

Of the great Christian leaders who have arisen in Asia, none has stood higher than Azariah of Dornakal (1874-1945). In 1912 he became the first Indian to be made an Anglican bishop. A writer of power, and a Christian leader of world stature, he led his diocese for over thirty years in a great program of evangelistic outreach.

Azariah's driving concern was that the entire church membership be won for evangelism. "It is our duty," he maintained, "to get every person who is attached to the church to go out as a witness for Christ" (1939:Vol. 3, 41). In his active, growing diocese, he vigorously promoted the slogan, "Every Christian a witness."

This was for him no stereotyped formula, but a conviction which grew out of his theological understanding of the Church. The Fourth

Gospel, he said, understands the Church to have been inaugurated by a creative act of Christ following His resurrection (John 20:21, 23). The Synoptics indicate that the parting message of the Lord after His resurrection consisted of the charge to evangelize given to the disciples, who stood as representatives of the Church of the centuries to follow. To the Church is given the task of carrying on the work begun by Jesus, namely, to reveal the love of God to the world, to save men. Azariah firmly believed that the Church is the "divinely appointed instrument of evangelism to the world" (1939:Vol. 3, 32-34).

It was the scattered Christians of Cyprus and Cyrene, he asserted, who founded the church destined to spearhead missionary work to the Gentiles (Acts 11:20). Such churches as those in Laodicea, Colossae, and Hierapolis were the result of the efforts of laymen, not of the apostles. (See Acts 19:10; Col. 2:1; 4:13.) With awesome energy Paul carried the Gospel to the leading cities of Galatia, Macedonia, Achaia, and Asia, but we should understand that the evangelism of the rural areas surrounding these cities was undoubtedly carried out by his converts rather than by the apostle himself (I Thess. 1:8).

The early history of the Church, Azariah held, affords evidence of the power of the New Testament teaching that all believers are called to be witnesses. He quotes Harnack and Latourette to prove that the phenomenal growth of the Church of the first centuries was due primarily, not to the work of professionals and regular teachers, but to the witness of ordinary Christians. Men witnessed as they carried on their ordinary occupations in the world. Everyone who took the faith seriously became of use in the propagation of Christianity's message. The verbal witness of these unknown believers was buttressed by the high level of life they displayed before a pagan world and by the charitable works of the Church. Azariah laid much stress on the duty of Christians to witness not only by their words, but by the quality of their daily lives. He attributed much of the growth of the Church in Dornakal to the impact made by the remarkable changes in the lives of even illiterate outcastes as a result of their conversion to Christ.

He was concerned that the Church everywhere recognize that its purpose for existing is to carry on the saving work which Christ, by His life, death, and resurrection, began. He expressed disappointment that the Conference on Faith and Order, meeting at Edinburgh in 1937, did not in its statements attain to this understanding.

> It is the Church's duty to concentrate all its energies to do the work of Christ. It is not just to worship; but it is to continue to do Christ's work with the help and the strength that we get in worship. Too much of the energies of ministers and churches is being spent in taking permanent care of hereditary Christians. The Church exists not to save itself but to save others (1939:Vol. 3, 42).

It is this conviction which lies behind his contention that once a mission has in a new place baptized and gathered a group of converts to form a church, it should place responsibility for the evangelism of that area upon the church. The mission should not leave the church to itself and independently continue the evangelism of the area. It should now recognize that it has a task "to perfect the saints unto the work of ministering." It must assist that church to recognize its evangelistic task and to be able to carry it out. Azariah labeled as disastrous the frequently encountered idea that the church should take responsibility for pastoral care and the mission for evangelism, and that the church should not attempt missionary work until it is able to pay for its own pastoral care.

He opposed, for the same reason, the employment of evangelists to do evangelistic work in an area in which a church had already been planted. It matters not, he held, whether the salaries of the evangelists are paid by the church or by some outside agency. The employment of evangelists in such situations suffocates the "spirit of voluntary evangelism" in the church. Paid evangelists should be sent to areas where there are as yet no churches.

Ministers must not think that their task is merely "taking care of hereditary Christians." They are to equip the believers to carry the Gospel to those who have not yet heard it.

> A man must consider his pastoral ministry so far a failure, if he does not see the people under his charge growing in soul-winning fervour, in missionary giving, and dedication to missionary service. Many churches are like refineries that are supposed to have done their task as soon as they refine enough oil to grease themselves with (1939:Vol. 3, 42)!

Not only did Azariah believe that in principle each Christian should engage in evangelism; he believed in devoting intensive efforts to actually achieve every-member participation.

> Let us make known to all our people the chief purpose for which the Church exists. Let us not be content until this duty is accepted by every communicant in our congregations (Graham 1946:11).

He directed all efforts to that end. He gave careful thought to how this priceless goal could be achieved. We may learn from the life of Azariah that it is not sufficient merely to be of the conviction that all Christians should be evangelists. The Church must exercise its ingenuity and properly channel its energies. It must adopt concrete ways of conveying this truth to the entire membership and of actually recruiting them to active evangelistic endeavor. What are some of the things Azariah did to realize this crucial objective?

He depended upon prayer. Arising daily not later than 5 a.m., he would bear up in prayer every person carrying important responsibilities in his diocese. As the diocese grew in numbers, the list of persons for whom he prayed grew accordingly.

He depended upon teaching, which he himself loved to do. Coupled with his knowledge of the thinking of village people was his firm belief that the simplest villager, including the outcaste, could understand the Bible. He believed, moreover, that if they were truly to live as Christians, they must understand it, and he devoted much effort to enabling them to do so.

He believed in the power of systematic teaching of the Bible to all Christians, and in the training of the believers for service and right living. *Christian Giving* is one of a series of books he wrote as part of his endeavor to foster this program of training. In his writings he sought to introduce to the Christians in his diocese the experience of the Church in Korea, Sumatra, Burma, and other countries.

He promoted the training of believers in evangelism. In his diocese, small groups of baptized persons were gathered and taught to go out into the villages and answer the simple questions of the villagers. He was convinced that even illiterate Christians could be effective witnesses, and contended that often such humble persons taught him ways of answering questions which were more penetrating than intellectualized formulations.

He was of the opinion that there is value in persuading Christians simply to identify themselves with public witness.

> The sharing of our experience with others adds to our joy and to our own Christian experience. Let some men just stand somewhere as Christians; let them just face a non-Christian crowd; let someone else do the preaching and someone else the singing; the experience of just standing for Christ will drive them to their knees before Christ (1939:Vol. 7, 41).

He used the rites of his Church, such as confirmation, to educate believers in their evangelistic calling. To the three vows commonly made by candidates (to renounce evil, have faith, and to obey), he persuaded his Church in India to add a fourth: to witness faithfully for Christ.

He believed that in baptism the candidate's life is dedicated to Christ, and that he is to be His faithful soldier until life's end. To be ashamed of Christ is to deny one's baptism, for every person who has been baptized should witness for Christ.

> I used to go around among the churches and have the baptized members place their hands on their own heads (as if in the act of baptism) and repeat after me, "I am a baptized Christian. Woe unto me if I preach not the Gospel" (1939:Vol. 7, 42).

He believed in the power of music and drama to implant ideas deep within people's lives. The words of familiar songs, he contended, would enable men to appropriate the truths of the Gospel when other methods failed. With his encouragement, Christian music of many kinds was written in the Telegu language, in which the life of Christ and other central articles of the Faith were sung. Morning and evening prayers came to employ canticles rewritten in Indian style and set to Indian melodies. Azariah also promoted the writing of biblical dramas, by which villagers could be helped to grasp more fully the meaning of the Gospel.

He inaugurated the custom, still carried on, of an annual great week of witness. This was planned for the hot season, when the villagers were least busy. He desired and worked for the participation of every communicant in this effort. He was not satisfied one year when the level of participation reached 36 per cent, even though this degree of involvement in active Christian witness is rare anywhere in the world. Clergymen and other salaried workers were expected to lead the people in preparation for the week of evangelism, but not to do any of the preaching. Ordinary believers were called on to do the speaking, as the thousands of Christians went out to the villages of their areas to witness for Christ. This annual campaign invariably resulted in requests for further teaching from a number of outcaste villages, in addition to which–as Azariah had, against much opposition, maintained would happen–numbers of high-caste people, influenced by the changed lives and verbal witness of outcaste Christians, would inquire into the Faith.

It must not be thought from all this that Azariah assigned light importance to the role of the clergy. When he became Bishop of Dornakal there were but eight Indian clergymen, but by the time of his death there were fifteen times that number. He made the training of able, dependable clergy his chief joy and care. He was concerned primarily with spiritual qualifications, and candidates for ordination had to be men who had already proved themselves. He unhesitatingly ordained humble village men as priests, though their educational qualifications might be slight. He trusted them as part of the Church's leadership, all the while working continually to improve the educational preparation of the clergy. By the time of his death he was seeing men ordained who had completed work in the arts and theology.

It would be a mistake to assume that everything in Dornakal progressed in accordance with Azariah's desires. Human frailty makes itself felt everywhere. He was, for example, in his later years distressed because second and third generation Christians did not manifest the zeal he had hoped for. Nevertheless, his work endured, and the Church continued its growth after his death.

This long and intensive ministry was carried on in a diocese which experienced immense growth during his tenure. When he became bishop of the small diocese of Dornakal in 1912, there were about 8,000 believers. In 1920, there were 86,000, and in 1930, 158,000. (A part of this increase was due to a portion of a neighboring diocese being incorporated into his.) By 1938, there were 220,000 Christians. Dornakal had been the smallest diocese in 1912, but at the time of Azariah's death in 1945, it had come to have the largest number of Christians in any diocese of his Church in India.

There can be no doubt that a major factor in this remarkable increase was the Bishop's lifelong endeavor to secure the involvement of the entire church membership in the work of evangelism. In this, he stands as an inspiration, an example, and a stimulus to the Church everywhere.

CHAPTER XI

TRAINING THE PEOPLE OF GOD

Training is a major secret of power. We have seen how Azariah insisted that if the power potential of the total membership of the churches is to be brought to bear upon the task of proclaiming the Gospel, much attention must be given to equipping Christians for their work.

There can be no question that if the churches are to move into an era of church multiplication based primarily upon lay evangelism, the training of the laity must be assigned high priority. Nor can there be any doubt that such training, if conducted in the right way, will lead to a new surge of power and enthusiasm within the ranks of the people of God.

We have also seen how Azariah sought to acquaint Christians in India with the experience of the Church in other lands, as a means of instruction and stimulus. This is an aspect of training which Christians everywhere would do well to adopt.

Let us now consider two Churches in which the power of training has been vividly demonstrated.

THE PRESBYTERIANS IN KOREA

In chapter six we traced the remarkable growth of the Presbyterian Church in Korea. It is now time to ask how that Church was able to develop the army of able leaders, the great majority of them unpaid, which spearheaded its aggressive program of evangelism and growth.

The Nevius Plan prescribed intensive Bible training for all believers. This policy is largely responsible for the vigorous lay participation which has characterized the evangelistic and church life of the Presbyterians in Korea.[1] The first training class was begun in 1890 in the study of a missionary, with seven men in attendance. In 1891 a rule was adopted requiring every missionary to "work out a course of Scripture instruction for each sub-station according to the general plan approved by the mission." During succeeding years the missionaries developed teaching procedures. Wide participation was assiduously sought. In 1904, 60 per cent of believers and catechumens participated in at least one class. By 1909, in the area of the Northern Presbyterian Mission, about 800 classes had a total attendance of 50,000 (twice the communicant membership).

This training program received considerable attention at the Madras Conference. Reports listed at least six ways in which Christians were trained, each of which (other than the seminary level) was used in the equipping of many thousands of laymen for service.

Each church had its weekly *Sunday School.* It was the custom for all church members, regardless of age, to attend.

Each of the 3,000 congregations conducted a *Bible class* once a year, and sometimes twice. These classes usually lasted from five to ten days, with separate provision for men and women. Elders, pastors, and other teachers taught the Bible in the morning. Visitation evangelism was frequently carried out in the afternoon, and in the evening they had old-fashioned, Moody-type revival services. Over 178,300 people attended these classes in 1937.

Next were district *mass classes,* held once or twice a year. Often as many as a thousand or more persons attended these short-term courses, paying all their own expenses. Those enrolled were taught in groups: new believers; catechumens; young, middle-aged and elderly baptized members; deacons; elders, and pastors. In 1937, no less than 130,000 people attended these district gatherings (the overall membership was 170,000). During a twenty-five-year period ending in 1936, the attendance at such assemblies was larger than the total membership of the Church in every year but three. It is not hard to believe that a Church with an annual training scheme of this magnitude grew!

Another level of training was *Bible institutes,* convened for six weeks annually for men and ten weeks for women. The annual sessions were part of a course designed for completion in five years. All the students were laymen. Their purpose in undertaking these rigorous studies was to become effective workers in their churches. In 1936, 4,509 persons studied. They bore all their own expenses.

Above this were the *seminaries* for the training of the clergy. Special schools were established to assist candidates who did not have sufficient school experience to enter seminary.

In addition to all these, a strong *Bible correspondence course* program was carried out. By 1938, 10,000 were enrolled and 5,000 had graduated.

Who did the teaching in this huge enterprise? In the beginning the missionaries were the only teachers, and through the years pastors and missionaries continued to participate in this capacity. But from early days it was the practice to recruit others to assume teaching responsibilities, and in 1938 it could be reported that "a large share of the work is done by volunteer workers and lay leaders who put aside their business to teach classes."

This amazing record of educating a large overall church membership in the Bible, in evangelism, and in effective church work, constitutes one of the great modern treasures possessed by the Church world-wide. J. Merle Davis wrote concerning it:

> The rapid growth of the self-supporting Church of Korea may be traced directly to the use of Bible-training classes and institutes. Under this system not only have scores of thousands of Korean Christians become thoroughly acquainted with biblical literature and truth, but very great numbers of laymen and lay women have been trained in church work and evangelism (1939:180-181).

THE C.M.A. CHURCHES IN THE PHILIPPINES

In 1950, a Christian and Missionary Alliance missionary assigned to the Sarangani District at the southern extremity of the Philippines surveyed the situation in which he found himself. There were few roads. The existing trails were impassable on horseback. He had no boat to travel along the long coastline to his nine churches served by a single Bible school graduate. Prayer was offered to God for some way of meeting the situation. Seven years later there had come into being over 50 churches with 5,000 baptized members! The congregations were led by 40 trained lay preachers (Hodges 1965:122-123).

What was the secret of this amazing growth? One factor certainly was that the populace was responsive to the Gospel. The Catholic Church is relatively weak in the area, and the prevailing religion is a form of animism. But without pastoral care and leadership not much would have happened, even in the midst of great opportunity. Acting upon the suggestions of an able lay Christian and former mayor, it was decided to rely upon trained laymen as a major contribution to the solving of the pastoral care problem. With earnest prayer and careful thought the Sarangani Institute was established (Ross 1963:3-5). The program was referred to as "Lay Preacher Training" and was designed to train as many laymen as possible, including some who did not plan to become preachers. The Institute conducted a one-week session every three months. Between sessions students engaged in home study and practical Christian work in their spare time.

The first session enrolled fifteen adult students. Two years later the first four graduates received diplomas. An advanced course was set up to enable graduates to continue their studies.

From the very beginning the training program led to new evangelistic outreach and spiritual power. As graduates came to act as unpaid pastors of new churches, which in many cases they themselves had founded, they began to bring forward pastoral problems for discussion, making the sessions even more challenging. A steady stream of new converts enrolled in the courses. A cell-like multiplication of new churches was the result.

The Sarangani Institute offered training at three levels: (1) the Literacy Course for illiterates; (2) the Standard Bible Course (the main course of the Institute), and (3) the Advanced Bible Course, which was designed for those wishing to prepare themselves to become lay workers. Individuals by special provision could continue studying beyond these levels.

The complete list of courses offered on these three levels is found in the booklet *Training Lay Workers* (Ross 1963), together with a brief description of each. In the Standard Bible Course, the general fields of study were: Old Testament books, sermonology, Sunday School, music, evangelism and basic doctrines, and hygiene. The individual courses listed under "Evangelism and Basic Doctrines" were Personal Evangelism, General Evangelism, Meeting the World Religions, Meeting the False Cults, Biblical Doctrine I, II, III, and IV.

Evaluation of work done was based on (1) class attendance and examinations, (2) book reports prepared between sessions of the Institute, and (3) a report of the practical Christian work done in the student's home area.

One credit was given for each class hour attended. A student could earn up to thirty credits a week. Five credits were given for the book reports and Bible reading done between sessions. Students had to attend at least two-thirds of the class sessions in order to receive credit for their field work. If they did not attend, no credit was given. For each of the upper two levels, 300 credits (including 200 from class sessions) had to be acquired in order to receive a diploma. The literacy course was designed for one year, and the others for two. An exceptionally diligent student might complete one of the upper-level courses in a minimum of one year. Many students whose work was very poor at the beginning showed much improvement later. New students were encouraged to pray about their studies and to persevere.

Students of both sexes and all ages participated. In addition to the class sessions, the opportunity to discuss their experiences in evangelistic work and to engage in recreation together enriched the fellowship.

A vigorous training program always calls for numerous and able teachers. In Sarangani, pastors and missionaries did a large share of the teaching, but able laymen also contributed their time as teachers. As time went on, some of the teaching was done by former students of the Institute. Missionaries and Filipino teachers (who had some other main occupation) contributed their time, but otherwise the program was self-supporting.

No assignments of work were made. The Institute operated on the theory that if volunteer workers are encouraged to seek and follow the guidance of the Holy Spirit, they will engage in far more difficult efforts, and without subsidy, than is the case when assignments are made.

The Christian and Missionary Alliance work everywhere in the Philippines makes wide use of laymen in the pastoral function. In 1951 in the Eastern Cobato and Davao district, there were only 21 paid workers laboring among a large number of churches. One pastor had oversight of 45 churches; another, over 25. Many churches were under the direction of faithful lay workers who had been trained by the pastors (Berg 1951:571). Training institutes are moved from place to place so that people from nearby churches can attend.

In 1963, the head of the Christian and Missionary Alliance Board in New York reported that the work of that Church in the Philippines had increased by 100 percent in ten years. Of over 500 churches, half had been founded and were currently led by trained laymen (King 1963:2). This Church is fully self-governing, and the churches are self-supporting. The growth of the work is indicated in the following statistics:[2]

Year	Ordained Clergy	Worship Centers	Baptized Church Members
1947	19	161	5,823
1949	20	160	6,874
1951	20	285	8,835
1953	34	264	8,932
1955	43	313	10,345
1957	57	404	13,186
1959	64	469	15,638
1961	76	575	16,795
1963	71	504	17,145

These statistics are encouraging and interesting in a number of respects. They call for careful analysis on the part of Christian and Missionary Alliance leaders in the Philippines. Only a study based upon a breakdown by area (statistics the writer does not possess) can reveal the full truth, but the figures recorded in this short section strongly suggest that a very considerable part of the total increase achieved by this Church from 1950 to 1957 was due to the expansion which took place in Sarangani. The rate of overall growth seems to have decreased as the Sarangani work changed in character in more recent years.

When I visited this district in 1966, I found that most of the churches which had been planted were still active, though a few had been lost to other groups. The training program described above had been discontinued after a decade of service, apparently for lack of leadership. However, many of the people who had begun work through its stimulus were still in service. The overall work of the district seemed to have suffered some loss of momentum and direction. Though the economy and the social milieu of Sarangani would seem to call for a skillful mixture of a few able and dedicated salaried clergy and many trained but unpaid lay workers, the tendency seemed to be to depend increasingly upon salaried leadership. Young pastors were being sent in who had trained at the Church's best school, but it appeared doubtful whether most of them would stay long. An attempt was being made to train salaried leadership at a new school within the Sarangani district, in the hope that graduates would not feel the cultural and economic strains so greatly as men coming in from the outside. But all in all, there remained in the district much to be encouraged about. Spiritual vigor, active lay evangelism, and a desire to win the district's populace were in evidence.

Quite aside from these reflections, the Sarangani story is a recent and impressive example of the power that training of the laity can generate when undertaken with competence, with confidence in the potential of ordinary Christians, and in earnest reliance upon the Holy Spirit. The people of God can be mobilized, far more than we ordinarily imagine, for the winning of the peoples around them.

PROBLEMS OF TRAINING IN JAPAN

Because Western missionaries introduced into Japan a clergy-centered form of church life, and because the true calling of the laity–co-equal in importance with the calling of the clergy–has not been recognized or emphasized, the training of the laity has been largely neglected, although there are some encouraging exceptions. Unfortunately, adults in the vast majority of Japanese Protestant churches do not attend Church School; there are not even classes provided for them. This makes the training of adults at once more necessary and more difficult.

By far the greater emphasis in Japan is upon the training of the clergy (which is, of course, a highly important matter). Yet growing Churches round the world are always Churches in which laymen actively are witnessing for Christ and bringing men to Him. Numerous Churches throughout the world which have a well-trained clergy are stagnant. But for a Church with a laity that is enthusiastically evangelizing relatives and neighbors to be static would be a contradiction in terms. Nothing is more crucial today for Japanese Churches than to recognize the pivotal importance of the laity, and to work for a well-trained and joyously witnessing army of lay Christians.

Few countries in the world are more advantageously equipped for engaging in a widespread lay-training program than Japan. All the people are literate. The Japanese are excellent organizers, and the planning and execution of a superior training program for laymen is quite within the capability of Japanese Churches to achieve. Further, the unusually large number of educated and able clergymen characteristic of Protestant Christianity in Japan provides a pool of potential teachers throughout the country. If these clergymen could be convinced of the need to train the laity and would learn how to do it, the way would be opened for unprecedented growth.

One of the factors which makes training difficult in Japan is scheduling. In the Philippine Islands some Churches are experiencing success with training programs in which students attend "school" one week in three months. But such a plan would be most difficult to implement in Japan. In the urbanized and industrialized society of this energetic island people, it is almost impossible to find persons with schedules flexible enough to permit taking time off so frequently. Even the farmers today often engage part-time in other occupations, so it is not easy to plan training sessions for their "slack" seasons as Kagawa used to do. A training program, to be successful, must cope with this problem. Although the rapidly improving road system and the increasing number of believers who own automobiles make for a new flexibility and mobility, the time factor requires that the place where training is carried out not be too distant from the place where prospective students reside.

Perhaps the best solution would be to develop short courses of about six sessions, to be held weekly or at times mutually convenient for small groups. Some individuals will find it possible to study regularly throughout the year on this basis. Others will be able to enroll in several such courses annually. Almost every believer ought to be able to make time for at least one short course per year.

The Lutheran Bible School in Kobe has had good success in its program of planning a week of lay training in March. This is school-vacation time in Japan, so university and high school students can attend. But it has also been found that some persons of all ages can manage to attend such a course. Here an important new avenue of service opens up for Bible schools and seminaries.

Happy is that Church which can agree together to undertake a systematic, continuous training program on several different levels. When such endeavors are planned cooperatively within a district, or when several churches (perhaps including those of different denominations) in the same vicinity formulate plans together, increased enthusiasm and greater competence are only two of the potential advantages. Under such circumstances, not only can several capable minds wrestle with the problems of curriculum and teaching materials, but the important matter of securing a sufficient number of able teachers can be more easily dealt with.

But, in any case, much of the teaching will have to be done on the local church level. Every pastor should be prepared to engage in training his membership and, in the beginning, to do most or all of the teaching on the local level. Even when his Church sponsors no systematic and cooperative training program, a pastor can accomplish a great deal himself.

In order to sustain a thorough training program in the local church, more than one teacher is needed. The pastor will want gradually to cultivate the abilities of promising teachers. Such persons may be led into sharing with the pastor the teaching of the catechetical classes, and in other ways given experience and prestige in the congregation.

Every occasion upon which believers gather for training should be regarded as an opportunity for the Holy Spirit to light fires of enthusiasm and the spirit of service in new hearts. Once these fires are burning, miracles of grace begin to appear. It is both surprising and encouraging to witness what takes place when believers are gathered for this purpose, even if only for a few short days.

WHAT TO TEACH

As stated above, the problem of setting up a curriculum can be more easily handled when a number of churches cooperate. The pastor in one church, however, can achieve much on his own initiative. The people of God must learn many things in order to be effective workers. The pastor must first reconcile himself to the truth that one training course will not be sufficient. He need not spend too much time trying to decide what to teach first, but should feel free to begin with any of several essential subjects.

This writer once visited a church in the United States in which a competent layman annually taught a course on the Church School and religious education. The course was taught during the Church School hour and lasted one year. All new church members, young and old, were expected to enroll in this course during the first few years of their membership, and every year saw an encouraging number of people complete it. The result was that in this medium-sized church almost all the members were thoroughly acquainted with the values and methods of the Church School. That church had no shortage of teachers.

Problems in Japan are somewhat different, but the pastor would be wise to decide upon a limited number of very important subjects which need to be taught, to teach them periodically, and to enlist the church's support in ensuring that every member at some time enrolls in each of these courses.

If church leaders are willing to begin small, and to recognize the value of teaching even two or three individuals, fervor and dedication will increase within the church, and the program will grow. If, as time passes, some of the teaching can be done by the pastor and some by enthusiastic laymen, the program will be more challenging and meaningful for all.

Any training program worthy of the name will stress systematic instruction in the Bible itself. But it will not stop there. In terms of the nature of the Japanese social situation today, a course in the value and method of house meetings would be most profitable. Another concerning the functions and values of small groups, such as Bible classes and prayer groups led by laymen, would also help prepare the church for growth. Laymen need to be taught how to maintain a regular and meaningful devotional hour in order to sustain the spiritual life. Instruction in Christian evangelism is essential. Once a training program is underway, the problem will not be so much to find something to teach as to find time to teach all that people want and need to learn.

TEACHING MATERIALS

Elsewhere I have referred to the *Shakubuku Kyōten* of Sōka Gakkai. This manual for instructing members in how to win other people to Sōka Gakkai has been a source of inestimable power for that movement. Christians sometimes laugh at the fact that Sōka Gakkai adherents in every part of Japan recite the same lines–ideas and phrases they have learned from the manual. But, in reality, it has been a major achievement to have placed in the hands of hundreds of thousands of humble but eager "evangelists" a manual which has aided the movement in the winning of so many converts. Even if the contents, including the somewhat unhinged attacks on Christianity, are completely unacceptable to the Christian, the method of propagandizing has been sound.

Throughout Latin America, Pentecostal Christians make extensive use of the *Reglamento Local* (Standard of Christian Doctrine and Practice). This short pamphlet (34 pages in English) contains teaching on important doctrines of the Church, on the life of the local church, and on witnessing. It is used for instructing new converts and provides a pattern for the life of the churches. So useful has it proved in El Salvador that missionaries attribute the impressive growth of the churches there to "two things, first the moving of the Spirit; and second, our *Reglamento*" (Hodges 1965:115).

A short and standard manual is needed for training converts and older Christians in Japan. A manual prepared in loose-leaf form might be most suitable. New sections could be added and old ones revised from time to time. If one basic but simple manual, which avoided eccentricities, could be prepared, then commentaries to meet special needs could be written later by Church leaders. This would provide a flexible and effective tool for the training of the laity.

Such a manual is but one example of the type of literature suited to this kind of training program. Whenever men embark on a program for training the laity, they soon encounter the problem of teaching materials. Japan is no exception. Unusually rich in books written for the clergy, and possessed of a considerable library of devotional and Bible study materials written for church members, the Church in Japan nevertheless is weak at the point of literature designed for membership training. Literature which is not too expensive or voluminous, which is practical and close to life, and which breathes the spirit of glad and fervent devotion to Christ, is an essential of effective training.

THEOLOGICAL SEMINARIES

This writer does not consider himself qualified to speak in detail of curricula, teaching methods, and similar matters relating to the planning of a seminary. But there are some principles about which all who are engaged in the work of church extension must be concerned.

The training of the clergy should be suited to the needs of the work of each Church. These needs differ widely according to time and place. Yet we tend toward uniformity of training. Sundkler writes of the I.M.C. commissions which have noted that theological training in Africa is largely an attempt to transfer to Africa the pattern of training familiar to the West (1960:211). Of course, since seminary training deals with the biblical revelation, the core common to us all, some similarities are inevitable. Nevertheless, protests were justly heard at Madras in 1938 against the imposition upon rural churches of a ministry trained according to Western traditions (Davis 1939:500). Western influence is strong in Japanese theological schools. Japanese clergymen are well acquainted with Western theology, and leading Western theologians. Many professors have studied in the West. The library shelves of Japanese clergymen contain many books by Western writers, frequently in Japanese translation.

This is to some degree inevitable and not necessarily evil, but there are great dangers. One is that books on the task of the Church and the work of the clergy written in the West are addressed to a vastly different situation from that which the Churches face in Japan. Not only are these books read in Japan, but they influence Japanese writers who write books in the vernacular on pastoral care. Thus an image of the Church and its ministry is fostered which may actually be detrimental to the needs of the Asian situation. The Protestant Churches in America could not triple their membership during the next ten years. There are not that many people in America who are not now church members. But the Churches in Japan could accomplish more than that and still compose less than 3 per cent of the population. The potential is different. Not only so, but they must achieve large-scale growth, or continue to be unable to disciple the nation. How important, then, that theological schools in Japan and other lands in which only a tiny percentage of the population is Christian include in their curricula studies on how to multiply new churches.

The churches in America must persuade their members to live like Christians (while not neglecting the evangelistic task). The Churches in Japan must first of all persuade people to become Christians (while not neglecting the task of building up the spiritual lives of those who are already believers). Seminaries in the West train clergymen to care for existing churches and to help Christians become better Christians. Missionaries who come from Western schools and nationals who go abroad to study are likely to be taught in these arts. Moreover, if the seminaries in Japan are modeled after those of the West, Japanese clergy will graduate with this concept of their ministry in mind.

But clergymen in Japan need to be expert in how to multiply new churches and care for people who are not yet believers in Jesus Christ—a very different task. Is it not clear that Japanese theological schools must resolutely face these Japanese issues?

Seminaries in the West train clergymen in the *one-paid-pastor-per-church* system. Books written on pastoral care in the West are written from this perspective. But the great need in Japan is to develop unpaid preachers, elders, and others who can share in pastoral responsibilities, especially in small new churches which cannot afford professional clergy.

If this kind of church life is to be realized, Japanese theological schools must orient the curriculum so as to train professional clergy who can inspire and train lay leaders. Clergymen must also be trained to lead a circuit of churches by enlisting and leading a corps of dedicated lay preachers and elders.

Anyone who has thought carefully about how to bring Christ to the myriad villages and small towns of countries like Japan, India, and China will have realized the impossibility of placing seminary graduates as pastors in all these communities. Ministers trained in seminaries in large cities like Tokyo will not go to villages. Even if they would, their education would probably not have equipped them for work among villagers. What is more, if suitable men were available, the villagers would not be able to pay them a living salary. These circumstances may change some time in the future, but for our day some other way must be found for providing leadership in rural churches.

There are, in fact, compelling reasons for thinking that Churches in Japan should set up separate departments to develop policies and procedures for the churches in rural areas and smaller cities. Strong and influential pastors almost inevitably gravitate to churches in the large cities. If these men set policies for the whole Church based upon the needs of the urban situation they know best, rural church life will continue to be weak and gasping, for the needs of these two types of society are different. Policies concerning such matters as educational preparation for pastors and qualifications for ordination, which may be appropriate for the city, can be serious impediments to the growth of the Church in other places.

The problem of pastoral care is central to the growth of the churches. While it is certain that in the kind of society in which the Church in Japan lives and serves, it needs many ministers with a full liberal arts and seminary education, it is not at all certain that every situation calls for this kind of man. Among the poor, and among rural people, other leaders may be able to do better work. The idea is for pastors to be educated somewhat more than the people they serve, but not too much more. They should not have so little training that they are unable to command respect or lead properly, nor so much that they are far beyond their people. Moreover, in pioneering new churches and providing pastoral care for small churches, a variety of leaders is called for.

As churchmen in Japan and elsewhere set themselves to provide a flexible and varied pastoral ministry, they need to reflect upon the fact that the Church's experience teaches that there is more than one way to train leaders.

Donald McGavran, in *How Churches Grow,* has left us in his debt for a fascinating glimpse of the training program for clergy of a great Anglican Church in Africa.

> The rapidly growing Anglican Church in Ruanda numbers about 100,000 people. It creates and supports its leaders in the following fashion. It has hundreds of village congregations–some big, some small. For its paid leaders, it seeks the best young men out of these village congregations. Up to the present time most of them have very little formal education. Some of them are not much more than literate when they first become church workers.
>
> The first appointment is to be an assistant in a small congregation. The worker gets free land from the village for cultivation. He–or more likely his wife–raises all his own food. He gets little besides. If he appears promising material, he is sent for a few months' instruction to his station school. If he passes, he gets his first Station Letter and goes back to a slightly larger responsibility. If he makes good, in a year or two he comes back for a second few months in the station school where he gets still further reading, writing, arithmetic, elementary Bible, and churchmanship.
>
> After he has served six or eight years and obtained his fourth Station Letter, he may be assigned to the supervision of eight or ten village churches. Making good here requires administrative ability. He will continue to farm village land for his food

> and receive contributions of cash and kind. There are scores of such supervising pastors, each tested for years in the service and found devout, loyal, and able.
>
> From these men the best are selected annually to go to the Warner Memorial College for a three-year course. While there they raise their own family food on the college fields and after passing the courses are ordained as fully qualified clergymen of the Church of England. The Church has secured for itself an elite corps of tested, trained clergymen, few if any of whom are even grade school graduates, whom the churches can support, and who are content with the recompense they receive.
>
> They do not desert the pastorate to go to highly paid commercial and government jobs. They are sympathetic to the system which produced them and are prepared to use it for the indefinite expansion of the Church. It provides abundant men who fit the incoming congregations. Systematic selection also provides top level leaders (1963:140-141).

This system could not be transferred to Japan, for conditions are very different in the two countries, but it shows (1) that ministers should receive training appropriate to the type of church they serve, (2) that not all ministers need the same training, and (3) that a leadership development program should be devised to fit local needs rather than some abstract standard such as one based on the practices of the Churches in the West.

In Latin America, among Pentecostals and among indigenous Churches, an apprenticeship system is widely followed for developing church leaders. Little formal training is given, but a man passes from very simple offices up a ladder of increasing responsibility. He may at 35 or 40 finally be given full responsibility for a church. Oftentimes a man is appointed pastor of the church in which he worships and serves, and undergoes a type of training which can be given as he serves the church.

SUMMARY

Few things are more important to the growth of the Church than training. We do well to profit from the experience of rapidly growing Churches in other lands. Lay training has received relatively little stress in Japan, but the Japanese Church by virtue of its large number of able clergy is particularly well equipped to carry out such a program. Practical solutions to the problem of scheduling classes in a busy industrialized society must be found. Cooperation between churches makes for more effective training, but the local church can and must do a great deal in its own right. Good teaching materials are important to effective teaching.

There is a strong tendency for seminaries in Asia to prepare men for the clergy along Western lines. One of the dangers of this tendency is that they will be trained for situations in nominally Christian lands, whereas the need in Asia is for the Churches to disciple their peoples. The education of prospective clergymen in a country like Japan, and the literature they read, often are shaped by the *one-pastor-per-church* system of the West, whereas what is needed in such a country are much more flexible patterns of pastoral ministry.

We close this chapter by calling attention to a principle we have referred to in other places: We teach more (for better or for worse) by what we do than by what we say. Church members learn their ways of conducting the church by seeing what procedures are in fact being followed. This means that our actual practice should be regarded as a teaching medium of great importance. We must carefully reflect upon what new Christians and old need to learn, and then structure church life so that believers may easily and naturally learn those things that are conducive to church growth, wide lay participation, and real missionary spirit.

CHAPTER XII

EVANGELISM AND JAPANESE SOCIAL PATTERNS

This chapter is admittedly written with the distinctive Japanese social milieu in mind. Its value for Christians in other lands is limited by this fact. But it is a sound principle, true in any land, that the Gospel should be proclaimed by the churches in ways which take advantage of the currents of national life rather than ignoring them or seeking to swim against them.

A COMPLEX SOCIETY

In the villages near Yonago, where this writer works, many people believe in possession by the spirit of the fox. This cult exercises a noticeable effect upon social status in the villages, and upon marriage arrangements both in the villages and in the cities. Yet people living in rural communities only thirty or forty miles away may consider such things absurd. Students who come to this writer's residence may be from homes where this belief is taken seriously, or from homes which reject all belief in spirits, gods, or any kind of unseen world.

Surveys consistently show that adherence to a religion is considerably lower among urban Japanese people than among rural. Yet it is in the cities and towns, rather than in the villages, that Sōka Gakkai has made most of its gains. Not the least of the problems of the Christian who seeks to lead men to Christ in Japan is that he must deal with so many different types of people. The religion of some is ancestor worship or spirit worship, while many have no personal faith at all, though they "practice" the household religion. Others are leftists who think all religion a curse, or atheists and skeptics who read Bertrand Russell, or materialists who believe religion irrelevant. Perhaps most common of all, and most disconcerting for Christians, are the many Japanese who believe all religions are good and basically *onaji* (the same), but none to be personally followed with ardor. The same kind of diversity is found in political and social attitudes.

There is much to suggest that one of the most promising ways of coping with this complex society is through the medium of small groups.

GROUP PSYCHOLOGY IN JAPAN

Every Japanese high school boy is familiar with the *habatsu,* the cliques that exist within business firms or government offices. These constitute a particular kind of group. Recent anthropological studies indicate that group psychology permeates Japanese society.

Vogel, who did an intensive study of a Tokyo suburb, finds that the basic cleavages in Japanese society are not along class lines, but between groups. The poor people of a village do not link up with the poor of other villages, but identify with their fellows in the village as over against the folk of other villages (1963:260-261).

Students of rural Japan are familiar with the dominant position that landowners have occupied in the lives of villagers. According to Matsumoto, however, recent studies show that as a result of the land reform after World War II, the power of the landowners has been reduced. As this has taken place, power has shifted to various groups, such as cooperatives united for economic purposes (1960:52).

Vogel finds that the salaried man, along with other Japanese, feels a sense of intense loyalty toward his own group, and intense hostility toward groups of which he cannot be a part. He speaks of the "tightly knit groups" in Japanese society, and of the "strong in-group feeling and suspicion of the outside world." Especially in urban centers, the old family system is rapidly breaking down. In Vogel's suburb, the people no longer fear expulsion from the *Ie* (the family line). Some of the people may even live with married daughters in their old age. A sharper departure from older customs can hardly be imagined. The group is often replacing the family for city dwellers.

Vogel addresses attention to a custom well known to anyone familiar with Japanese social life: Whereas at a cocktail party or social hour in America one may converse with two or three persons in personal fashion, in Japan these are group affairs. A circle is formed; speeches are made, songs are sung, jokes are exchanged, and people air their *nayami* (troubles).

In his investigations in a Tokyo suburb, Vogel found that loyalty (along with competence) occupies a primary position in the value system. The two main groups for these people are the nuclear family and the work group. Loyalty may require that the individual place group interests above his personal interests. He is expected to accept group goals as his own, to cooperate willingly when there is group consensus, to avoid embarrassing the group, and to join in presenting a united front against the outside world.

Group solidarity is dependent upon maintaining the exclusive loyalty of members. Life is organized so that group loyalties do not conflict. Because most salaried men spend their lives with one firm, they find their closest friends and social relationships there. Men do not easily, even apart from this, change groups. When they do change, they do not usually approach the new group directly, but through a go-between.

Japanese think of "success" in a less individualized sense than Americans. Probably as a result of the ancient emphasis upon the family, success is often related to one's group (Baker 1956:14).[1]

Dore also calls attention to the group orientation of the Japanese, though he finds that individualism has increased somewhat in the postwar period. He distinguishes between the pattern in which persons merge themselves into the life of the group and another important pattern in which people surrender a part of themselves to authoritarian leaders in society. In either case, the result is different from the individualism of the West (1965:387-389).

It is likely that the group psychology of modern Japan has been structured partly by the psychology nurtured by life in the *buraku*, where most Japanese resided until modern times.

In *Village Japan*, authors Beardsley, Hall, and Ward show that although the *buraku* Niike is related to the *mura* (see Glossary) and to other administrative units, by far the most intense and basic loyalty is to the *buraku*. Thus religious meetings are held in the *buraku* the twelfth day of each lunar month, to which each household sends representatives since community matters are also discussed. Ditch-cleaning and road-repair activities are *buraku* projects. Although the Youth Association is formally related to the *mura* Association, it is *buraku* activities which are considered more important. Life is so organized that habit conditions people to group loyalty; that is, loyalty to the *buraku,* with conflicting group loyalties being kept at a minimum.

> The people of Niike feel their main attachment to their *buraku* and are not merely less intimately attached to their *mura* but regard it with a certain amount of suspicious reserve (Beardsley 1959:248-251).

Cornell also deals with the strong spirit of solidarity within the *buraku,* and the reluctance to call in authorities from the outside to deal with *buraku* problems (1965:62-65).

Familiarity with this group orientation is important for understanding the forms which religions in Japan assume, whether Christian or otherwise.

THE SMALL CHURCHES OF JAPAN

We have earlier referred to the fact that virtually all Japanese churches remain small. This phenomenon baffles both Japanese pastors and missionaries. Many highly competent Japanese pastors, who in other countries would be leading large churches, struggle along in Japan with Sunday congregations of 70, 80, or 100. A few reach 200. Why do Japanese churches remain small?

Probably one reason for this nationwide pattern is that Japanese do not become Christians, as a rule, by families or social groups, but as isolated individuals. In America, a church of 100 members may be drawn from 25 to 40 homes, and many of these will be interrelated. But a church of the same size in Japan may be drawn from twice that many homes or more, and relatives will be few. Obviously the pastoral care required per member will be much greater in the latter type of church.

Another factor which needs consideration is the hunger for fellowship on the part of the people. Many churches grow to the point of having 30 to 50 active members, and then experience severe difficulty getting beyond this point. This number of people is about the maximum for intimate fellowship. Japanese churches–though there are many encouraging exceptions–are weak in the area of small auxiliary groups in which people can know and be known. This is especially true for men. Would Japanese churches grow larger if they multiplied small groups in which people could enjoy satisfying fellowship at other times than when the whole church body assembles?

But we must reckon with the group psychology described above as a most important factor limiting the size of Japanese churches. There are many reasons for thinking that Japanese social organization, religious and otherwise, prefers the smaller face-to-face kind of association to the more impersonal atmosphere of large groups.

This would seem to be supported by the phenomenal growth of Sōka Gakkai, the neo-Buddhist sect which exploits, among other things, the use of the small group. The movement is worthy of attention.

SŌKA GAKKAI

In attempting to analyze the reasons for the amazing growth of this bizarre religion, several factors are important and obvious. The crass materialism and self-seeking to which the religion appeals are a factor, but the same approach by other of the New Religions has much less effect. Much more important are Sōka Gakkai's superb organizational structure, its ability to identify and use the leadership potential in each community, and its ambitious training program.

Fitting into all of this is a plan for gatherings suited to today's Japan. Japan is in a period of transition in which all the old values are under attack. Because the old communal patterns are breaking up, many Japanese are for the first time undergoing the unnerving experience of having to live as individuals. The warm fellowship of Sōka Gakkai and certain other of the New Religions which emphasize the small group, provides relief from loneliness and a sense of social support.

The house meeting is the right technique for Japan today. A study of Sōka Gakkai, and of certain other newly risen religions such as PL Kyōdan and Seichō No Ie, indicates that the small house meeting has power to make possible a religious atmosphere which is congenial to the Japanese today. All over modern Japan, millions of people are gathering in the homes of their neighbors for religious meetings. The ever-increasing urban and industrial structuring of society leads to the mechanization and depersonalization of life. The resulting emptiness is further aggravated by the breakdown of the communal and family patterns of the past. The swift growth of these religions is in large measure due to their ability to fill the void left by these modern phenomena. The loneliness and lostness of people draw them to the warmth of the small gathering, where they sit face to face and are recognized by other men.

We should not allow the popularity of the monster rallies of Sōka Gakkai to hide the basic fact that the foundation on which the society is built is a very great number of small groups.

THE CHURCH AND SMALL GROUPS

Christians should with alacrity and joy shape their evangelistic efforts to this aspect of Japanese culture. The first Christian churches were all house meetings. This is our heritage. The Church in Japan needs to develop skill and conviction in the use of the small house meeting as a means of enlarging established churches and of rapidly multiplying new ones.

Pastor Murai, the founder of the Spirit of Jesus Church, declares that there are 7,000 members of the Church in Tokyo. When he was asked how so many people could gather when the church building had only a small seating capacity, he replied that a number of services were held at the church both Saturday and Sunday. Meanwhile, many house meetings all over the city gather every week under the leadership of members or Bible school students.

This writer's limited experience verifies the effectiveness of the house meeting. Japanese people, except those in the larger cities, find it difficult to enter a Christian church. An elder of the church begun by me, a man in his forties, approached the church entrance on eight different occasions before he finally came in and introduced himself. Japanese often work and are otherwise busy on Sundays and feel they cannot attend church. But if they are won to genuine faith in house meetings, they gradually come to find it somehow possible to devote Sunday morning to worship.

House meetings are good preparation for evangelistic meetings. Many pastors and missionaries are discouraged by the meager results accruing from such gatherings. In part this is due to dubious expectations. In a country like Japan where people do not possess the knowledge of God and Christian concepts that even ungodly men have in Western lands, it is too much to expect that most people can be won to a deep conversion upon hearing the Gospel for the first time in an evangelistic meeting. Moreover, a false impression of the church is often received by people whose first contact is the evangelistic meeting, with its large crowd, good music, exciting atmosphere, and skilled speaker. When they attend regular services of the church, which are to the superficial eye much less glamorous, there is a natural letdown, and many drift away. But if people have for several weeks or months attended a small house meeting, perhaps occasionally visiting the church itself, and then attend evangelistic meetings, the situation is quite different. Now they recognize the meetings for what they are: a special occasion. Moreover, the evangelist can make his appeal to those who have acquired some background of knowledge. In such a situation, the Holy Spirit can use evangelistic meetings to bless the church with converts whose conversions will last.

Once the possibilities of house meetings are seen, any believer who desires may be encouraged to begin one in his own home. Church leaders need not hold back for fear men may not be qualified for such work. Experience and the hard knocks of real life will reveal that.

Two or three Christians who are congenial may sponsor a house meeting as a missionary effort. A rule that other Christians may attend *if* they bring non-Christian friends may avert the tendency toward "just one more gathering of believers" and serve to preserve the evangelistic purpose.

The first half of the Book of Acts makes it very clear that the Holy Spirit is pleased to work in groups of believing men. In their midst, the Spirit of Christ is at work to guide, to empower, and to use men. Groups of Christians may confidently anticipate that when they join together for fellowship and service, the power generated among them will be much greater than the sum total of their abilities as individuals.

House meetings may open the door for ministering to the lower classes, who do not easily find their way into ordinary churches. House meetings may make it easier to win families. They may be the key to planting the church in a new community. If two or three different house meetings can be begun in a community, it should eventually be possible to organize a church. Such meetings, led by people of the community, may make it easier to penetrate villages and rural towns. Rural people tend to be suspicious of outsiders, and it is difficult for missionaries or city-bred Japanese pastors to gain acceptance. But if the initiative is taken by village residents themselves, then there is a contribution the clergyman from the outside can make, as we saw in the case of Sawadani in *Upon This Rock* (Gosden 1957).

A literature in Japanese on the techniques of small groups needs to be built up. In recent years a large number of excellent publications on the role of small groups has appeared in English, but a literature born out of actual Japanese experience is needed.

Clergymen should seek to cultivate knowledge and skill in this area and should instruct church members in the secrets of effective small groups. It is especially necessary to train members to hold meetings without the pastor's presence. If a large number of such groups can be established, the pastor can encourage and stimulate them through occasional visits. At least some of the groups should be challenged to develop into independent churches.

SMALL GROUPS AND INDIGENEITY

Small groups meeting in the homes of believers and led by the natural leaders of the community can greatly aid in making Christianity more Japanese in its flavor.

Especially in places where a dialect is used, small house meetings can supply an atmosphere where humble people can talk about faith in Christ using the same language in which they love and laugh and fight and weep. As a missionary, I have felt that though I can contribute much to such meetings, the necessity of using standard Japanese because I am present acts as a damper upon intimacy. I have also noticed that Japanese pastors who come from other parts of Japan experience similar problems. If the missionary or pastor visited such meetings occasionally, while local residents were in charge most of the time, this difficulty would not occur.

The Japanese *sanbika* (hymnal) in most common use in Protestant Churches in Japan is an excellent work. It incorporates fine hymns from all over the world, some by Japanese writers. But many of the hymns are difficult for ordinary Japanese unaccustomed to church life. For small meetings, to which people new to Christianity are invited, a hymnal using melodies familiar to all Japanese is badly needed. Japanese Christian poets should be encouraged to listen again to their national folk songs and popular music. Some of these which contain lovely or haunting or martial music will suggest Christian themes which the melodies can carry.

One of the major sources of church music in many lands has been just this kind of use of familiar melodies, but little has been done in Japan along these lines. In the diocese of Bishop Azariah in India, the Gospel has released an outburst of melody and joy expressed in indigenous forms. Christian lyrics have been set to native tunes, and these songs are sung in worship, in the fields at harvest time, and on other occasions. Old village dances, purged of heathen connotations, are enjoyed by great crowds at festival time. Bishop Azariah enthusiastically supported the expression of faith in forms familiar to people. He gave keen attention to music, and also to scriptural drama, for which he often suggested themes and offered praise or criticism arising out of deep interest and concern.

JAPANESE SOCIAL STRUCTURE

It is important that Japanese pastors be trained in the knowledge of social structure. Some parts of society will be found to be more responsive to the Gospel than others. For example, in the early years of Protestant missions, it was the *samurai* who were responsive to Christianity.[2] From them came many of the dauntless and capable Christian leaders of that day. Some sections of society may call for a different approach than others. Hopeful experiments are underway at present in an attempt to minister to workers in industry, who in Japan as in other countries are somewhat resistant to ordinary Protestant evangelism. The efforts of Japanese Christian social scientists to acquaint the Church with the nature of modern society must be valued.

CHAPTER XIII

AN EXPECTANT OUTLOOK

Japan is reputed to be one of the most difficult countries in Asia for Christian evangelism. Moreover, the situation is widely held to have become even more difficult since 1952. How deserved is this reputation? Masao Takenaka expresses the thoughts of many observers:

> With a few exceptions, the progress of most of the Protestant Churches in the last four years is not so rapid as was anticipated in the period immediately after the war. We are entering a new stage, passing from the years of naive optimism to a time of sober realism, in developing true conversation with the existential issues in Japanese society rather than carrying on a one-sided spiritual monologue (1964:203-204).

Certainly everyone familiar with the conditions of the past twenty years knows that it is more difficult to attract newcomers to churches today than it was fifteen years ago. No one who has at first hand engaged in evangelism and church building in Buddhist Japan would assert that the Japanese are flocking into Christianity. Nevertheless, in this chapter we wish to take strong issue with the pessimism that characterizes so much writing about evangelism in Japan today.

The article referred to in the above quotation causes concern at this point. Does Takenaka mean to assert that because evangelism meets a slight response, Christians must reduce emphasis upon direct evangelism and turn to such matters as the social problems which afflict Japanese society today? In the same article he refers to the "hard fact" that Christians are a tiny minority in Japan. He contends that as a minority Christians must be neither a minority in a ghetto nor a minority which conforms to the secular world, but a creative minority "constantly maintaining a distinctive secular presence in the ordinary Japanese society, thus to become the salt and light of the world" (1964:205). We may cordially agree that Christians must be the salt of the earth; they must exercise an influence for good in society. But if it be proposed that Christians resign themselves to their minority role, concentrating not on the task of winning large numbers of men to the faith, but upon playing a creative role in society, we must strenuously demur.

DANGER OF STAGNANCY

It is possible for Churches to become stagnant and, because they do not grow, to play a steadily decreasing role in society as the overall population increases.

In Jamaica in 1950, four old-line Churches (Methodist, Baptist, Presbyterian, and Moravian) were at work. They then composed a total of about 60,000 communicants, who constituted 4.3 per cent of the total population. One hundred years earlier these same four Churches numbered 54,000 communicants, who constituted 13.5 per cent of the population. During a full century these Churches, assisted by missions from England, increased from 54,000 to 60,000, but had decreased from 13.5 per cent to 4.3 per cent of the population (McGavran 1962).

We cannot assume that Protestant Christianity was up against a stone wall in Jamaica, because some other Churches ranging from small Baptist groups to Pentecostal and Seventh-Day Adventist Christians were all growing. (So were the Roman Catholics.) These newer denominations, all of which began work after the turn of the century, in 1956 numbered over 94,000 members (McGavran 1962).

In 1910 seven familiar Protestant denominations who entered Mexico before 1900 were at work there.[1] During the period 1910 to 1938, these Churches, with the exception of the Baptist groups, did not grow.

Churches	1910 Communicants	1938 Communicants
Methodist	12,470	10,300
Presbyterian	5,700	5,300
Congregational	1,540	600
Friends	670	200
Christian Church	900	600
American Baptist	1,202	3,440
Southern Baptist	1,428	2,442
	23,910	22,882

Meanwhile, Churches which entered Mexico after 1906 were having a very different experience in precisely the same 28 years:

Churches	1910 Communicants	1938 Communicants
Mexican Indian	0	560
Assembly of God	0	6,000
Seventh-Day Adventist	70	4,000
Pentecostal Holiness	0	1,300
Pilgrim Holiness	0	1,200
Nazarene	0	2,000
Swedish Pentecostal	0	4,000
	70	19,060

Some of the older Churches, however, made considerable progress in the years after 1938, as did the newer ones listed above. (The following figures do not include some fast-growing very new Churches.)

Churches	1910	1938	1962
Methodist	12,470	10,300	33,000
Presbyterian	5,700	5,300	42,000
Congregational	1,540	600	600
Friends	670	200	100
Christian	900	600	1,000
American Baptist	1,202	3,440	5,000
Southern Baptist	1,428	2,442	7,640
Mexican Indian	0	560	6,000
Assemblies I & II	0	6,000	15,000

Adventist	70	4,000	22,000
Pilgrim Holiness	0	1,200	5,700
Nazarene	0	2,000	5,700
Swedish Pentecostal	0	4,000	15,000

At least three things are suggested by a story like this: (1) Churches can become stagnant, or nearly so, with the result that their influence in the country is steadily reduced;[2] (2) Churches which have been stagnant over several decades can come alive and achieve renewed growth, and (3) when some Churches are growing rapidly but others are not, under the same conditions, the reason for slow growth may very well lie in the non-growing Churches themselves, rather than in the conditions in the country.

The third point deserves special attention. Evidence from many countries and times shows that Churches which have in the past had good growth sometimes enter into long periods of stagnation. In explaining such lack of growth, missionary and church leaders often say that political and social conditions are hindering advance. Or it may be argued that a period of consolidation is required. In some cases such explanations are valid, but in many cases they are put in serious doubt by the fact that other Churches working in the same general area under the same conditions go on growing, even increase their rate of growth.

The dire effects of stagnation or regression must not be overlooked. Whether we define the Church's role in the sense of participation in the evangelism of a country or in the sense of being a creative and dynamic factor in the stream of social change, or both, it is clear that a tiny Church which does not grow can hardly fulfill its role. The Friends (Quakers) have often left mankind in their debt owing to their quickened social conscience. In recent times Congregationalists have increasingly focused their interest upon social action. But what happens to their impact upon a vast and rapidly multiplying population in Mexico when their members shrink in number over the years to 100 and 600 respectively?

Stagnation and little growth should not be accepted as normal or even desirable, some writers notwithstanding. Such rationalization of defeat is not a constructive way of interpreting the situation. Few situations require pessimism.

THE MEIJI ERA

Historians agree that the 1880s were a great period of growth for Protestant Christianity in Japan. Recent repressions forgotten, people were flocking into the churches. For example, in 1884 the Congregational Church reported a 60 per cent increase over 1883, and the rate of increase in the following year was 53 per cent (Cary 1909:172). Some enthusiasts predicted that Japan would soon be Christian.

But then the tide turned. The flood of new converts receded, and a much more difficult period followed. Latourette writes of the great difficulties of the 1890s (1944:396). Cary lists several reasons for the slowing down of Protestant growth: There was a strong reaction against the acceptance of Western civilization. The Buddhists took on new life. Important political events excited the minds of the people and made it harder to persuade them to consider Christianity (1909:212-215).

It would be idle to deny that there was a considerable difference in the atmosphere of the 1880s and the 1890s. But the analysis of the situation found in the histories as sketched above is by no means the whole story.

For one thing, the historians give the impression that the 1880s were a time of growth for Protestants in general. Cary, in the work cited, does not draw attention to the Churches in which growth was occurring. Winburn Thomas writes of the "spectacular growth" of the years 1883-1889, but does not differentiate between the growth rates of the several denominations (1959:161-181). The fact seems to be that most of the growth was taking place in two Churches, the Congregational and the Presbyterian. The former increased from 1,000 to 18,000 in this period. In less than ten years both achieved a ten-fold increase. The Methodist Church was enjoying moderately good growth during this period, while the Episcopal Church, the American Baptists, and the Disciples of Christ were either standing still or growing only slightly (Yamamori 1963).[3]

What about the "difficult" 1890s? After 1887 the Presbyterians, the Congregationalists, and the Disciples of Christ hardly grew at all for a number of years. However, the Methodists continued their advance. The Baptists grew more than they had during the "wonderful" years. The Episcopal Church began to move rapidly forward in what Bishop Tucker has called an "era of notable progress" for Episcopalians. The Orthodox Church, under Nicolai, reported an 1882 membership figure of 7,611. The 1890 figure was 17,000, and that for 1900 was 26,000 (Neill 1964:446; Latourette 1944:379-381).

It is clear from facts like these that in Japan, as in other places, the growth of the Church is often affected as much by internal factors operating within the Churches themselves as by prevailing social and political conditions.

THE YEARS SINCE WORLD WAR II

After World War II, the door was opened as never before for the evangelism of Japan. As Hiyane put it,

> Shrine Shinto was separated from the Government, the Religious Body Law was abolished, and the new Constitution guaranteed unconditional religious freedom. Thus opened an unprecedented epoch in the history of the religions of Japan (1965:525).

A period of rapid Christian growth ensued. Ariga points out that baptisms within the United Church increased from 11,386 in 1948 to 15,765 in 1951 (1958:372). Then they began to drop:

1952	11,985	1958	7,860[4]
1953	9,965	1960	6,515
1954	8,800	1962	6,232
1955	7,879	1964	7,719
1956	8,538	1966	6,055
1957	7,521		

After 1951, says Ariga, the United Church entered a "period of consolidation." As justification for this interpretation, he refers to the problems this Church has had to face as a body formed through the merger of a number of denominations. We concede a degree of legitimacy to this argument, but was not that problem present also between 1948 and 1951, when annual baptisms increased by over 4,000?

Ariga feels that another highly important factor in the slowdown in the number of baptisms lies in the changed situation after 1951. In that year the peace treaty between Japan and the Allied Powers was concluded. The strong pro-Americanism of the postwar years receded, and periods of anti-American feeling occurred. Moreover, as the shock of the war defeat faded, the people, who had seemingly rejected traditional Japanese religious values, again began to appreciate their heritage, and national self-consciousness was strengthened. This meant they could choose more deliberately from among the many ideas and doctrines available to them. It is against this background, says Ariga, that the decline in the number of baptisms in the United Church must be viewed. "Christianity in Japan has now entered a new period in its history" (1958:372-380).

On the surface this seems convincing. Yet this analysis is open to the same objections we have noted to the explanations made for the "slowdown" in the 1890s: Ariga's article tends to lump all Protestants together and to take insufficient notice of the fact that growth rates of the postwar Churches vary considerably, though all must contend with the same social situation. Compare the annual number of baptisms in the United Church (p. 170) with four other Churches during the same period:[5]

Year	Lutheran Bodies	Southern Baptist	Spirit of Jesus	Roman Catholic
1949		506	300	18,905
1951		1,037	302	21,665
1953	1,015	983	978	24,865
1957	952	1,052	5,419	20,305
1959	917	1,339	5,085	19,665
1961	996	1,073	4,220	15,349
1963	882	1,053	3,154	15,361

These figures warn us both against naive optimism and unnecessary pessimism. That they do not show a steady rise in each Church indicates that Japanese Christians do face many difficulties. But there are also reasons for sober optimism. Note that some Churches were able to increase the number of baptisms subsequent to the time when United Church baptisms began to decline. Others have been able substantially to maintain their momentum through the years. Note also that the Protestant groups listed, while among the larger denominations, are far smaller than the United Church, so that the number of baptismal candidates per thousand church members is considerably larger in these groups. These facts suggest that the goals, methods, and spiritual vitality of the different Churches are factors which often are of even greater importance than the social and religious conditions of the society in which they work.

Iglehart takes a somewhat more optimistic view of the rate of growth in the postwar period. He concedes that the growth has not been as rapid as many had expected, but he considers that we should not expect mass accessions to Christianity from a people like the Japanese who rule their own destinies and possess an integrated religious system. But Iglehart's analysis also suffers from the fact that he lumps all Protestants together in describing the postwar picture, though he is aware that the Churches have grown at different rates (1959:334-344).

It is my opinion that we are entitled to be much more hopeful concerning church growth in Japan than is often thought. There are at least four reasons why we may believe that the conditions prevailing in Japan today do not have the power to prevent the Churches of Christ from moving ahead much faster than they are at this time.

The first reason is the rapid growth of the Spirit of Jesus Church. Appendix C consists of two maps which graphically portray the rapid spread of this Church. Its growth is reminiscent of the kind of growth seen among the Presbyterians in Korea, the Pentecostals in Brazil, the Lutherans in New Guinea, and the Anglicans in Dornakal, India. The *Kirisutokyō Nenkan* (Christian Yearbook) has recorded in its various issues the rapid growth of this Church:

Year	Members
1948	436
1952	1,132
1954	3,399
1958	23,534
1960	33,446
1962	41,244
1964	46,870

As yet too little is known about this movement. It is beginning to attract attention among students of church growth in Japan, both Protestant and Catholic, although most pastors and missionaries are still astounded when told that it is now one of the largest Christian bodies in the nation.

Evaluations of the movement vary considerably among Japanese observers. Some call attention to the "doctrinal heterodoxy" of this new Church. It practices baptism for the dead. It does not affirm the doctrine of the Trinity, though it does believe in the deity of Christ. Its members speak in tongues. Some Christian leaders deny that it is Christianity at all. Its adherents, it is said, do not live like Christians. Others maintain that there are genuine Christians, known personally to them, active in the Spirit of Jesus Church.

In attempting to assess, however, the potential response to the Gospel of the Japanese today, it must not be forgotten that this Church is avowedly Christian. Regardless of how men may estimate its right to that claim, the point is that it has been able to find and win a very large number of people. These people were not averse to entering a movement which unhesitatingly identifies itself as Christian.

It is a mistake to allow reservations concerning the doctrinal stance or standard of Christian living of this indigenous Church (there are no foreign missionaries) to hide from us the significance of its rapid advance. Here is a professedly Christian movement which seems to be laughing at the difficulties in the way of its exuberant growth. Already it has passed the Episcopal Church to become the second Protestant body in Japan. If this Church, working in the same social milieu as others, can win as many converts as it has, is the slow growth of other groups correctly attributed to conditions in society?

It is of considerable interest to note that the Spirit of Jesus Church attributes its progress to lay witness. It stresses house meetings. Its leaders receive no monetary aid, either for their education or for their efforts at church planting.

The second consideration has to do with the growth of the Lutheran, the Baptist, and the Holiness Churches during the years 1949 to 1963. The United Church and the Episcopal Church long were the two largest non-Catholic bodies. If, during this period, they had grown at the rate of the average increase of the above three groups, the Protestant total for 1963 would read 464,853 instead of the 251,718 reported, assuming that all other groups grew as reported (*Kirisutokyō Nenkan* 1964:340-341).[6] It may be objected that the three former groups have been aided by a large influx of missionaries, and this is true, at least in the case of the Baptists and Lutherans. But it is also true that the factor which actually increases membership totals is the multiplication of new churches. A major emphasis of this book is that multiplying churches is not the special task of officials in Tokyo or of foreign missionaries, but it is the task of each pastor and each church. We have striven to show how, by the adoption of less rigid ideas concerning such things as the ministry and buildings, new congregations can be begun by ordinary Christians anywhere in Japan. If the United Church and the Episcopal Church set themselves to multiplying new churches, they can enter into an era of new triumph and growth which would be of great significance to the total cause of Christ in Japan.

The third observation is strictly subjective. Having attempted in a small way to do personal and church evangelism in both the United States and Japan, it seems to me that it is somewhat less difficult to win converts in Japan from among persons unrelated to the church than it is in the United States. True, one must add that the social pressures in Japan pull people out of the church, and unless converts are thoroughly grounded and enabled to find a warm supporting fellowship, they drift away rather easily. Nevertheless, Japanese people can be won to Christ. But–and this must be stressed–apart from certain wonderful exceptions, they do not come searching for Christ's salvation.

We do not insist upon fixed evangelistic procedures. Let each Church settle on the ways of evangelism it thinks most effective, but let it vigorously exercise them. Too frequently Christians do not practice visitation evangelism, do not distribute tracts, do not draw new people to evangelistic meetings, do not significantly touch non-Christians with the Gospel, but only wait for the non-Christians to come to them. When they do not come, they write articles about the poor response to the Christian gospel. People can be won, but they must be sought out by hearts which burn with genuine love for men (not just for another number to be added to the statistics).

The fourth consideration has to do with the growth of the New Religions, and especially Sōka Gakkai (which now claims over 13 million adherents). Christians in Japan are often heard to speak–some half-despairingly, others half-contemptuously–of the appeal of Sōka Gakkai to the credulous masses. But there is another way of looking at this matter. Whatever the appeal to which they are responding, it is clear that millions of Japanese people today are ready to make a religious change. Something over 15 million Japanese have become adherents of one or another of the New Religions since World War II, although many of them have drifted out again. It is evident that whatever the religious or nonreligious background from which these people have come may have been, it was not strong enough or satisfying enough to hold them. Herein lie both the challenge and opportunity presented to the Church. Millions of people in Japan today are drifting. They do not know why they were born, why they are living, or where they are going. Many of them are afraid not only to die, but to live. All of those who would respond to Christ's Gospel ought to be given that opportunity.

It is the position of this book that the Japanese, while certainly not the most receptive people in the world to the Christian Gospel, can nevertheless be won in far greater numbers than is now the case. The Church is today, in the providence of God, being given a magnificent opportunity to persuade many Japanese of the truth of Christ's claims. If one million can be won, a second million will follow close behind. Empowered by the Holy Spirit, willing to utilize flexible forms of the ministry and church organization, Christians of the burning heart can in our day win great victories for Jesus Christ in Japan.

CHAPTER XIV

BLUEPRINT FOR A GROWING CHURCH

Christian leaders ought to dream dreams, and from the dreams develop hard, bold, aggressive plans for planting churches. This chapter attempts to draw together the major ideas of the book as a whole; however, because it is not possible to cover all aspects of church life, we will concentrate on a few selected themes. An attempt has been made to limit proposals to methods which have been successfully used by important Churches in a number of countries, including Japan.

The method used is to present a "survey report" made by an impartial observer who examines the work of a hypothetical "district" in some part of Japan.[1] We shall assume that it is fifteen years since this "district" adopted a new strategy along lines suggested in these pages.

THE DISTRICT

The district dealt with in this report is spread over a considerable area between the sea and the central mountain ranges. By ordinary train it takes two hours to traverse the length of the district. The total population is 850,000. District headquarters is located in a city of 250,000. Three other smaller cities have populations averaging 65,000. A number of towns are in the 10,000 to 25,000 category; others range in size from 1,500 to 10,000, and there are many *buraku.*

ORGANIZATION

The national organization and its work is beyond the scope of this report. The district is governed by a delegate body composed of clergy and lay representatives. Each professional ordained clergyman is entitled to a vote. Each church is entitled to a vote. Each church is entitled to one lay delegate for every fifty active members. It is required that the number of lay delegates be at least as many as the number of professional clergymen.[2] The district is responsible for overall policies and administers funds through the circuits. It maintains a loan fund for church structures, and a health insurance plan and retirement fund for clergymen. Circuits pay the salaries of circuit pastors and sometimes partially subsidize a pastor of a local church. Ordination matters are handled by the circuits under policies drawn up by the district in cooperation with the national body. The district participates in the assignment of clergymen.

The territory now is divided into three circuits. The geographical area and the population of each circuit are about the same. The number of churches in the youngest circuit is considerably less than in the other two. Each circuit is administered by a representative body which meets several times a year. It is made up of the professional clergymen, the lay preachers, and lay delegates (elders) from churches of ten or more active members.

KINDS OF WORKERS

As a part of a concentrated effort to secure as widespread participation as possible in the life and work of the churches, the district has created a number of roles to which believers are appointed.

Fully ordained ministers of the church (*seikyōshi*). Their ordination is recognized everywhere. Candidates for this office must have fulfilled standard educational requirements, including study at a theological school.[3] It is the custom that ministers be present when any of the several kinds of ordination rites are conducted. These men are highly respected throughout the district, and a continuous effort is made to secure able men for this office. Since there are several other roles which earnest persons may play, less qualified individuals are not encouraged to seek appointment to this office. There are several ministers in the district who are recognized as specially able and devout men. A conscious effort is made to ensure that these men are freed from time-consuming routine work, and that their gifts and abilities are shared so as to bless all the Christians in the district. As in other parts of Japan, the preparatory office for *seikyōshi* is *hokyōshi* (preparatory ministers).

Pastor-teachers (bokkai-kyōshi) are a new rank of ordained leaders, whose ordination is effective within the district only. To qualify for this role, candidates must have completed prescribed training which includes both courses taught by qualified teachers and correspondence study. Candidates with two years of theological school training are sometimes appointed to this position. In certain cases, pastor-teachers who have completed many years of effective service, and a rigorous course of theological studies, may be selected by the district for ordination as full ministers *(seikyōshi).* Most pastor-teachers serve without pay; some serve on a part-time basis. However, they may serve as full-time pastors, and several are at present serving churches in the district. This role has opened up leadership functions in the churches to highly qualified persons. One church is pastored by two Christian psychiatrists who serve the church without salary. Two doctors, four factory workers, five businessmen, three farmers, twelve school teachers, four salesmen, three bank officials, and seven other men of varied occupation are serving in the district as pastor-teachers. Usually these men, unless they have studied at theological school, do not lead a church alone, but share pastoral functions with one or more other persons. Pastor-teachers conduct the sacraments. It is expected that the number of persons serving in this way will steadily increase.

Professional clergymen serve in three capacities in the district. Some are the full-time pastors of large churches. Some serve as pastors of smaller churches with a portion of their time given to itineration within a circuit.

Others serve as circuit pastors (salaried). Each circuit has a circuit head pastor, and in two of the circuits additional circuit pastors are active. Only men who are willing to itinerate are appointed to this office. These men are the key to the success or failure of the circuit.[4] Aside from their own preaching and pastoral functions, the circuit pastors have the important task of recruiting and training lay preachers and drawing up their monthly preaching schedules. It is also part of their work to encourage and counsel with elders and other leaders of small churches.

Lay preachers are the other secret of the vitality of the circuit system. They are of all ages (but the youngest are at least 24) and many different occupations. There are now 180 lay preachers in the district. Usually they preach in a different place each week. The circuit seeks to arrange their schedules so that they need prepare a new sermon only once in six weeks, although some may prepare new messages more frequently. Lay preachers are recruited from churches large and small. It is a matter of pride in the district that each church with more than ten members has at least one lay preacher. When the men are from very small congregations, they are usually scheduled for evening appointments rather than Sunday morning. The frequency of preaching appointments is based on the amount of leisure time a lay preacher has. Some preach once or twice every week, others only twice a month.

Among the lay preachers in the newest circuit, the people of the circuit are particularly appreciative of the service of three men. One is an insurance company executive. He is so busy that he can manage to prepare only one sermon a month, but his joyous life blesses all the congregations. A second is a university professor, who has a wonderful ability to present the Gospel in a way to which young people respond. He has a bubbling kind of humor, yet is a serious Christian. The third is a farmer, and no one can explain quite why his sermons are so effective. He speaks rather quietly, and if what he says were written down it would seem quite ordinary, but when he speaks people are profoundly moved. All these men have humbly accepted training in preaching from the professional clergy, partly to encourage others who are being instructed for appointment as lay preachers.

Persons who feel a call to preach are first appointed as *exhorters.* They accompany lay preachers to their appointments and assist in various ways. They are allowed to preach occasionally, under observation, in circuit churches. If they serve acceptably they are next appointed *preachers on trial.* The district has drawn up standards of character, knowledge of spiritual things, personal appearance and bearing for these positions. Preachers on trial are persons who desire to serve as lay preachers, to which position they may be appointed after two or three years of acceptable service. Young candidates continue in this role until they are at least 24 years of age. Courses of study are required and examinations must be passed for each of these levels of service.

Young people fill these positions with enthusiasm and verve.

Some of the *exhorters* are only 17 or 18 years of age. Not only do the churches benefit from the efforts of these zealous young people, but the experience they gain prepares them for added responsibility as they grow older. Some of the best professional clergy are men who began serving as exhorters during their high school or university days.

In order for lay preachers to be able to carry out their ministry effectively, the understanding of the professional clergy is essential. As a major method of fostering this understanding, it is the policy of the district that all candidates for the professional clergy in this district must first become lay preachers–a requirement that is vigorously enforced. When clergy come into the district from other parts of Japan, they are asked to undergo a regime of reading designed to acquaint them with the purpose and function of lay preachers.

Every church, if possible, has at least one *elder.* These men must be at least 30 years old. They are chosen jointly by the congregations and the circuit pastors. Usually one elder for each 25 members is elected. Elders in this district may be ordained, and may then conduct the sacraments. They perform important pastoral functions in their churches. Their ordination is effective in their own church only. Whenever possible, elders serve terms of three years and are rotated in office. Except in special cases approved by the district, they may not serve for more than six consecutive years. Elders in this district are respected men. A study program must be completed before an elder may be ordained and given authority to conduct the sacraments. The district draws up the qualifications for the office. It seeks to ensure that men are not elected to this office as a face-saving device, but because they have a spiritual contribution to make.

When new churches are begun, the circuit pastors frequently appoint suitable persons as *preparatory elders.* Such persons often become elders subsequently. Some men in their late twenties are appointed to this office. It is notable that when laymen are given this kind of responsibility in new churches they carry it out in most cases with vigor and enthusiasm.

Deacons are also appointed in many churches. They assist the pastors and elders, serve on the finance committee and conduct services in the homes of believers. They also lead small groups in the church. Both men and women serve as deacons. In a new church, if there are no qualified persons old enough to be appointed elders, younger men may be appointed deacons and perform some of the functions of an elder.

Women also serve as *Bible Women.* Some are employed full-time or part-time by larger churches. Others serve without pay. They are especially effective in visiting homes and hospitals, and in children's work. Some are also capable of providing musical training.

The district encourages the ministry of small groups, both as a means of strengthening existing churches and of planting new congregations. There are two kinds of groups. In the larger churches there are groups for Christians, each headed by a deacon, or sometimes an elder. If one or more persons from a family is a full church member, that family is considered a church family. Each deacon has ten families under his care. When the number exceeds ten, a second deacon is elected. When it exceeds 20 a third deacon is appointed, and so on. A deacon acts as a little pastor for his group. He visits the sick, congratulates family members (whether Christians or not) for their successes, and sympathizes with them in their difficulties. He seeks to assist the believers in winning the unsaved members of their families. He consults with the minister about his families. If there is no minister, or if he is very busy, the work of the deacons is supervised by one deacon who has been elected *steward.* The groups meet at least monthly if possible. The composition of the groups and the times at which they meet vary from church to church. These groups are effective in maintaining the spiritual life of church members.

Other types of small groups are used for evangelistic purposes. These vary according to the church. A manual, such as the one suggested on p. 150, ought to be prepared as skills in using small groups led by laymen for evangelistic purposes are developed. This manual should also cover the subject of house meetings.

Training coordinators are appointed in many churches of the district. They cooperate with the pastors in promoting the training program in the church. They keep a record of studies members have completed. They prepare (or post) promotional material for training classes in which members can enroll. District semi-annual gatherings of the training coordinators are held, at which they are helped to develop better programs in their churches, exchange experiences, and learn about training programs planned by the district and the circuits. In small churches an elder or a deacon may carry out this task.

Missionaries play an active role in the district. The role of the missionary has been the subject of debate in recent years in Japan and other lands, but in a district in which the multiplying of new churches is recognized as a paramount goal, there is plenty for missionaries to do. There are three missionaries in the district. The policy is to involve them in the program of establishing new churches. One missionary acts as a circuit pastor. Another is an effective speaker at evangelistic rallies, and devotes much of his time to answering calls from district churches to preach at small evangelistic meetings (10 to 75 people). (At larger evangelistic rallies, the preaching is done largely by Japanese leaders.) His services are particularly appreciated by small, struggling groups who do not yet have very great financial strength. He has responsibility for about 20 per cent of such meetings annually in the district. His Japanese is excellent. He is also a leader in youth work. The third missionary is assigned to assist Pastor Tanabe.

Tanabe is the able and aggressive leader of a large church which is busy establishing new congregations. In the past seven years this strong church alone, with its six bands of trained laymen, has started fifteen congregations. Most of these are still small, but two are now growing churches with their own paid pastors. Both of these have now started new congregations of their own. Tanabe uses the missionary to preach for him when he is away serving at a branch church. The missionary is used extensively in training the laymen of the church and accompanying them in their work in the branch churches. Says Tanabe:

> Our missionary's Japanese is not very good, and I think Christians in small groups can listen to him more patiently than non-Christians would. Though he doesn't preach to non-Christians very much, he is a fruitful evangelist because he trains many laymen to do evangelism, and imparts his evangelistic passion to them.

This missionary also is effective in helping laymen fulfill their vocations in the secular world. The district justifies assigning a missionary to one pastor because this pastor is an effective church planter. Tanabe requested the assistance of the missionary and takes time and thought to see that his abilities are fully utilized. The relations between the two men are excellent.

In the days when the changeover to the present system was being debated, three arguments against the idea of having churches without paid pastors, led by laymen, were frequently heard. They are not so often raised within the district nowadays, although outsiders occasionally mention them. This reporter interviewed Pastor Yoshida, one of the veteran leaders in the district, in this regard. The gist of his remarks follows.

> One argument was: Such a system may work in foreign countries, but not in Japan. There was bound to be trouble between the pastors and lay leaders. But we answered that even under the system of *one-paid-pastor-per-church,* some clergymen strongly believe in the ministry of laymen. They trust laymen to carry out many responsibilities, and leave churches in their care when they are away for evangelistic meetings, travel abroad, and for other reasons. We also pointed out that we Japanese need not yield to such feelings of inferiority. If people in other lands can work in this way, Japanese Christians, led by the Holy Spirit and fired with resolve, can do it too. We challenged the objectors to shake off their negative thinking, and to exercise their ingenuity in finding ways of making a better pattern for accomplishing Christ's purposes succeed in Japan.
>
> The other two objections were rather similar. Some argued that "under the *one-pastor-per-church system,* someone is always in the church building when people in trouble want to go for guidance and comfort. But a church building to which lay leaders and clergy only came for meetings would be a cold and unattractive place." Others pointed to the "warm intimacy which pastors in Japan enjoy with their members. When members feel the need of fellowship and strength, they can go and confer with the pastor. But under the circuit system, this would be lost."
>
> To these two objections, our basic answer was that they represented a very luxurious attitude. It is true that a clergyman cannot maintain quite the same intimacy with believers when he has from five to ten congregations to think about instead of only one. And it is also true that it is not as convenient for the believers to contact the pastor when they cannot simply drop into the church at any time.

What is not realized by many Christians in Japan, however, is that this kind of intimacy can be enjoyed only at very high cost indeed. It is possible only because churches in Japan are so small. If, as in many other countries, a church has a membership of 300 or even 500, such intimacy is not possible even though there be a full-time pastor in the church. People in a church that size cannot go and spend an hour with the pastor any time they like. Appointments must be made. Actually, members of small churches in a circuit can enjoy more intimacy with the circuit pastor than members of such large churches can with their pastor.

Secondly, the luxury of having a pastor almost always present in the church is possible only at the expense of the people in nearby communities which have no church at all. People in those communities need the Gospel too. But it is impossible to find, train, and finance enough able men to make that kind of intimate church life possible for all the people in the country. Only when salaried pastors are serving larger areas and more people in the lands of Asia and Africa will church life and the grace of God come to every community.

What is needed is for the experience of fellowship to be enjoyed more between believers, and not so exclusively between individual believers and the pastor. Believers must be trained to bear more responsibility for each other, to open their hearts and homes to each other, to be able to give Christian guidance to one another in times of trouble. Moreover, it needs to be emphasized that under the circuit system, the pastor is not, after all, so very far away. His residence is close enough that members in any of the congregations can readily contact him in times of real need.

These are some of the objections and the ways in which we met them.

MULTIPLYING CHURCHES

Fifteen years ago the district identified the multiplication of new congregations as a chief goal of the Church's work in the world. Recognizing the need to clear away obstructions to the achieving of that goal, it introduced new flexibility and originality into its organizational structure and methodology. The result has been an era of remarkable expansion. The growth in the total number of Christians in the district during the first decade was 100 per cent. At the present rate of increase, the second decade will see an increase exceeding 130 per cent. The number of churches has increased by 70 per cent during the past five years.[5] Of course, many of these churches are small.

The multiplication of churches is not a mechanical thing. It takes place as the lives of many individuals are transformed. The tragedy, the beauty, and the pathos of human life are present in all their forms as loving and sacrificial evangelistic efforts lead to conversions and infant churches. Over it all is the brooding, searching love of God. The ways by which new churches are planted in the district are several.

The fastest and most efficient method of establishing new churches is for an existent church to divide, cell-fashion, into two churches. Then both groups endeavor to grow to the strength of the original church. It is difficult to persuade pastors and churches to take this step, but several of the stronger churches in the district have been formed in this way, especially in the cities.

A second way in which new churches are established, especially in cities, is for believers who belong to rather distant churches, but live in the same vicinity, to be formed into a new congregation. When a survey reveals that there are a considerable number of believers (sometimes unknown to each other) living in a neighborhood where a church is needed, an attempt is made to interest them and the churches to which they belong in praying and working for the creation of a new church. This method requires courage and missionary vision on the part of both these members and their churches, but when the new church takes its place in the district, all concerned share the joy and satisfaction of the achievement.

Many of the churches sponsor cottage meetings and other types of small groups which meet on weeknights in homes. Some of these grow in numbers under the blessing of God. When such a group is a considerable distance from the sponsoring church, it has in a number of cases proved possible to constitute the group a new church.

One of the most effective methods is the use of the evangelistic band. Usually about eight persons compose a band, the majority being young people. Large churches may have several. When churches are very small, sometimes members from two or three churches form a band. Usually at least two members of a band are able to preach. These bands are trained in such things as visitation evangelism, literature evangelism, and conducting evangelistic and regular meetings. These bands are given recognition and prestige in the district as well as in their own churches and circuits.

In Japan today, except in highly resistant places, it is possible to get a group of converts anywhere if loving, winsome evangelism is energetically carried out. Even in rural communities it is possible to get crowds of forty or more listeners to special evangelistic meetings (although converts are more difficult to win).[6] Some churches in the district lay careful plans for a campaign in a new locality as much as a year ahead of time. Funds are gathered, and prayers are offered weekly for the coming effort. Visitation evangelism and literature evangelism are carried out by the members, and a preaching campaign is conducted. Strong emphasis is placed upon following up converts and inquirers won by the special evangelistic efforts. One-third of the budget for special meetings is apportioned to follow-up efforts. Leaders are trained in ways of enabling the converts to assume a considerable share of the responsibility for the growth of the new congregation resulting from the campaign. Often efforts of this nature are combined with one of the other methods described in this section.

In one circuit, three strong churches have pooled their resources to employ a missionary pastor. His work is to train the members of those churches in the work of church planting, and then to lead them in the work of planting new congregations in the area of the sponsoring churches. This work is separate from, but coordinated with, the work of the circuit. Five small churches have resulted in the three years since the program was begun.

Many of the new congregations which have been started during the past fifteen years have been initiated by one or two laymen. In one case, for example, two laymen have recently begun a new effort in a small town where there is no church. The pastor visits this work only occasionally, at the request of the two leaders. He relates with some amusement how one of the laymen even "repaired and explained" his sermon upon one occasion. But that pastor rejoices because he knows that when laymen become so concerned for the salvation of people under their care that they long for them to understand the message, then fruit will be borne.

It is a recognized part of district strategy that one highly effective way to found new churches is to inspire laymen to do this work. Not only does this emphasis result in the message of Christ reaching new people, but it strengthens the spiritual muscle of the sponsoring churches. A considerable number of laymen in the district have now begun congregations. There are in the district three laymen who have each been instrumental in the starting of four or more congregations in the past ten years. It is an accepted principle in the district that the man the Holy Spirit has used to begin a congregation should in most cases continue–for the time being at least–to exercise leadership in that place, rather than turn the work over immediately to a professional clergyman.[7]

One of the most interesting episodes in the history of the district has to do with the work of a man named Yamaguchi, who was converted at 47. He was a part-time farmer who also owned timberland which yielded him a steady profit. Three years after his conversion, he was appointed a lay preacher. He began to manifest unusual ability in evangelism. When he was 52, he became burdened to begin evangelism in a part of the countryside in which there were no churches. His own resources permitted him considerable freedom in the use of his time. Soon three small churches sprang up. Yamaguchi ministered to these, with the assistance of lay leaders from among the congregations. His methods were rather unusual, and there were some in the district who criticized his work. However, since the work was growing, the district did not interfere. In seven years, five hundred people were baptized, and the number of churches grew to ten. Many families were won. Some proposed that the work be formed into a circuit with a professional clergyman in charge. However, since the work had been established through one man and was growing rapidly under his leadership, the majority in the district thought it would be a mistake to smother this spontaneous expansion. Cordial relations existed between Yamaguchi and his churches, and the district leaders. He frequently sought the aid of professional clergymen in evangelistic meetings and in training new believers. The work is still growing. As Yamaguchi has grown older, he has come to feel he can no longer handle the work alone. He recently requested that two salaried pastors be assigned to the largest churches, and to assist him in leading the others. Two young pastors who were among Yamaguchi's early converts were dispatched to these posts, and the entire work continues to prosper.

The Japanese are today a highly mobile populace. The district seeks to turn this oftentimes disconcerting reality of modern urban life into an opportunity for planting new churches. When, because of employment transfers or need of new housing, church members move to a new locality, it has sometimes been found possible to establish a new church in a needy neighborhood with such individuals (in some cases a family) acting in the beginning as the responsible local leaders. On occasion, their own church has subsidized part of the cost of an apartment to enable such Christians to secure living quarters large enough to accommodate meetings. Evangelistic efforts of various kinds are undertaken, and a new congregation comes into being. Pastoral leadership is usually provided at first from the mother church, and perhaps later from the district. In two cases, several zealous young Christians have intentionally moved into a new locality for the purpose of beginning a church.

The professional clergy play a large part in the multiplication of churches. Directly or indirectly they are related to the beginning of most of the new churches in the district. Pastors now take deep satisfaction in being able to develop laymen who can start new churches. Several older pastors who had become somewhat discouraged pastoring one church with a small average attendance have had the joy of seeing new churches planted. They say they have recovered the missionary fervor they felt when they originally received the call to the ministry. In some cases when their lay members were not yet ready to join in church-planting efforts, two pastors have met frequently to pray together and to discuss the missionary calling of each Christian and each church. They locate and write literature on the subject for Christians to read. Sometimes the two of them devote one night every two weeks to trying to start a new congregation. When the time is right, they begin to preach sermons on the subject and then assist each other in conducting training sessions for their church members. They may invite a challenging speaker from outside to inspire and instruct their congregations. As the help of the Holy Spirit is sought, the way is opened for believers and pastors to plant new churches.

Even very small churches can start other churches. When the leaders have a busy schedule, even meetings held once a month may result in the formation of a group of believers in a new place. The rest of the time meetings in the preaching station can be conducted by laymen who reside there.

In addition to the above, there are three other methods of establishing new churches which were described in notable articles recently in the *Kirisuto Shinbun*.[8]

During the past fifteen years, district leaders have devoted much thought to the problem of how to circumvent the financial barriers to the establishment of new congregations which have so often thwarted expansion in Japan. The district has sought to work out a set of procedures aimed at making it financially feasible for any church to start a new church with or without outside aid. Close scrutiny has been given to one of the main points of the Nevius Method, which has so signally fostered growth among Korean Presbyterians:

> Self-support, with all places of worship provided by believers, each group as soon as founded beginning to pay towards the circuit helper's salary; even schools to receive only a partial subsidy, and no pastors of single congregations to be provided for by foreign funds (Beyerhaus and Lefever 1964:92).

This policy, formulated by missionaries for Korea, has been "translated" by district leaders to make it appropriate for a missionary program in Japan sponsored by Japanese churches. The principle of not subsidizing pastors of single congregations, and of gaining the support of a large percentage of the salaried clergy from the several congregations of circuits, has been implemented.

The recognition of the ministry of lay preachers and other unpaid leaders has opened the way to the rapid multiplication of churches in this district. Once it was recognized that real churches can carry on without a salaried pastor and an expensive building, it became possible to plant numerous congregations in unchurched parts of cities, in small towns, and in villages. Each new group is trained by the circuit leaders in its responsibility to be God's agent for winning the whole community. So long as constant attention is given to the recruiting and training of lay leaders, it has not been necessary to place any restrictions upon the establishment of new congregations. A way can be found to provide pastoral care for every new group.

The circuits are constantly making decisions concerning pastoral care. Key leaders move away and must be replaced. New congregations frequently are formed, and pastoral care must be planned. Each situation calls for a new decision. One congregation may be led by a pastor-teacher and an elder, both of whom serve without pay. In another place, a pastor-teacher on half-salary may be solely in charge. In still another, three unpaid elders may exercise responsibility for the work under the direction of the circuit pastor. A small group may be led by a deacon, with lay preachers doing most of the preaching. The circuit decisions take into consideration the needs of each congregation large or small, the personnel available, and the growth potential of the communities in which work has been undertaken. The varied roles played by workers, paid and unpaid, enable circuit leaders to employ a flexible approach to the problem of providing pastoral care for each group in its territory.

As new congregations contribute to the treasury of a circuit, additional salaried clergy can be employed to train volunteer workers and to cooperate with them in providing pastoral care for all the congregations. In a growing and evangelistically minded district, there is no shortage of candidates for the professional ministry. Finding satisfactory quarters for the meetings of new congregations is a constant problem in a land suffering from a chronic housing shortage, but a flexible and prayerful approach to this problem enables some kind of solution to be found in each case. (See pp. 98-100; also p. 188.)

Any church or group of Christians has the freedom to begin a congregation on its own initiative, provided it takes responsibility for the work until it has grown large enough for the circuit to assume responsibility. The circuit takes over only when requested to do so. The district takes the position that it is better not to interfere with the initiative of laymen, even though their methods are occasionally unconventional, on the grounds that spontaneous expansion is so precious a thing that it is worth the price of some inconvenience and anxiety.

DEVELOPING THE YOUNG CONGREGATION

The district gives careful thought to the matter of how to develop the initiative, independence, and power potential of the nucleus of believers in a new place of evangelistic endeavor. It is constantly emphasized that these people are called to be the chief workers for Christ in their community. Every effort is made to avoid their developing a spirit of dependence, or simply of passively receiving the grace brought by clergy and other workers from outside.

The notion that once a congregation has formed, no more outside help is needed, and that such assistance may even be harmful, is regarded as extreme. The leadership and encouragement and inspiration provided by outside workers who come regularly or from time to time to the new congregation, are held to be essential. But a constant effort is made to ensure that their contribution is so devised as to build up the new believers into men and women who can themselves be active and effective workers for God.

From the very beginning the believers are given as much responsibility as they are able to assume. Leaders coming in from the outside endeavor to make it their practice to avoid doing for new converts what they are able to do for themselves. As soon as is feasible, new congregations are persuaded to hold meetings themselves on days when outside leaders do not come. Simple ways for ordinary people to conduct meaningful meetings are taught.

A treasurer from among the members of the new congregation is elected at the earliest opportunity. The circuit leaders also oversee the appointment of temporary local leaders of various kinds suited to the stage of development of the work. From the first, prayer is offered that God will raise up lay preachers from among this new body of believers to participate in the work of the district. When this takes place, it usually acts as a great stimulus to the young congregation.

Every attempt is made to involve new converts in evangelistic endeavors. It is regarded as harmful to the future of the church to allow a time gap between conversion and the moment when a convert begins actively to serve Christ. Candidates in baptismal preparation classes are encouraged to pray (during class) for specific persons, to witness to them, and to endeavor to bring them to church. Church members are led to engage in visitation evangelism, literature distribution, and other evangelistic activities. Experienced Christians occasionally come from other churches to help the new group get started in such endeavors.

A definite effort is made to bring the new believers into the circuit fellowship. Based on the conviction that an enthusiastic faith is usually caught more than it is taught, it has been found fruitful to bring the members of the young congregation into warm contact with earnest Christians of the circuit at retreats and other inspirational gatherings.

Careful thought is given to training. A list of essential courses has been drawn up, and an intensive effort is made to enroll all members in these courses. They are invited to district and circuit training sessions. Training in the local meeting place is also given high priority. Members are encouraged to participate in the Bible correspondence study program.

TRAINING PROGRAM

The training program is a major factor in the vitality and progress of the district. Candidates for all leadership positions described above are expected to complete a standard course of instruction designed by the district for that position. These courses include both classes taught by qualified teachers and correspondence study. Each of these courses includes some material on the methodology and spirit of the district. This is very important in the case of laymen, since they form half or more of the delegates to the district assembly and the circuit meetings.

A large old farmhouse has been secured in which many of the training sessions are held. It is called the Institute for Lay Training. Here retreats and youth and missionary rallies are also held. At the latter, the evangelistic successes and needs of the district are movingly presented. Earnest prayer for the district's evangelistic effort is made. Many of the lay preachers of the district have heard and answered the call of God at these rallies.

It is a goal energetically pursued throughout the district that every church member complete at least one study course each year. The courses are usually taught in units of six sessions each. Over 50 per cent of all courses are conducted in local churches, about 30 per cent at the Institute, and the remainder in courses in which two to five neighboring churches cooperate. Inquirers are also encouraged to enroll in these courses. For the past five years, total enrollment in all courses taught in the district has each year exceeded the total district communicant membership. This is a goal the district had sought for a long time to achieve.

In order to enable clergymen to renew their inspiration, to develop new skills, and to keep abreast of a changing world, the Institute for Lay Training arranges courses from time to time for the professional clergy. The goal is to develop a program providing for clergymen intermittent training over a lifetime.

One of the essentials of a good training program is quality study materials. A literature appropriate for short courses has gradually been built up. Some suitable material was already in print and some has been translated, in addition to which district pastors and laymen have written a number of short textbooks.

The district accepts the principle that we teach more by what we do than by what we say. It strives then to adopt concrete procedures to teach the overall membership the methodology upon which district growth is based. Since the idea that only churches led by salaried clergy are genuine churches has been very deep-rooted in Japan, the district each year rewards the three churches without salaried clergy which have been most outstanding. The awards emphasize that such churches are very important to the evangelization of Japan. As one means of teaching the theology of the laity, once each year Holy Communion is celebrated in all the churches on the same day by unpaid elders or pastor-teachers who have not studied at theological school. On this day the professional clergymen sit with the people in the congregation.

The district accepts the principle that most successful training enterprises have small beginnings. In many churches, pastors frequently teach short-term courses to small classes of two or three persons. As church members see the value of training, enrollment in the classes steadily increases.

Every course, large or small, is looked upon as an opportunity for the Holy Spirit to work in the hearts of believers, awakening them to the possibilities of the life lived for Christ. Many Christians have caught fire in instruction classes, and have been used to transform the atmosphere in their churches.

Pastor Ito, head of the training program, has written:

> Spiritual fervor that endures is indispensable to church growth. This kind of fervor comes only from the Holy Spirit. Christians need to be instructed in the truths pertaining to the Holy Spirit. There are many strange notions concerning the Spirit. It should be emphasized that the Holy Spirit is the Spirit of Jesus Christ. He will do always that which is true to the character of Christ, and only that. If this principle is observed, many of the excesses erroneously associated with the Holy Spirit will be avoided. It should be recognized that the Holy Spirit works according to His sovereign will, in varying ways in different people. Some persons are naturally demonstrative, for example, while others are naturally reserved. We should not forbid men to speak in tongues (I Cor. 14:39), but those who speak in tongues should not insist that others must also do so (I Cor. 12:30), or imply that those who do not speak in tongues are not filled with the Spirit. Spiritual

fervor is rightly expressed in various ways, but if Christians are not fervent they are spiritually ill, and should implore the Father for the gift of the Holy Spirit (Luke 11:13).

PROBLEMS OF GROWTH

Frequent problems occur organizationally and otherwise when new churches are being rapidly brought into being. This is true in the district. A few leaders have called for a slowdown in the pace of multiplying new churches and a tightening and refining of organizational lines. But the argument which has prevailed is that the problems caused by rapid growth are the kind of problems the Church wants to have. A church which has a smooth-running organization but does not grow is a far greater problem than a church which has organizational difficulties caused by rapid growth.

FINANCIAL CONSIDERATIONS

A most noteworthy aspect of the life of the churches in the district is that they have swept past the barriers which have long retarded the multiplication of churches: clerical salaries and expensive buildings.

This should not be interpreted to mean the district has no financial problems. Money is always in short supply. Continuous effort must be expended to secure sufficient funds for the salaries and expenses of the circuit pastors and the traveling expenses of the lay preachers. Training in stewardship is stressed constantly. Offerings are taken in new congregations from the beginning. From the first, at least 25 per cent of these offerings, and if possible up to 50 per cent, is sent to the district treasurer. However, these percentages are sometimes reduced when a church is paying a pastor's salary or paying building costs. It is the practice for the district to pay part of the salary of a pastor of a local church when his church is establishing new congregations which contribute to the district treasury, and when his church is financially pressed.

The district has adopted a firm rule that no subsidy is extended for a salaried clergyman to serve as pastor of a single church when the average Sunday adult attendance is less than 20, or when the church cannot pay at least 80 per cent of the salary. Even then, subsidies are not continued for more than 30 months (48 months in certain difficult rural situations). When funds for subsidies are available, the policy is to extend them to men who itinerate in a circuit. In the first years after this policy was adopted, some young pastors disagreed with it and each took part-time employment so he could act as the pastor of one church. But the comparative results of the two approaches were so different that almost all younger pastors today gladly work on the circuit itineration pattern.

The widespread use of trained laymen to cooperate in providing pastoral care has eased somewhat the demand for salaried clergymen. One result has been that the district does not feel compelled to subsidize candidates of doubtful ability. Rather it counsels such persons to seek ordinary employment. They are encouraged to endeavor, during their leisure time, to begin new churches or to assist in established ones that desire their services. Over the years, some of these men have demonstrated genuine ability in pastoral work and evangelism and are now full-time salaried clergy. The district endeavors to welcome and recognize the efforts of men of this kind, and to approve them as salaried clergy when their work justifies such action.

DISTRICT EMPHASES

In concluding this report, we should mention certain goals and emphases which the district endeavors to keep continually before all the churches.

The district constantly works at maintaining a spirit of advance and adventure among the Christians of the churches. It knows that if it directs too many demands at the people, or sets impossible goals which no one really expects can be reached, enthusiasm will eventually be dampened. It attempts always to keep challenging but realizable goals before the people, and to inculcate the feeling that the Church is on the march.

Numerous small new churches are being planted and it would be difficult for pastors of larger churches to get around to all of them and conduct the sacraments in each place. Circuit pastors regularly perform this service, and their efforts are supplemented by the work of ordained elders. Every congregation in the district is able regularly to enjoy the blessing of participation in the communion service.

It is a district goal that lay preachers considerably outnumber congregations. It is made a matter of pride for each church to have at least one unpaid preacher; larger churches are expected to supply more. It is also a goal of the district to see that there are several times as many churches as there are professional clergymen.

Another goal of the district is to increase the number of its churches by at least 100 per cent each decade. This means that for each ten churches, one new church per year must be established. All three circuits are maintaining this pace, although this was not true during the first three or four years of the program. The oldest circuit is actually establishing new churches at the rate of two per year for each ten churches. If small churches of eight or more members are counted, quite aside from the question of whether they have paid pastors or buildings, such a goal is not unattainable.

The district constantly surveys what is happening in its territory, both in its own churches and those of other denominations. The district keeps careful statistics and knows whether or not it is growing. When other denominations are growing faster, it seeks to learn from them. It is interested in whether any particular segment of society is especially responsive to evangelism and attempts to concentrate the greater part of its strength on the people most likely to become Christians. Every-member surveys conducted once in two years help to indicate the groups from which new converts are coming. The district also seeks to determine what kinds of persons are most likely to leave the Church, and whether anything can be done about it.[9]

It is the purpose of the district to plant congregations in every community in its territory where no Christian church is found, or where the number of churches is inadequate to serve a large population. Recognizing that other denominations are also part of Christ's one true Church, and seeking to live in brotherhood with all who love Christ, the district recognizes its responsibility for the spiritual destiny of all the people in its territory who do not yet believe in Jesus Christ.

* * * * *

Not everyone will dream the dream in the same way. Moreover, it is highly unlikely that a Church in the real world will turn out just like the "district" described in this chapter. Readers are encouraged to refashion the dream according to the differing situations they face in each land and Church. But some realities cannot easily be changed.

One of the realities of our day is that spiritual receptivity and the freedom to preach in numerous places in the world are such that great hosts of people could and should be won for Christ. Another is that all too often the Church is encumbered by growth-hindering traditions of leadership and organization which prevent her from meeting these enormous challenges.

Still another and more hopeful reality is that some large and growing Churches have learned to leap over perennial obstacles to growth. They have carved out flexible patterns of church life which release great new waves of power. Such Churches succeed in recruiting large numbers of people to fill a variety of unpaid leadership roles. They learn how to rally a large part of the believing community to the task of evangelism. The call today is for God's people to act upon the knowledge these Churches provide, and to carry out in the power of the Spirit the unchanging mandate delivered to them by their Lord.

NOTES

CHAPTER I

[1] Japan's most famous Christian. During the first half of the twentieth century Kagawa engaged in countless endeavors for social uplift. He was, at the same time, Japan's most effective evangelist, conducting mass evangelism campaigns in every part of the country.

CHAPTER II

[1] Calculations based upon figures in *Kirisutokyō* Nenkan (1964:341). In calculating the Episcopal figure, I did not assume any total membership enlargement in the older churches, so that the projected "increase" derives wholly from new congregations, for whom I assumed a membership average of half that reported for all Episcopal churches in 1963.

[2] The Burma Methodist figures are taken from records on file at the Methodist Missionary Society headquarters in London. The Brazil Baptist figures are based upon Crabtree (1953). I have not had exact Baptist figures at hand, but have had to rely upon Crabtree's graphs. However, the figures listed, while approximations, are sufficiently reliable for purposes of the argument.

[3] Provided by the *Christian Yearbook (Kirisutokyō Nenkan).*

[4] Since 1955 most *buraku,* villages, and small towns have, for administrative purposes, been amalgamated into larger units, though most of these places retain much of their former social consciousness as separate communities. *The Japan Statistical Yearbook 1964* lists the number of cities in categories beginning with 10,000 to 19,999, and by degrees working up to 499,999. In each category the 1955 figures are nearly double those of 1950. Meanwhile, units of one to 1,999, and of 2,000 to 4,999 population are listed as much fewer in 1955 than in 1950. The pattern is clearly for smaller communities to be absorbed into larger ones for administrative purposes, although no dramatic

change has occurred in the actual locations in which people reside. There is, however, a steady population decline in rural areas everywhere in Japan.

[5] Stephen Neill (1957:158-159) also draws attention to the damage done by separating the work of the Churches (pastoral) and the mission (evangelism).

CHAPTER IV

[1] Except as otherwise noted, this account is based upon Sweet: 1946.

[2] Neill (1964:353) believes the population may approach four million, but other sources give lower estimates.

[3] This account is indebted to three sources: Kuder (1952), Frerichs (1957), and Vicedom (1961).

[4] School teachers, whose salaries are paid by the congregations of the circuits.

[5] Unless otherwise noted the following account is based upon Davis (1938), Davis (1939), Neill (1964), Warneck (1911), and Beyerhaus and Lefever (1964).

[6] No statistics were kept before 1935, so figures for those years are estimates. The "net growth" figures have been arrived at by subtracting 20 per cent from the "cumulative baptisms" figure to allow for losses. The "net growth" figures have been found to compare well with Brazilian government census figures since 1957. Further, the number of believers reported by the *Congregacao* in various communities compares favorably with the rapidly increasing number of buildings constructed and owned by the Church. This Church now has structures seating 5,000 or more people in over 15 Brazilian cities.

CHAPTER V

[1] The source of much of the information contained in this section was Douglas Webster's *Patterns of Part-time Ministry* (1964).

[2] The *World Christian Handbook* (1962) reports an estimated 12,000 communicants in the Plymouth Brethren Church. Among Protestants, only the Baptists (312 meeting places and 12,813 members) and the *Svenska Fria Missionen* (250 places and 13,000 members) are listed as larger.

CHAPTER VII

[1] Writing several decades ago over against a situation in some respects considerably different from that of our day, Allen's arguments are almost entirely directed to missionaries and their sending Boards. In Japan today, as is proper, planning for church expansion in established Churches is primarily the responsibility of Japanese leaders, so that Allen's works must be "translated" as they are read, into the situation of today.

[2] The El Salvador story is based upon Hodges' article and supplemented by information found in the files of the Institute of Church Growth.

[3] Dr. Alan Tippett informs me that in 1960, in the Australian Methodist

Church in Melanesia and Polynesia, the ratio of active ordained ministers to local preachers was 1 to 54. Ministers in training or on probation were approximately three times the number of ordained men, and class leaders were nearly twice the number of local preachers. This reveals a strongly participant laity.

CHAPTER VIII

[1] Gore thinks that by "others" in verse nine, Jesus meant the apostles, but he concedes that in the parallel passage of Matthew 21:33-46 the reference is probably to "the Church of the believers in Jesus."

[2] This section is largely based upon Kraemer's provocative book on the vocation of the laity.

[3] The idea of the totality of the Church is met in the New Testament picture of the congregation of the redeemed in Rev. 5:9 and 7:9. In Heb. 4:9 the term *people of God* is used for the total group. The term *my people* occurs in II Cor. 6:16, and of the Gentile converts in Rom. 9:25. In Rom. 15:9-14 Gentiles are incorporated in the *people of God* with participant responsibility (v. 14). Of course, I Pet. 2:9-10 binds all this together in a specific all-inclusive community to be known as the *people of God.*

[4] According to William Ramsay, the use of *laos* to mean the congregation as distinguished from the clergy is latent in writings dated as early as 218, while by the time of the *Lycaonian* inscriptions (third and fourth centuries) the distinction is clearly expressed. He adds: "It is true that the words were in Christian use from the beginning; but not hardened in the technical sense of contrasted orders of society" (1908:387-389).

[5] *The International Critical Commentary* renders: " 'with a view to the perfecting of the saints unto the work of ministering,' " but then, oddly, goes on to remark: "But in a connexion like this, where offices of the Church are in question, *diakonia* can only mean official service; and this does not belong to the saints in general." But whether that is so is precisely one of the major issues.

CHAPTER IX

[1] See Titus 1:5-7. Leon Morris lists the evidence for the contention that these two terms refer to the same office (1964:73-74). The *Catholic Encyclopaedia,* pointing to Titus 1:6-7 and Acts 20:17 and 28 (note that the word translated "guardians" in the latter verse is the Greek word for "bishops"), concedes that these words "are to some extent interchangeable." The Catholic practice of distinguishing between the offices of bishop and presbyter is defended on grounds that by the end of the second century there was an unquestioned and "universal" tradition that the bishops had superior authority.

[2] Morris believes that the later office of deacon was a development from the account of Acts 6, but he doubts whether Luke there intended to record the creation of an order.

[3] As Gwatkin in *A Dictionary of the Bible* evidences, "it is not easy to trace in the New Testament any precise form of ordination or consecration to

ecclesiastical office" (1950:631). Edwards, in the *International Standard Bible Encyclopedia,* says, "The New Testament throws but little light on the origin of the later ecclesiastical rite of ordination" (1943:2199).

[4] To this definition ought to be added the thought that the rite is symbolic of the transmission of the Holy Spirit for an assigned task.

[5] Even so, there is serious reason to believe that the cry for a more educated ministry endangers the identification of minister and congregation in many situations. The wider the educational gulf between them, the more real the danger. An educated ministry is needed for one task but it is a disadvantage for another. The Church will neglect the lower levels of ministry at her peril.

[6] The idea of rotation of elders is practiced in some places in Japan. The United Presbyterian Church in the U.S.A. provides that ruling elders be elected for a term of not more than three years and that they may not be "elected for consecutive terms aggregating more than six years." Before such a man may be elected again, at least one year must elapse (Blake 1965:23).

CHAPTER X

[1] This well-known statement grows out of the work of the Latin American Mission and the program it originated known as "Evangelism in Depth." The man most responsible for this dictum and the program which has developed was the late R. Kenneth Strachan. Evangelism in Depth has in Latin America succeeded in rallying a larger portion of the membership of a wide number of Protestant Churches of all kinds than any other contemporary movement. It has inaugurated a remarkably effective evangelistic ministry and deserves serious study by all concerned about the subject of this chapter.

[2] See also Webster (1964:45). Of the rapid growth of churches in South America, he says: "Basically their growth is the result of lay witness, not clerical activity."

[3] This account is based upon the following: Azariah (1939:Vol. 3, 32-47); Graham (1946); Neill (1954:9-26); Neill (1957:72-74, 128).

CHAPTER XI

[1] Concerning the training program described in the following paragraphs, see C. A. Clark (1939:159-161); Davis (1939:369-373); Soltau (1954:54-56).

[2] Included in a letter to the writer from the Christian and Missionary Alliance, New York, March 11, 1966. The reason for decrease in the number of ordained clergy and worship centers in 1963 is not known. Overall membership shows a gain.

CHAPTER XII

[1] It should be noted that there is in this analysis no disposition to place Japanese social patterns in an unfavorable light. All human patterns are the expression of man's nature, which having been made in the image of God reflects the glory of the divine, but which being infected in every part by sin,

reflects also the dark shadow of the demonic. If some aspects of Japanese group psychology are destructive in their influence, other aspects are closer to the Christian way than the excessive individualism of the West.

[2] Thomas states that 30 per cent of the converts during 1883-1889 were *samurai,* although this class composed only 5 per cent of the total population (1959:161).

CHAPTER XIII

[1] The following analysis is based upon McGavran (1963:126-130). The reader's attention is drawn to McGavran's cautions (pp. 22-23) concerning the difficulty of securing accurate church statistics for Mexico. The Mexican statistics above are used in the conviction that their veracity is sufficient for the purpose of the argument.

[2] It is notoriously difficult for twentieth-century Christians to maintain a balanced view of the Church's role in society, though we are in a better position to do so today than a few decades ago when men held out either for the "individual" gospel or the "social" gospel. Few will deny that the Christian is to live a life of love and good works in the world, and it will also be readily conceded by most that this mode of living itself constitutes an important and even essential testimony. The problem becomes more acute when the question is asked as to how much the Church as such should concern itself with social action. William Temple held that nine-tenths of the Church's work in the world is carried out by believers who accept their responsibilities in the world (1950:23). Perhaps this ratio might well serve as a rough rule of thumb. This writer holds that the Church must at some points engage in social action, but that it is essential it not neglect its task of making disciples. There is little to commend the position that social action is itself a form of evangelism, and none at all for the idea that social action should be substituted for discipling the peoples.

[3] The statistics upon which Yamamori's analysis (1872-1960) was made were painstakingly compiled from records of the denominations, church histories, and statistical compilations, and are reliable. His investigations included interviews with responsible Japanese church leaders.

[4] Figures for 1958 and after supplied by *Kirisuto Shinbun.*

[5] Statistics are from *Kirisutokyō Nenkan* (1950, 1952, 1954, 1958, 1960, 1962, 1964).

[6] The United Church figure for 1951 was used instead of that for 1949, as the latter figure seems to be in error.

CHAPTER XIV

[1] "District" is a term widely used by the Methodists. Another word could have been chosen. Each reader should substitute terms familiar to him as he reads through the chapter.

[2] No attempt is made in this chapter to detail an organizational structure or to insist on a given form of church polity. Each denomination determines these things for itself, but the principle of having as many lay delegates as clerics ought seriously to be considered by all.

[3] Again the requirements are left ambiguous here. Each denomination establishes its own standards as a matter of course.

[4] For duties of the circuit pastor not mentioned here, compare pp. 00-500.

[5] Such rates of growth are very rare in Japan in the present century, and I may be overly optimistic. However, faster growth than this is experienced in many places throughout the world and is not unknown in Japan.

[6] Even in conservative Tottori Ken, the author has observed this on many occasions, in his own denomination and in others. Of course, it is important to have respected Christians in the community. Personal invitations are more effective in getting an audience than posters and loudspeaker announcements. The type of meeting held affects attendance the next time meetings are planned. Evangelists must love the people to whom they preach, and respect their dignity as human beings. In this section, I do not intend to argue that evangelistic rallies are the most fruitful of the methods of evangelism, much less that they are the only way of conducting evangelism. They are one way.

[7] Lesslie Newbigin writes out of the experience of planting churches in a previously unevangelized area of India, largely through the ministry of laymen. When converts were baptized in a new place, the temptation to send in a salaried worker in the usual fashion was resisted. Rather, the sovereign act of the Holy Spirit in using some humble layman was respected, and he was, at least for the time being, recognized as the one through whom the Spirit would lead the new converts. He was assisted by trained leaders, but not replaced. An era of unusual growth ensued in the area in which this practice was followed. In twelve years, the number of congregations increased from 13 to 55 (1964:71-72).

[8] Here room is left for methods suited to the particular conditions of Japan and the characteristics of the Japanese, including the originality of Japanese clergymen. The foreign missionary must gladly recognize that the Holy Spirit will lead Japanese Christians in a manner suited to their consciousness as Japanese, sometimes in ways not likely to occur to persons of Western ancestry. *Kirisuto Shinbun,* sometimes translated *Christ Weekly,* is the periodical founded by Kagawa.

[9] Because of space limitations, this chapter has emphasized expansion and the multiplication of new churches. Of course, in any healthy district, much attention should be given to how to strengthen existing churches, how to stimulate believers to deeper and more worthy Christian living, and how to fulfill the vocation of the Church and its members in the ongoing life of the community.

APPENDICES

APPENDIX A

Glossary of Japanese Words

bokkai-kyōshi. In this book suggested as a title for a level of ordained minister, below *seikyōshi.*

bokushi. Pastor.

buraku. A primary rural community consisting usually of fewer than one hundred homes.

habatsu. A word used of the cliques which often exist within business firms and government departments.

hokyōshi. The office preparatory to becoming a *seikyōshi.*

ie. House. Often used to refer to the family, including the ancestors.

kyōdan. Literally, "teaching organization." It is used of many religious organizations, including Christian denominations. The word is often used by missionaries to refer to the United Church.

mura. Village. Now used officially for the smallest unit of local government. It may include several *buraku.*

PL Kyōdan. One of the New Religions. PL stands for "perfect liberty." This religion seeks to interpret life as art, claims to be monotheistic, and to have over 600,000 adherents.

samurai. A warrior. The warrior class.

Seichō no Ie. One of the influential New Religions. It is syncretistic and organized around the founder, Masaharu Taniguchi. Many meetings are held in homes.

seikyōshi. Used in many Protestant churches in reference to fully ordained ministers.

sensei. Term of respect used of any kind of teacher. It is the term used when addressing or referring to a pastor.

Sōka Gakkai. Militant neo-Buddhist sect, now claiming over 13,000,000 adherents.

APPENDIX B

About Statistics

Church statistics present many problems. The meaning of the term "church members" differs among the Churches. Moreover, it is sometimes defined in more than one way by the same Church at different times and in different parts of the world.

Some Churches count as members persons who make contributions, or who attend at least occasionally, while others count only those who commune. Some Churches count all who have been baptized, including infants, whether they attend or not; others include only those who are baptized as adults and who are active.

Some Churches maintain records for several classifications of members. The Episcopal Church of Japan, for example, compiles statistics for four classifications (active communicants, total communicants, active members, total members). If one wishes to compare in a meaningful way the size or growth of this Church with that of another, a membership classification of the latter must be chosen which is defined similarly to one of the four Episcopal classifications. Moreover, when gathering from various sources statistics pertaining to a given Church over a period of years, it is essential that all figures be taken from the same membership classification. Unfortunately, this rule is not always observed.

Not only do the Churches define "members" in different ways, but the word "church" as used in statistical reports is understood in more than one way. The *World Christian Handbook* uses the more accurate classification "worship centers," which makes it possible to include organized and unorganized churches, as well as preaching places.

The ways in which church leaders are classified also are varied, though to a lesser extent.

Caution is certainly necessary, but it is extreme to declare that church statistics are useless. Statistics compiled by the same Church over many years are reliable as indicators of size and growth. Even if occasional inaccuracies intrude, they are corrected by succeeding years, and the general picture such statistics yield is accurate and reliable.

I have sought to use the most accurate and reliable statistics available. The sources have been cited, and cautions inserted where appropriate.

In a few cases, especially with older statistics, it is difficult to know whether available figures are to be understood as meaning communicant membership or Christian community. Such statistics have been used only to give a general impression of the size of a movement, or (more accurately) to chart the growth of a Church over a period of years.

In the case of Figure Two, the figures for the Protestant Episcopal Church (U.S.) were taken from the *World Christian Handbook 1952.* The Christian and Missionary Alliance statistics come from the annual reports of the Christian and Missionary Alliance, New York. The Presbyterian Church (Korea) figures are found in *World Christian Handbook 1957.* Those for all Protestants in the Philippines were taken from Davis (1939). The figures for the Methodists in Great Britain come from *World Christian Handbook 1962.* The statistics for the Assemblies of God in Brazil were supplied from an Assemblies booklet (Erasmo Braga and Norman Grubb, *Republic of Brazil*) cited by Read (1965). The 1882 and 1900 figures for all Japan Protestants were taken from Cary (1909). The 1963 figures for Churches in Japan are set out in *Kirisutokyō Nenkan 1964* (Christian Yearbook 1964).

A comparison of this kind is subject to uncertainties, since in some Churches a considerable number of ordained ministers are not in charge of churches, and some Churches do not report salaried leaders who are acting as pastors but are not ordained. The early Japanese statistics do not, it seems, list preaching stations, which suggests that the number of "worship centers" would have been larger than the number of Japanese ministers. But this is offset by the fact that our figures do not include the number of foreign missionaries, who were more numerous than Japanese ordained ministers. I am convinced that the impression given by Figure Two is true to the real situation, and that the literature supports this conclusion.

Figures on page 51 were acquired during an interview in July 1966, at the Local Preachers' Department, 1, Central Building, Westminster, London, S.W. 1. British Methodists often employ their circuit and lay preacher system overseas also. Statistics for 1957 include the following: Rhodesia–35 ministers, 143 full-time lay evangelists, and 2,069 local preachers serving 672 worship centers; Nigeria–47 ministers, 275 evangelists, and 3,948 lay preachers serving 1,333 worship centers; Burma–13 ministers, 32 evangelists, and 518 local preachers serving 105 worship centers. These figures do not include missionaries, who tended to outnumber the ministers somewhat. Statistics are from annual reports on file at the Methodist Missionary Society, 25 Marylebone Road, London, N.W. 1.

Since Batak Church statistics in English are difficult to locate, we have listed the sources used. The 1866 and 1876 figures are from Neill (1964:349). The 1911 figures are from Warneck (1911:22). The 1930 figures (the actual statement is "over 273,000") are from Kraemer (1958:*Mission Field,* 50). The 1938 figures are from Davis (1938:5). He reports 800 churches in that year. The 1891 and 1950 figures are from Beyerhaus and Lefever (1964:74, 85). The latter vary moderately from the *World Christian Handbook,* which lists the membership at 502,855 (1952:52). The 1962 figures are from *World Christian Handbook* (1962:163). Thomson (1964:252) reports a figure for 1960 of 691,000, so that the 1962 *Handbook* figure is probably too small. The "teacher-preacher" office in 1938 differed somewhat from that of 1911. The sub-title *presbyter* is, of course, equivalent to the *elder* of many churches.

APPENDIX C

The two maps showing the distribution of the churches or worship centers of the Spirit of Jesus Church were prepared by Mr. Mitsuyoshi Yamada and are based upon the 1952 and 1964 issues of the *Kirisutokyō Nenkan.* The actual addresses of the Spirit of Jesus worship centers are found in this yearbook.

Each dot on the maps represents one worship center. There were so many Tokyo area addresses in the 1964 yearbook that Mr. Yamada was obliged to use a number in lieu of placing the large number of dots which would have been required.

DISTRIBUTION OF WORSHIP CENTERS

SPIRIT OF JESUS CHURCH — 1951

one dot equals one worship center

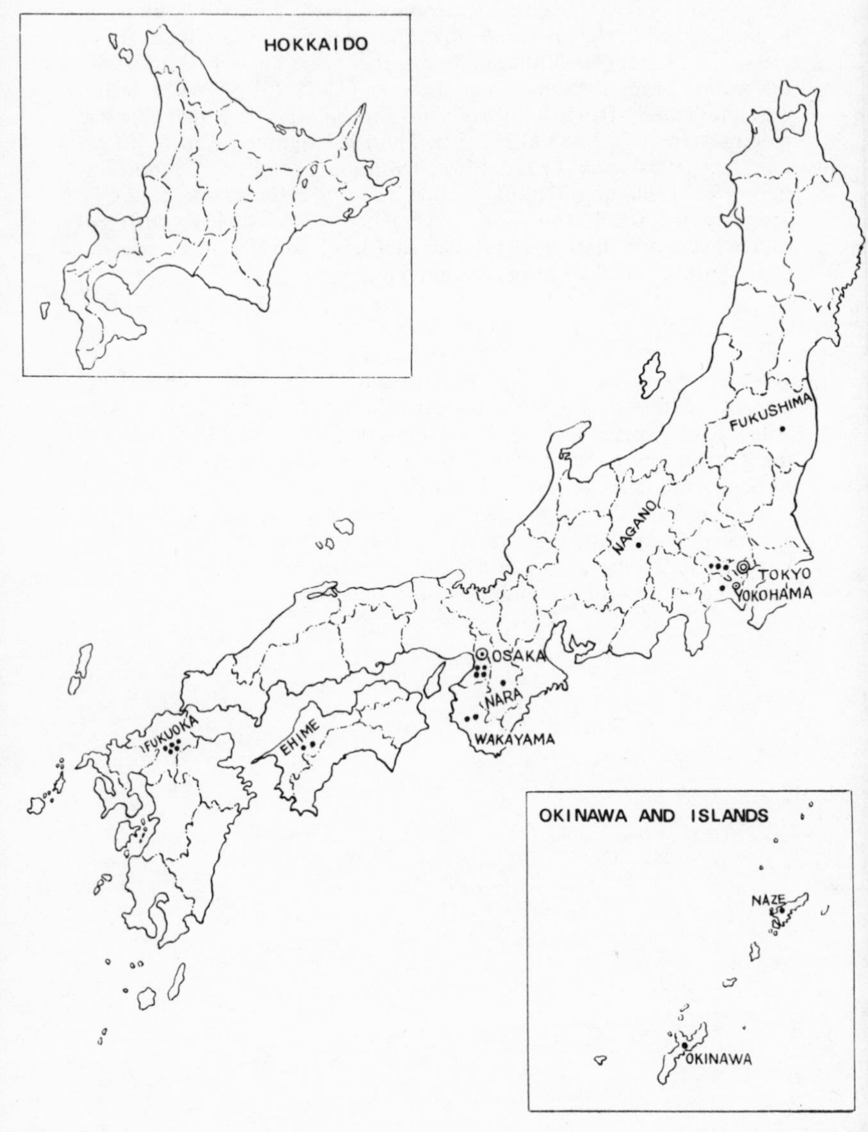

DISTRIBUTION OF WORSHIP CENTERS

SPIRIT OF JESUS CHURCH — 1963

one dot equals one worship center

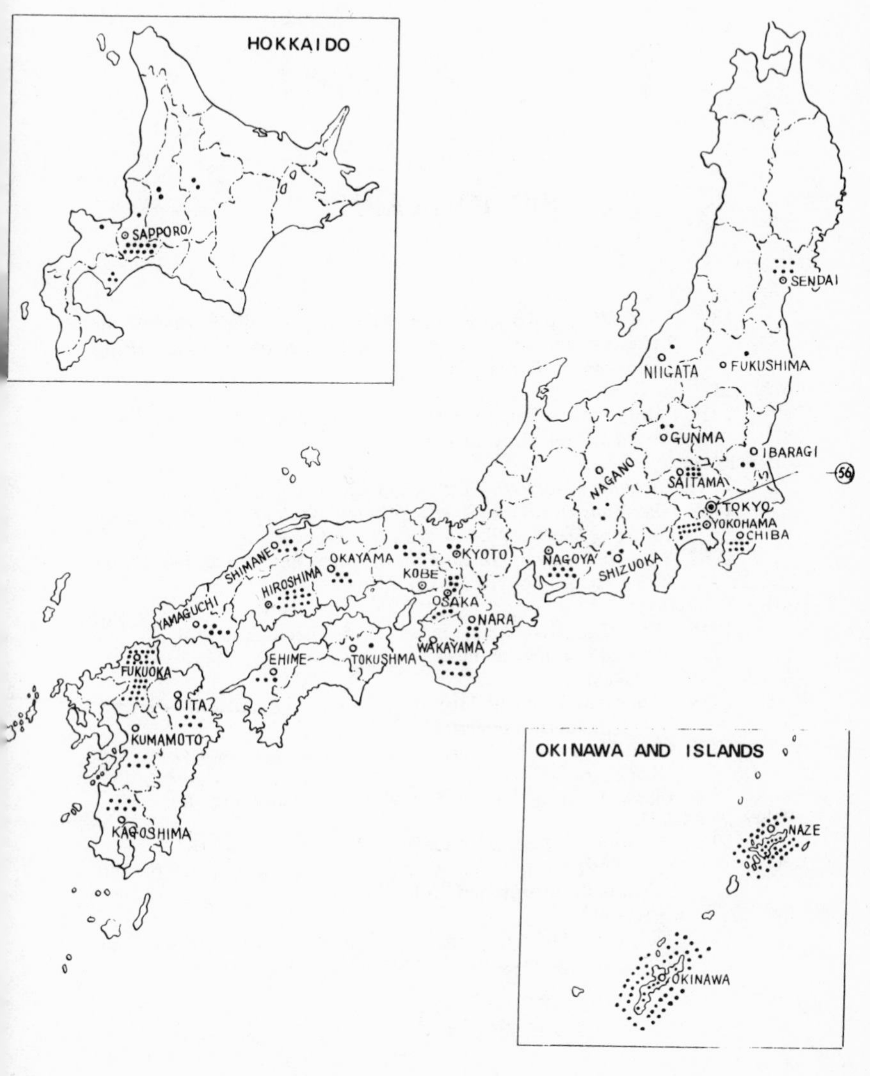

BIBLIOGRAPHY

Abbott, T. K.

1897 "A Critical and Exegetical Commentary on the Epistle to the Ephesians and to the Colossians," in *The International Critical Commentary,* T. & T. Clark.

Ahaus, H.

1911 "Holy Orders," in Charles C. Herbermann, *The Catholic Encyclopedia,* Vol. XI, Appleton.

Allen, Roland

1962 *Missionary Methods: St. Paul's or Ours?* Wm. B. Eerdmans.

1962 *The Ministry of the Spirit: Selected Writings of Roland Allen,* edited by David M. Paton, Wm. B. Eerdmans.

1962 *The Spontaneous Expansion of the Church and the Causes Which Hinder It,* Wm. B. Eerdmans.

Ariga, Tetsutaro

1958 "Christian Mission in Japan as a Theological Problem," in *Religion in Life* (Summer).

Azariah, Vedanayakam

1939 "The Church and Its Mission," in *Addresses and Other Records,* Vol. VII, *Tambaram Series.*

1939 "The Place of the Church in Evangelism," in *Evangelism,* Vol. III, *Tambaram Series.*

1954 *Christian Giving,* United Society for Christian Literature.

Baker, Wendell Dean

1956 "A Study of Selected Aspects of Japanese Social Stratification: Class Differences in Values and Levels of Aspiration" (unpublished Ph.D. dissertation, Columbia University).

Barclay, Wade Crawford

1957 *Widening Horizons,* Vol. III, *History of Methodist Missions,* Board of Missions of the Methodist Church.

Barres, Oliver
1964 "The First Missionary Deacon," in *World Mission* (Winter 1964-65).

Bates, M. Searle, and Wilhelm Pauck (ed.)
1964 *The Prospects of Christianity Throughout the World,* Charles Scribner's Sons.

Beardsley, Richard K., John W. Hall, and Robert E. Ward
1959 *Village Japan,* University of Chicago Press.

Beare, Francis W.
1953 "The Epistle to the Ephesians (Exegesis)," in *The Interpreter's Bible,* Vol. X, Abingdon-Cokesbury.

Berg, William L.
1951 "The Philippine Church Progresses," in *The Alliance Weekly* (September 12).

Beyerhaus, Peter, and Henry Lefever
1964 *The Responsible Church and the Foreign Mission,* Wm. B. Eerdmans.

Blake, Eugene Carson (ed.)
1965 *Presbyterian Law for the Local Church,* The United Presbyterian Church in the United States of America.

Boschman, Paul W.
1964 "Church Growth in Miyazaki Prefecture" (A mimeographed report prepared at the Institute of Church Growth).

Bowman, John Wick
1943 *The Intention of Jesus,* Westminster.

Bratcher, L. M.
1938 *Francisco Fulgencio Soren, Christ's Interpreter to Many Lands,* Broadman.

Brauer, Jerald C.
1953 *Protestantism in America,* Westminster.

Braun, Neil H.
1964 "A Second Look at Roland Allen" (A mimeographed report in English and Japanese based upon three books by Roland Allen: *The Spontaneous Expansion of the Church and the Causes Which Hinder It; Missionary Methods: St. Paul's or Ours? The Ministry of the Spirit: Selected Writings of Roland Allen).*

Brown, Arthur Judson
1921 *The Mastery of the Far East,* Charles Scribner's Sons.

Cary, Otis
1909 *Protestant Missions,* Vol. II of *A History of Christianity in Japan,* Fleming H. Revell.

Christianity Today
1966 "Babies and the 'New Birth' Rate," *Christianity Today* (April 29).

Clark, C. A.
1939 "The Presbyterian Church in Korea," in *The Growing Church,* Vol. II, *Tambaram Series.*

Clark, Sidney J. W.
1928 *The Indigenous Church,* World Dominion Press.

Cole, Fay-Cooper
1966 "Batak," in *Encyclopedia Britannica,* Vol. III.
Cornell, John B.
1962 "Buraku Social Organization and Community Life," in Bernard S. Silberman (ed.), *Japanese Character and Culture,* University of Arizona Press.
Crabtree, A. R.
1953 *Baptists in Brazil,* Baptist Publishing House, Rio de Janeiro.

Davis, J. Merle
1938 *The Batak Church,* International Missionary Council.
1939 (ed.), *The Economic Basis of the Church,* Vol. 5, *Tambaram Series.*
1943 *How the Church Grows in Brazil,* International Missionary Council.
d'Espine, Henri
1961 "Ordination and the Diversified Ministries of the Church," in Robert Clyde Johnson (ed.), *The Church and Its Changing Ministry.*
Dore, R. P.
1965 *City Life in Japan,* University of California Press.
Drummond, Richard H.
1958 "A Missionary's Outlook," in *Japan Christian Quarterly* (July).
1961 "Hendrik Kraemer in Japan," in *International Review of Missions* (October).

Eastwood, Cyril
1960 *The Priesthood of All Believers,* The Epworth Press.
Edwards, D. Miall
1943 "Ordain, Ordination," in James Orr (ed.), *The International Standard Bible Encyclopaedia,* Vol. IV.
Eguchi, Takenori
1965 "Nihon Dendō no Kōsō" (Planning Evangelism in Japan), in *Fukuin to Sekai* (Gospel and World) (September).
Evangelism-in-Depth
1961 *Evangelism-in-Depth,* Moody Press.

Fanning, Wm. H.
1911 "Baptism," in *The Catholic Encyclopedia,* Vol. II.
Felton, Ralph A.
1938 *The Rural Church in the Far East,* Baptist Mission Press (Calcutta) for I.M.C.
Frerichs, Albert C.
1957 *Anutu Conquers in New Guinea,* The Wartburg Press.

Gaustad, Edwin Scott
1962 *Historical Atlas of Religion in America,* Harper and Row.
Gerrish, B. A.
1965 "Priesthood and Ministry in the Theology of Luther," in *Church History* (December).
Gibbs, Mark and T. Ralph Morton
1964 *God's Frozen People,* Westminster.

Gore, Charles
1924 *The Holy Spirit and the Church,* John Murray.

Gosden, Eric
1957 *Upon This Rock,* Marshall, Morgan and Scott.

Goshi, Zoji
1939 "The Church of Christ in Japan," in *The Growing Church,* Vol. II, *Tambaram Series.*

Graham, Carol
1946 *Azariah of Dornakal,* S.C.M. Press.

Grant, Frederick C.
1955 "Organization of the Early Church," in Lefferts A. A. Loetscher, *Twentieth Century Encyclopaedia of Religious Knowledge,* Vol. II.

Grimley, John B. and Gordon E. Robinson
1966 *Church Growth in Central and Southern Nigeria,* Wm. B. Eerdmans.

Guy, Robert C.
1965 "Directed Conservation," in D. McGavran (ed.), *Church Growth and Christian Mission.*

Gwatkin, H. M.
1950 "Ordination," in James Hastings (ed.), *A Dictionary of the Bible,* Vol. III.

Hamilton, H. F.
1912 *The Church,* Vol. II of *The People of God,* Oxford University Press.

Hanson, A. T.
1965 "Shepherd, Teacher and Celebrant in the New Testament Conception of the Ministry," in David M. Paton (ed.), *New Forms of Ministry.*

Hara, Ryozo
1964 "The Awakening of the Church in Japan," in *Religion in Life* (Winter).

Hesselgrave, David John
1965 "A Propagation Profile of the Sōka Gakkai" (unpublished Ph.D. dissertation, University of Minnesota).

Hiyane, Antei
1965 "Japan," in *Religion in Life* (Autumn).

Hodges, Melvin L.
1965 "Developing Basic Units of Indigenous Churches," in D. McGavran (ed.), *Church Growth and Christian Mission.*
1966 "Spiritual Dynamics in El Salvador," in *Evangelical Missions Quarterly* (Winter).

Hort, R. F. A.
1898 *The First Epistle of St. Peter,* I.1–II.17, Macmillan & Co.

Iglehart, Charles W.
1959 *A Century of Protestant Christianity in Japan,* Charles E. Tuttle.

International Missionary Council
1928 "Constitutions of Some Recently Developed Churches on the Mission Field," in *Younger and Older Churches,* Vol. III, *Jerusalem Series.*

Ito, Kyojun

1961 "Sokagakkai wa Naze Sakan ni Naru ka?" (Why Does the Sōka Gakkai Flourish?), *Sekai Bukkyo* (March).

Jackson, Samuel M. (ed.)

1910 "Ordination," in *The New Schaff-Herzog Encyclopaedia of Religious Knowledge*, Vol. VIII.

Japan Statistical Yearbook 1964

1964 Tokyo: Bureau of Statistics.

Johnson, Robert Clyde (ed.)

1961 *The Church and Its Changing Ministry*, The General Assembly of the Presbyterian Church in the United States of America.

King, Louis L.

1963 "Introduction," in Byron W. Ross, *Training Lay Workers.*

Kirisutokyō Nenkan (The Christian Yearbook)

Tokyo: Kirisuto Shinbunsha. This yearbook is published every two years.

Kraemer, Hendrik

1958 *A Theology of the Laity*, Westminster.

1958 *From Mission Field to Independent Church*, S.C.M. Press.

Kuder, John

1962 "The Lutheran Mission in New Guinea Today," in *International Review of Missions* (July).

Latourette, Kenneth Scott

1944 *The Great Century in Northern Africa and Asia*, Vol. VI, *A History of the Expansion of Christianity*, Harper and Bros.

1961 *The Nineteenth Century Outside Europe*, Vol. III, *Christianity in a Revolutionary Age*, Harper & Bros.

Lawson, John

1955 *Green and Pleasant Land*, S.C.M. Book Club.

Lightfoot, J. B.

1901 *The Christian Ministry*, Macmillan & Co.

McGavran, Donald A.

1962 *Church Growth in Jamaica*, Lucknow Publishing House.

1963 *How Churches Grow*, World Dominion Press.

1963 (with John Huegel and Jack Taylor), *Church Growth in Mexico*, Wm. B. Eerdmans.

1965 (ed., with Robert C. Guy, Melvin L. Hodges, and Eugene A. Nida), *Church Growth and Christian Mission*, Harper and Row.

McKinnis, Velma

1953 "Lay-Workers Do It in Sarangani," in *The Alliance Weekly* (July 29).

Manson, T. W.

1948 *The Church's Ministry*, Hodder & Stoughton.

n.d. *Ministry and Priesthood, Christ's and Ours*, John Knox.

Matsumoto, Yoshiharu Scott

1960 *Contemporary Japan, The Individual and the Group*, The American Philosophical Society (January).

Morris, Leon

1964 *Ministers of God*, Inter-Varsity Fellowship.

Neill, Stephen
1954 "Vedanayagam Samuel Azariah, 1874-1945," in V. S. Azariah, *Christian Giving*, United Society for Christian Literature.
1957 *The Unfinished Task*, Edinburgh Press.
1963 (ed., with Hans-Ruedi Weber), *The Layman in Christian History*, Westminster.
1964 *A History of Christian Missions*, Penguin Books.

Newbigin, Lesslie
1953 "The Ministry of the Church–Ordained and Unordained, Paid and Unpaid" (An unpublished document, prepared in Madura, for the consideration of the dioceses, March 1953).
1964 *Trinitarian Faith and Today's Mission*, John Knox.
1965 "Preface," in David M. Paton (ed.), *New Forms of Ministry*.

"New Guinea"
1966 *Encyclopaedia Britannica*, Vol. XVI.

Nida, Eugene A.
1965 "Culture and Church Growth" (pp. 87-108) and "Dynamics of Church Growth" (pp. 170-192), in D. McGavran (ed.), *Church Growth and Christian Mission.*

Norwood, Frederick A.
1966 "Methodism," in *Encyclopaedia Britannica*, Vol. XV.

O'Grady, Desmond
1963 "Religion and Politics in Japan," in *America* (February 2).

Paton, David M.
1953 *Christian Missions and the Judgment of God*, S.C.M. Press.
1965 (ed.), *New Forms of Ministry*, Edinburgh House Press.

Paton, William (ed.)
1939 *Evangelism*, Vol. III, *Tambaram Series.*
1939 *The Growing Church*, Vol. II, *Tambaram Series.*
1939 *The Life of the Church*, Vol. IV, *Tambaram Series.*

Pezzotta, Antonio
1965 "The Unserviced Millions in the Philippines," in *World Mission* (Fall).

Pickett, J. Waskom
1960 *Christ's Way to India's Heart*, Lucknow Publishing House.

Porter, H. Boone
1965 "Modern Experience in Practice," in David M. Paton (ed.), *New Forms of Ministry.*

Priestly, Eber
1956 "The New Pattern of the Church," in *International Review of Missions* (October).

Ramsay, W. M.
1908 *Luke the Physician*, Hodder and Stoughton.

Read, William R.
1965 *New Patterns of Church Growth in Brazil*, Wm. B. Eerdmans.

Ream, W. G. B.
1956 "The Support of the Clergy in the First Five Centuries A.D.," in the *International Review of Missions* (October).

Richardson, Alan
1958 *An Introduction to the Theology of the New Testament,* S.C.M. Press.

Ross, Byron W.
1963 *Training Lay Workers,* Christian and Missionary Alliance.

Shearer, Roy E.
1966 *Wildfire: Church Growth in Korea,* Wm. B. Eerdmans.

Silberman, Bernard S. (ed.)
1962 *Japanese Character and Culture,* University of Arizona Press.

Soltau, T. Stanley
1954 *Missions at the Crossroads,* Van Kampen Press.

Streeter, Burnett Hillman
1920 *The Primitive Church,* Macmillan & Co.

Sundkler, Bengt G. M.
1960 *The Christian Ministry in Africa,* S.C.M. Press.
1961 *Bantu Prophets in South Africa,* Oxford University Press.

Sweet, William Warren
1946 *The Methodists,* Vol. IV, *Religion on the American Frontier,* University of Chicago Press.
1964 *The Baptists,* Vol. I, *Religion on the American Frontier,* Cooper Square Publishers.

Takenaka, Masao
1964 "Japan," in M. Searle Bates and Wilhelm Pauck (ed.), *The Prospects of Christianity Throughout the World.*

Temple, William
1950 *Christianity and Social Order,* S.C.M. Press.

Teranishi, Eiji
1966 Letter to the writer (February).

Thomas, Winburn T.
1959 *Protestant Beginnings in Japan,* Charles E. Tuttle, Tokyo.

Thomson, Alan C.
1964 "Indonesia," in M. Searle Bates and Wilhelm Pauck (ed.), *The Prospects of Christianity Throughout the World.*

Tucker, Bishop Henry
1951 *Exploring the Silent Shore of Memory,* Whittet and Sheperson.

Turner, H. E. W.
1953 *Jesus, Master and Lord,* A. H. Mowbray.

Vicedom, G. F.
1961 *Church and People in New Guinea,* United Society for Christian Literature.

Vischer, Lukas
1965 "The Ministry and a Secular Occupation," in David M. Paton (ed.), *New Forms of Ministry.*

Vogel, Ezra F.
1963 *Japan's New Middle Class: The Salary Man and His Family in a Tokyo Suburb,* University of California Press.

Warneck, John
1911 "The Growth of the Church in the Mission Field: I. Among the Bataks," in *International Review of Missions.*

Weber, Hans-Ruedi
1963 *The Militant Ministry,* Fortress Press.
Webster, Douglas
1964 *Patterns of Part-time Ministry,* World Dominion Press.
Westcott, Brooke Foss
1952 *St. Paul's Epistle to the Ephesians,* Wm. B. Eerdmans.
Williams, R. R.
1957 "Laying On of Hands," in Alan Richardson (ed.), *A Theological Word Book of the Bible,* S.C.M. Press.
World Christian Handbook
A statistical summary published every two years by World Dominion Press.
World Council of Churches
1963 "The Growth of the Church" (A statement drawn up at a Consultation on Church Growth convened at Iberville, Quebec, July 31–August 2, 1963. By the Department of Missionary Studies, WCC).
n.d. A Tent-Making Ministry, Division of World Mission and Evangelism, WCC.
Yamada, Hiroshi, and Doyle M. Bethel
1964 "The Spirit of Jesus Church," in *Japan Christian Quarterly* (July).
Yamamori, Tetsunao
1963 "A Century of Church Growth in Japan" (An unpublished paper prepared at the Institute of Church Growth).

INDEX

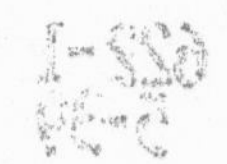